Headhunting and the Social Imagination in Southeast Asia

CONTRIBUTORS

Jules De Raedt

Kenneth M. George

Janet Hoskins

Allen R. Maxwell

Andrew McWilliam

Peter Metcalf

Anna Lowenhaupt Tsing

HEADHUNTING
and the Social Imagination
in Southeast Asia

Edited by Janet Hoskins

STANFORD UNIVERSITY PRESS
STANFORD, CALIFORNIA 1996

Stanford University Press
Stanford, California
© 1996 by the Board of Trustees of the
Leland Stanford Junior University
Printed in the United States of America

CIP data appear at the end of the book

Stanford University Press publications are distributed
exclusively by Stanford University Press within the
United States, Canada, Mexico, and Central America;
they are distributed exclusively by Cambridge
University Press throughout the rest of the world.

The second essay in this volume, by Kenneth M. George,
is reproduced by permission of the American Anthropological
Association from *American Ethnologist*, vol. 20, no. 3.
© American Anthropological Association, 1993.
It is not for sale or further reproduction.

Preface

This volume did not come from a conference, and in fact its contributors have never met. Our common concern with the history of headhunting and how it has been reimagined as a form of state predation on indigenous peoples emerged through correspondence. During the years that the volume has been in preparation, the task of bringing together authors scattered all over the globe, from Norway to Australia and New Zealand, from the Philippines and eastern Indonesia to California and Massachusetts, has often been formidable. I am grateful to the contributors for their patience and their continued commitment to this somewhat unlikely project.

An original call for papers went out in 1990, and I wrote my own contribution and a first draft of the Introduction at the Institute for Advanced Study in Princeton, New Jersey, as part of an interdisciplinary research group convened by Clifford Geertz and Joan Scott on the historical turn in the social sciences. I drew at that time on field materials collected during a six-month period of fieldwork in 1988, funded by NSF Grant no. BMS 8704498. Revisions of the introduction were done at the Institute for Social Anthropology in Oslo, Norway, and received helpful comments from Signe Howell and Olaf Smedal. The final compilation of the manuscript was completed at the University of Southern California, Los Angeles, in the period 1993–94. Additional archival research in the summer of 1994 was funded by the Small Grants program of the Southeast Asian Studies Committee at the University of Michigan, Ann Arbor. I am grateful for all of this assistance.

Muriel Bell and John Feneron at Stanford University Press

helped to bring the book together and guide it through production. Sherry Wert skillfully copyedited the entire manuscript, and two anonymous readers who reviewed the manuscript provided thoughtful and reasoned commentary on each paper.

My greatest thanks go to the contributors, who have waited through the long process of bringing this collection into print, and generously agreed to share their thoughts and experiences with a wider audience.

J. H.

Contents

Contributors

Jules De Raedt, Research Associate, Cordillera Research Center, Baguio City, the Philippines

Kenneth M. George, Assistant Professor of Anthropology, Harvard University

Janet Hoskins, Professor of Anthropology, Monash University, Melbourne, Australia

Allen R. Maxwell, Associate Professor of Anthropology, University of Alabama at Tuscaloosa

Andrew McWilliam, Postdoctoral Fellow, Northern Territory University, Australia

Peter Metcalf, Professor of Anthropology, University of Virginia

Anna Lowenhaupt Tsing, Associate Professor of Anthropology, University of California, Santa Cruz

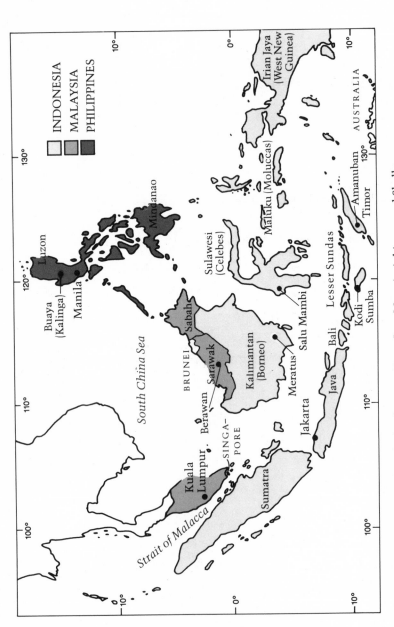

Countries and major islands and island groups. From Jane Monnig Atkinson and Shelly Errington, eds., *Power and Difference: Gender in Island Southeast Asia* (Stanford University Press: Stanford, Calif., 1990).

Headhunting and the Social Imagination in Southeast Asia

Janet Hoskins

Introduction: Headhunting as Practice and as Trope

Headhunting is a subject that has long had a great hold on the imaginations of both European and Southeast Asian peoples. Nineteenth-century travelers and explorers published a series of accounts of encounters with headhunters in the jungles of Southeast Asia that were widely read and discussed (Bock 1881; Furness 1902; Haddon 1901; Hose 1927). Anthropologists, following with some trepidation in their footsteps, have provided ethnographic accounts that also give prominence to martial traditions and headhunting lore (Barton 1919, 1938, 1949; Freeman 1970; Jones 1907–9; Metcalf 1982; M. Rosaldo 1980; R. Rosaldo 1980; Rousseau 1990). Popular accounts bestow upon the headhunter a place alongside the cannibal and the noble savage in constituting an image of the exotic for Western audiences. The fascination is not limited to Westerners: recent field researchers in Southeast Asia report that even in areas where headhunting has been suppressed for several generations or seems never to have been practiced, rumors circulate about contemporary headhunters who raid living communities and terrorize whole populations (Drake 1989; Erb 1991; Forth 1991; George 1991).

Who is this headhunter who has cut his way so fiercely into the social imaginations of such different cultures? Is he the epitome of the savage warrior, who severs the head of his victim to rob him of any dignity in death? Such an image is often found in European writings. Could he instead be a brave man, crazed by grief and acting to achieve emotional release? Or a local hero, championing indigenous autonomy and defending the boundaries of traditional territories? Such counterimages are advanced by some of the descendants of famous headhunters. Or is the modern headhunter now more likely to be a government official, the representative of a Japanese petroleum company, or a European missionary? Recent reinterpretations suggest a postcolonial recasting of headhunting as a form of violence perpetrated not by isolated forest people but by exploitative business interests and a predatory state development program.

Given the long fascination with headhunting in popular thought, it is surprising that no comparative study of headhunting has been undertaken. A few critical essays, highlighting aspects of specific headhunting practices and controversies about their interpretation, have been published (Downs 1955; McKinley 1976; Needham 1976), but there has never been either an edited volume that specifically addresses the topic, or a critical discussion of the history and imagery of headhunting in Southeast Asia.

The present volume is only the beginning of the long process of analytic synthesis concerning the practice and significance of headhunting. We define headhunting as an organized, coherent form of violence in which the severed head is given a specific ritual meaning and the act of headtaking is consecrated and commemorated in some form. The contributors to this volume have all done ethnographic fieldwork in living cultures in Southeast Asia, where headhunting, although perhaps no longer practiced, is still of great symbolic importance. They join original fieldwork materials with historical and archival documents. Each contributor has worked intensely in an indigenous language and collected oral histories, ritual texts, and memories of the past in context. As a result of this closeness to the lived experiences of those touched by headhunting, each takes the position that the material "facts" of headhunting cannot be understood independent of its symbolic and ritual elaboration.

In taking this stance, we here place ourselves in opposition to most of the recent anthropological literature on war and violence (Ferguson 1984; Ferguson 1988; Ferguson and Whitehead 1992; Foster and Rubenstein 1986; Haas 1990; Turner and Pitt 1989), which emphasizes materialist and evolutionary models. We do not treat headhunting as a form of "primitive warfare" on a ladder of evolutionary stages leading to more complex formations, nor as an expression of "man's aggressive nature" or the "inevitable" violence that occurs in stateless societies because of competition over scarce resources. We do, however, draw on some of the insights that have emerged in studies of the relationship between expanding states and indigenous warfare to historicize the phenomenon of headhunting and place it in a wider regional perspective (Drake 1989; Gibson 1990; Ferguson and Whitehead 1992).

The theoretical approaches used in these essays are eclectic, ranging from literary and symbolic analyses to studies of political economy and ethnohistory. Still, seven themes emerge as important in a number of papers: (1) headhunting, slavery, and trade; (2) headhunting and state formation; (3) heads as political symbols; (4) heads as gendered symbols; (5) headhunting and human sacrifice; (6) "headless" headhunting rituals; and (7) headhunting scares and rumors as part of the "culture of state terror" that emerged after pacification and transformed the meaning of the headhunter in Southeast Asia. These seven themes, in turn, link the papers in this volume with a wider literature.

Headhunting, Slavery, and Trade

The study of any cultural practice must always recognize its changing historical circumstances. Few accounts of headhunting in Southeast Asia go back further than the nineteenth century, a time when all indigenous peoples had been deeply affected by interactions with a variety of states, from coastal Malay sultanates to Hindu kingdoms to the Netherlands East Indies administration. The notion of a "precontact" period has never had much meaning for a part of the world where relations of trading and raiding across great distances predate the period of colonial control by at least several centuries (Reid 1988). But until the beginning of this century (and sometimes much more recently), the peoples discussed in these studies retained a certain degree of tribal autonomy over internal political and ideological systems, and responded creatively to a changing set of political and economic forces.

The most important precolonial institutions in Southeast Asian political economy were slave-raiding and coerced trade (Reid 1988). As peoples connected by water but separated by land, Southeast Asians had a dense network of relatively rapid maritime trade connections at a time when few coastal peoples had ever traveled over the rough terrain of the interior. States, located near the coast, could try to compel trade with inland peoples through military threats, or entice it with gifts, trade opportunities, and pledges of political support. The peoples of the interior wanted to receive metal tools, weapons, gold, jewelry, porcelain, and cloth, and they traded food, forest products such as camphor, sandalwood, and benzoin, and human captives. Slaves were one of the most important "local products" exchanged from the hinterland for sale in entrepôts along the coasts, and they were usually obtained by raiding inland communities:

Before indentured labor was developed in the nineteenth century, the movement of captive peoples and slaves was the primary source of labor mobility in Southeast Asia. Typically it took the form of transferring people from weak, politically fragmented societies to stronger and wealthier ones. The oldest, and demographically most important movement was the border raiding against animist swidden cultivators and hunter-gatherers by the stronger wet-rice cultivators of the river valleys. . . . There seems little doubt that the majority of the Southeast Asian urban population prior to about 1820 was recruited in a captive state. . . . Slavery was an important means whereby animistic peoples were absorbed into the dominant Islam of the city and coast. (Reid 1983: 28–29, 170–71)

Because much of Southeast Asia was underpopulated until the eighteenth and nineteenth centuries, the key to political control was the control of labor power. Land was relatively abundant, but society was held together by bonds of debt, obligation, and obedience. Most forms of slavery in Southeast Asia seem to have originated in debt bondage, but they have gradually diversified into complex "closed" systems of enduring social stratification and "open" ones of slaves captured primarily for external trade (Watson 1980; Reid 1983).

The history of Southeast Asian states is recorded primarily through their impact on regional trade. From the seventh century to 1025, the Srivijayan state dominated the western part of the archipelago, until it was defeated by the Chola dynasty of South India. The earliest rulers were content to provide a neutral commercial facility for the exchange of Western, Chinese, and Southeast Asian products, but later ones became more active in seeking out products from the interior to trade on the international market (Hall 1985: 210). For two hundred years, Arab, Indian, and Chinese traders tried to negotiate directly with spice growers and forest dwellers to get products for which there was a growing demand in southern China and Europe. By the thirteenth century, local intermediaries had become more important in the trade, and foreign merchants had begun to deal with coastal go-betweens who provided goods for the international trade.

The explosive growth of the Sulu state of the southern Philippines during the eighteenth and nineteenth centuries derived from the use of slave labor to extract forest and sea produce. The isolated interior peoples of the Bisayan islands and Luzon provided this labor (Warren 1981). On the Malay Peninsula, it was the small, dark-skinned peoples known as Orang Asli who were often kidnapped and enslaved by the Malay populations ruled by the sultan (Endicott 1983). The coastal sultanates of Bima and Goa were centers of an extensive slave trade that drew primarily on Bali and the islands of Nusa Tenggara Timor, purchasing people from communities of shifting cultivators and using them in irrigated rice cultivation and as domestic servants (Needham 1983).

Many of the shifting cultivators themselves participated in slave-raising and slave-trading. In central Borneo, a class of aristocrats was freed from subsistence production to engage in long-distance trade because they owned a number of hereditary slaves (Rousseau 1990). The Iban, perhaps the most famously predatory group in Southeast Asia, took prisoners as well as heads, and used their captives for ransom, sale, or adoption. Success in headhunting was marked by tattoos and an ascending sequence of renown-building rituals for the greatest warriors. As in West Sumba, the overall ethos was one of achieved ranking, in which every individual was expected to prove himself on the warpath. Even war captives were eventually ritually enfranchised and adopted into the household (Freeman 1981: 47). The frequent headhunting raids of the Iban have been interpreted by Vayda (1969) as a form of predation motivated by the need for territorial expansion, but this "need" was constructed out of social and political circumstances and cannot be understood as purely "ecological."

Although many isolated shifting cultivators made violence an important part of their culture and self-concept, some did not. Headhunting was not limited to a single subsistence type or ecological niche that produced a "primitive warrior" complex. Some more stratified peoples, such as the Toraja, took heads on the

Illus. 1. A Kayan party sitting in the gallery of a longhouse. From Hose and McDougall 1912, plate 68.

warpath and also had large proportions of their own populations who worked the rice terraces as slaves and could be exported as well (Bigalke 1981; Reid 1983). The different historical experiences of a wide range of peoples in relation to violent raiding, coerced trade, and debt bondage combined to produce their present evaluations of violence and aggression. Some hinterland peoples, such as the Buid of Mindoro (Gibson 1990) or the Semai of Malaysia (Robarchek 1990), responded by retreating altogether from any violent encounter.

Both Gibson and Robarchek argue that the absence of violence in the societies they studied did not stem from an absence of natural scarcity or individual sentiments of anger, grief, and rage. Instead, these groups chose to flee violent encounters because they thought they had little to gain, and much to lose, by retaliating. Violence is one possible response to the exploitation of a weaker group by a stronger one, but so is flight. Military expansionism and aggression are now totally alien to the Buid, Gibson argues, because they have spent centuries retreating from external aggressors infinitely more powerful than themselves. Their current emphasis on egalitarian sharing and peacefulness is as much a product of history as is the glorification and celebration of violence by those groups who profit by it:

It is quite inaccurate to characterize members of [nonwarlike] societies as "submissive": They do not respond to efforts to dominate them with violence as do the Ilongot and Iban, but they are just as insistent on the maintenance of their political autonomy. . . . Any explanation of the role of violence and domination in the social lives of insular Southeast Asia shifting cultivators must be sought in terms of their relations to the regional political economy. . . . In political economies based on the coercive extraction of surplus value from neighboring societies, inter-group violence may even be fetishized as a product of mystical vitality itself. Thus violence is neither a necessary part of social life, nor is it necessarily seen as evil; there are societies which systematically devalue it, just as there are societies which view it as the ultimate good when exercised in appropriate contexts against the right opponents. (1990: 145)

The account by Tsing of the Meratus of Kalimantan in this volume presents a view of headhunting from "the victim's perspective"—that is, perceived by those who were primarily prey rather than predators in the system. Heirs to an oral tradition about raids from precolonial kingdoms into the interior, the Meratus talk about violence as a product of the state, and believe the Indonesian government has headhunters in its employ. Many small-scale peaceful societies in the hinterland have images of headhunters as forms of spirit beings or afflictions. Among the Wana of Sulawesi, "headhunting spirits" give you headaches and piercing pains in the skull (Atkinson 1989). The Manggarai of Flores say that black-robed forest spirits (*gorak*, reminiscent of Catholic missionaries) and headhunters (*penyamun*) kidnap children and put their heads under churches (Erb 1991: 121).

Another perspective on the problem of tribes and states comes from the oral epic that describes the founding of the sultanate of Brunei and includes extensive descriptions of bloody headtakings from indigenous peoples in the interior (Maxwell, this volume). In some distant, pre-Islamic past, the sultan's ancestors were presented as headhunters, and the epic is still performed as a charter for the present monarchy. In this way, the state acknowledges and even exaggerates the violence involved in the conquest of the interior. Those groups from whom heads were taken were placed in a subordinate, tributary relationship to the ruler at the capital. The superiority of the center was shown by Awang Halak Batatar's refusal to accept heads from his victorious forces. He would take only booty and plunder, placing himself above the exchanges of heads that continued in the hinterland. Many centuries later, in 1849, James Brooke used Iban troops to put down rebellious Malay groups and followed a similar strategy of hiring headhunters but refusing their trophies.

Heads were involved in complex ceremonial exchanges that would seem to give them an "exchange value." In northern Luzon, a Chinese Ming jar could be accepted as the compensatory payment to end a feud following a beheading (Cole 1912: 15). In Timor, Dutch officials received recently smoked heads as tribute and "proof of a righteous bond with the Company" (McWilliam, this volume), and in Borneo, a British district officer volunteered to keep an inventory of severed heads, which he allowed to circulate for ritual purposes, so that the indigenous people could continue to hold traditional ceremonies without taking new heads (Metcalf, this volume). The exchange of firearms for human heads is reported from many parts of the world, from sale of shrunken Jivaro heads for rifles in Amazonia (Bennet Ross 1984) to accounts of a similarly gruesome trade between Sumbanese rajas and Endehnese pirates, or the consecration of guns as a replacement for heads by Wona Kaka, a Kodi headhunter who raided Dutch forces (Hoskins 1987).

Headhunting and State Formation

The historical contrast between the perspectives of predators, prey, and the overseeing state must be evaluated carefully. Working on materials from tribal societies in Burma, Jonathan Friedman has argued that "societies practicing headhunting, competitive feasting, continual warfare, with tendencies toward reciprocal exchange, the dissolution of chiefship and even the establishment of anti-chiefs in isolated village communities were structural transformations of societies based on large scale politically expansive theocratic chiefdoms, that took slaves instead of heads, maintained a system of strictly asymmetrical marriage and tended via the extension of tributary relations towards state forms of organisation" (1985: 123). His argument is based on an assessment of the various historical constraints placed on the "expansionist-accumulative kind of tribal reproduction." One type of society, exemplified by the Kachin, tried to expand production and to convert the goods produced into rank through feasting. Thus, the slaves they accumulated were eventually assimilated into "grandchildren" and became part of the labor force. Another type of society, exemplified by the Naga, took heads instead of slaves and converted the heads into "ancestors," who were supposed to maintain fertility and bring good crops: "Ancestral force is thus siphoned off from one group to another in an inexorable struggle to maintain or restore declining fertility" (Friedman 1985: 125).

Friedman opposes slavetaking systems, which he says emphasize an accumulation of labor, to headtaking systems, which emphasize an accumulation of "soul force" (Friedman 1979, 1985). In doing so, however, he commits the familiar error of assuming that there must be a term that mediates between heads captured on the warpath and fertility. Kruyt (1906), trying to describe what motivated Toraja headhunting, suggested that there might be a "soul substance" or "life fluid" inside the skull, although he admitted this was not a native category. Needham (1983) criticized Kruyt roundly for confusing an association with a causation. His article makes a fair point, but has perhaps done the field of comparative studies of headhunting a disservice by discouraging others from exploring the connections between fertility and violence so evident in the ethnographic material. Fearful of overreading native metaphors concerning heads, few people have attempted any broader analytic synthesis of *why* severed heads embody some form of vitality.

Applying Friedman's model to the societies of Borneo, the Philippines, Sulawesi, and Eastern Indonesia surveyed in this book, we do not find such a sharp distinction between slavetaking and headtaking. Most peoples took both, although in varying proportions. The more egalitarian societies of Borneo and the Philippines integrated captives into the society, whereas in Sulawesi, Timor, and Sumba there were classes of hereditary slaves. Only in parts of Eastern Indonesia (Timor, East Sumba) was asymmetrical marriage associated with the shift to stratified state systems. It is quite possible, however, that an intensification of the slave trade in Eastern Indonesia in the late eighteenth and early nineteenth centuries (Needham 1983; Reid 1983) increased the number of raids carried out by inland peoples, and thus also the number of heads taken and perhaps the degree of political centralization.

Headhunting plays an important role in two quite different political systems on Sumba. In East Sumba, it is associated with territorial conquest by noble lords, who seek to encompass both captured heads and subservient populations as "subjects," whereas in West Sumba it is part of a more competitive system of raids concerned primarily with revenge. It seems reasonable, given strong cultural similarities, to suppose that the two systems are, as Friedman suggests, "structural transformations" of each other, and the presence of strictly asymmetrical marriage in the east but not the west also fits his model well. State formation was always precarious in the precolonial period, however, and it was not until Dutch political control became a reality at the beginning of this century that the aristocratic privileges of the nobility became more permanent.

Any model of the shift from competitive raids to state tribute and incipient hierarchy must take into account the contingent circumstances of colonial contact and regional political conditions. Some aspects of Friedman's model are relevant to the argument McWilliam presents that "the ritual management of ceremonial violence served as the creative basis for attaining autonomous political power" for the Nabuasa clan of Southwest Timor. Looking at the imperialistic ambitions of one particular warrior clan in the nineteenth century, he shows how the clan members articulated a

Illus. 2. An Iban war party in the jungle. From Hose and McDougall 1912, plate 99.

diarchic political order in which conceptually male and female functions overlay a complex of unstable and shifting alliances (McWilliam, this volume).

Though earlier commentators have seen Timorese heads taken as a kind of "tribute" to invisible ancestral spirits (Middelkoop 1960: 70), McWilliam argues that success in headhunting had important political and historical consequences. Nabuasa headhunters managed to usurp a position of political centrality through their management of war, and were at the peak of their power just before the Dutch took administrative control of Amanuban in the first decade of the twentieth century.

"Pacification" itself caused a fall in prestige for the headhunters, but the long period of indirect Dutch intervention in the political process during the nineteenth century seems to have intensified armed conflict and thus the importance of war ritual. By signing treaties with as many specific rulers and claimants to power as came forward, the Dutch legitimated many rival chiefs and encouraged the fragmentation of opposing political forces. Male ritual authority over warfare became crucial at the turn of the century because of contingent historical circumstances that destabilized most of the island. It gave a new cast to the diarchic theory of power, placing warrior leaders at the head of an incipient state formation. After pacification, the end to raiding resulted in the greater importance of female ritual authority over the management of agriculture. One form of incipient state, based on achievement in combat, was displaced by another, based on the generalized and shared links to the land, in a form more acceptable to the new colonial government.

The Head as a Political Symbol

The taking of a head as a trophy of combat and proof that a person has been killed is a practice found all over the world, but it does not fit our definition of headhunting unless the head is the focus of ritual attention. Attempts to preserve heads and bestow upon them a particular ceremonial role have, in different societies, begun with a separation of the flesh from the skull. North American Indians preserved only the scalp, roughly dried, whereas lowland South American Indians perfected techniques that used the complete outer covering, carefully dried and molded into shape, to produce the famous boneless "shrunken heads" of the Jivaro (Bennet Ross 1984; Siverts 1975). Though Maori warriors managed, in a more temperate climate, to dry the whole head, almost all the peoples of Southeast Asia preferred the more hygienic alternative of preserving only the bone. Thus, on Borneo, heads were skinned by privileged village women, on Sumba they were boiled, and on Timor they were smoked until no flesh was left.

A great number of accounts report that taking heads was associated with certain positive benefits that accrued to the whole group, in terms of either status improvement, better health, or a release from mourning. Individual participants could also cross the threshold to manhood, become eligible for marriage, or be released from debt. In many headhunting societies, any head would do—and the most frequent victims were older people, pregnant women, and children because they provided easy prey (Freeman 1970; Rousseau 1990). In other societies, like those of both East and West Sumba, where anxieties about rank were more prominent, the head of a nobleman had to be taken to avenge the death of an important leader, and women and children were taken captive rather than killed.

Headtaking is often interpreted as a form of insatiable violence. McKinley notes, "One is tempted to believe that the discovery of this custom was immediately welcomed by the various Euro-American powers of the last two centuries as living proof that there were indeed blood thirsty savages in their tropical possessions" (1976: 92). But ethnographic accounts of Southeast Asian headhunters indicate that the ritual importance of severed heads may in fact have acted as a constraint on raiding. Geddes offers one case from Borneo:

> The value placed on heads itself actually tended to limit warfare. Presentation of the heads to the gods had to be made on pain of misfortune otherwise, but presentation, with its accompanying festivities, was costly in food and effort. There was little temptation, therefore, to collect heads randomly or often. . . . The balance of power within the Land Dayak world usually restricted headcollecting to small encounters which the losers would break off at the first loss to await an occasion more favorable to themselves. (Geddes 1973: 53)

Kruyt's ethnography of the Toraja of Sulawesi, reanalyzed by Downs, presents a similar case, showing that heads were taken largely to keep crops from failing and to avert sickness, without an idea that a great accumulation of heads was necessary for ritual purposes: "The *tanoana* [life force] of the enemy was taken to weaken them, not to strengthen their attackers. The fact alone that a single head was sufficient for victory indicates that it was a symbolic act and not a matter of gathering a life-giving substance" (Downs 1956: 64).

The question of why enemy heads should be treated as ritual objects is a complicated one. Maxwell (1992: 52) surveyed sources on headhunting for 23 Borneo groups and came up with ten different reasons for taking heads. The most common ones given by informants were to suspend mourning for important men, to impress a potential bride, to display one's honor and prowess, to prevent sickness or famine, to promote better crops, and to even the score in feuding. Somewhat less common reasons were to mark an initiation into manhood, to increase the fertility of village women, to gather slaves for the afterworld, and to atone for adultery. Most groups cited several reasons in combination, and they are difficult to distinguish clearly.

McKinley, surveying the ritual beliefs associated with Borneo headhunting, noted that war raids were associated with cosmic journeys. The head became a companion on these journeys, and was treated with great friendliness once it arrived in the village: it was fed with meat and rice wine, fires were lit for it on cold nights, and women even coddled and nursed it like a baby. McKinley interprets this as the "ritual incorporation of the enemy as friend." It was particularly important to bring home the face of the victim, since it signified his "social personhood" (1976: 94). Building on Mary Douglas's idea of ritual pollution as "matter out of place," McKinley argues that the humanness of the enemy is out of place, so his head must be severed and put "back in place" in the home of the victor. He concludes:

To celebrate a head feast is to declare that much of what is alien and threatening—what lurks beyond the edges of a tribal life-world—can be successfully absorbed by the tribe. . . . One main crime of the enemy is that he is so strikingly human yet he lives in a region that has been zoned as non-human. . . . A relocation of the enemy's humanity is a needed correction.

The most telling point about headhunting is that killing alone is insufficient to do away with the phenomenological threat posed by the headhunter's categorical enemy. He, or his most human qualities, must be brought into the fold to further totalize the headhunter's society as the only human realm. (1976: 123–26)

McKinley argues that headhunters conducted their raids because of a "humanistic moral philosophy" that nevertheless "fell short of encompassing the brotherhood of man" (1976: 126).

The idea is intriguing, and McKinley's is certainly the most sympathetic analysis of headhunting in print, but this interpretation is hard to apply beyond Borneo. Headhunters on Sumba, Timor, and Sulawesi do not treat their heads with such "friendliness" (Hoskins 1989a; George 1991; McWilliam, this volume), nor are the groups that they raid categorically outsiders to such a degree. In fact, alliance alternated with hostilities in much of East-

Illus. 3. A Kayan woman dancing. In her right hand she carries a head dressed in leaves. From Hose and McDougall 1912, plate 102.

ern Indonesia and Irian Jaya (McKinnon 1991: 8; Valeri 1990a; Van der Kroef 1969). Applying McKinley's thesis to the Amaya people of the Moluccan island of Damar, Sandra Pannel (1992) argues that severed heads are ritually incorporated and appropriated by local peoples in ways that parallel the fascination with skull collecting and measuring shown by Western naturalists.

The Amaya say that they took heads because it was "customary," but also because the head was more portable than the whole body and could clearly encode the identity or otherness of the enemy. They thus confirm McKinley's point that the face must be taken in order to appropriate the physical symbol of social personhood. The head itself was not described as a friend but as a piece of "rotten fish," which they brought back from other islands to feed to the ancestors. The "fish" was cooked and smoked until the flesh, the hair, and, most importantly, the face were consumed, so the ancestors could incorporate the corporeality and identity of the other: "The bare skull, removed from the village and displayed upon stone platforms, in this context, does not encapsulate the identity of the other in the same way that the face does but functions as a tangible trophy of the act of appropriation" (Pannel 1992: 171–72).

At the same time that Amaya were hunting heads on Wetar and other islands, British naturalists A. F. Wallace and Henry Forbes were measuring and collecting heads as "specimens" to reconstruct the history of human racial differentiation and classify the peoples of the eastern archipelago within an evolutionary model of a common biological past. Pannel argues that both the Amaya and the Western scientists constructed narratives of headtaking that involved "travelling to other worlds"—for the Amaya, travel to a world of ancestral power; for the naturalists, time travel into their own primitive past (Pannel 1992: 173).

In both cases, the appropriation of the other also entails the incorporation of the other. The Amaya incorporated heads into the ancestral order by cooking them and turning an "external social person" into an "internal social person" (McKinley 1976: 120). Wallace and Forbes did so by displaying the skulls collected from the Tanimbar Islands of the Moluccas as evidence of earlier stages of human development in a hierarchical order determined by "scientific investigation."

The skeletal remains of non-Western peoples are arranged to demonstrate how different they are from us, and to reduce their personhood to a series of generic "racial characteristics." Pannel calls the description of the anatomical features of each of the "early races" a form of "discursive dissection" that pays no attention to the face as a total configuration of referents (Pannel 1992: 177). Relocated to museums, catalogs, and archives, these skulls are removed from their historical context in a society where ancestors are important, and are turned into evidence of a "timeless" state of primitive savagery. Once entangled in the processes of colonial representation, the heads, exported to Australia, Europe, and the United States, assume new meanings as trophies of the Western appropriation of indigenous history and personhood (Thomas 1991).

The complicated history of exchanges between local peoples and foreign powers must be situated within the parameters of indigenous notions of exchange. Headhunting has been explained primarily through exchange theory ever since Van Wouden's early synthesis of Eastern Indonesian materials (originally published in 1935, translated in 1968). Scholars trained within the Dutch tradition argued that headhunting had value because of the place it occupied in the reciprocal relations between groups (de Josselin de Jong 1937; Downs 1955). Peter Metcalf applies a version of this idea to the Berawan of Sarawak (this volume), arguing that death is "exported" through the taking of heads, because "the jealousy of the recently dead becomes someone else's problem." The explanation builds on the elaboration of mortuary rites through the practice of secondary burial, and can therefore apply to a number of Borneo societies, but not all of them. It also builds, however, on a more sophisticated reading of the imagery of headhunting and its own power to generate both a colonial mythology of the "ignoble Savage" and a countermythology in which the white man is equally implicated in perpetrating regional violence and preying on those who are largely defenseless.

Recent work, including Metcalf's essay, has gone beyond representing the complex as "a hermetic system linked to the antagonistic exchange of victims and souls" (George 1991: 538) to analyze it in relation to the historically situated interdependencies of coastal and hinterland societies, expressed in patterns of labor and trade exchange. George analyzes a story from the Salu Mambi that explains headhunting as originating in a violation of the moral relationship that binds siblings to one another. When the brother on the coast hoarded his goods and did not exchange them fairly, his counterpart in the highlands began to exact his own reciprocal payments in heads. Contemporary highland rituals reenact this bloody settling of scores to "present an ideal vision of exchanged relations that could be recalled and put into conscious tension against the real order of things" (George 1991: 557).

Tsing (this volume) studies a similar system from a different vantage point, arguing that Meratus highlanders who have often been the prey of coastal headhunters do not discuss violence in relation to exchange: "A victim's perspective looks out toward wider configurations of power rather than to the reciprocal equivalence of social units." The systematic deployment of violence at the borders of state rule has created a political strategy of craftiness and "fierce eyewitnessing" that both acknowledges the highlanders' vulnerability and resists intimidation.

Heads are ambiguous political symbols, and we do not want to lift headhunting out of history and make it into something discrete, essentialized, and timeless. There is no reason to assume a single explanation for all cases where heads are taken in raids or warfare. Instead, what all of the contributors to this volume try to do is to situate local meanings of the practice in relation to the contingent social and political factors that make headtaking a potent ritual act.

Heads as Gendered Symbols

The connection between the taking of heads and both human and plant fertility has provided a classic problem for anthropological interpretation. Recent feminist theory forces a rephrasing of this old problem in new debates about the relationship of masculinity and violence. On the one hand, the ritualized taking of life is seen in many societies as an essential component of masculinity, and headhunting is institutionally linked to initiation or the ability to marry. On the other, there is evidence that women play important roles in ceremonies held to welcome heads, and the rites as a whole celebrate a more generalized idea of fertility, not just a glorification of male aggressiveness.

The papers in this volume, when placed in a comparative perspective, show that more complex notions of masculinity and femininity must be used to understand how human reproduction is linked to the taking of human lives in these societies. We must first recognize the variety of ways headhunting is represented. Comparing Ilongot notions of gender with those of the Wana of Sulawesi, Atkinson notes, "For the Ilongot, women and men share the same basic humanity, but through headhunting, men (up until the early 1970s) could achieve a form of transcendence not available to women" (1990: 65). The Wana, who were usually the heads, not the headhunters, in the regional game of headhunting, do not link anger, courage, and masculinity in the same way. There were fewer activities that were exclusively male or female, and sexual differentiation was less marked.

The Huaulu of Seram, like the Wana and the Ilongot, are a small-scale people who live on hunting, gathering, and horticulture in the rain forest, but they have sharply differentiated roles for men and women. The elaborate taboos that apply to headhunting oppose men's exclusive prerogative to shed blood to women's bleeding at menstruation. The husband of a woman menstruating or giving birth is considered sufficiently polluted to be disqualified from any ritual activity, including headhunting. Valeri hypothesizes that "contact with bleeding women stunts the power of warriors by turning them from bleeders of humans into humans bleeding (just like menstruating women)" (1990b: 247). Women are not allowed to touch any of the weapons used in hunting or headhunting, since the active repression of points of similarity between the two terms (both involve bleeding) is necessary to sustain the contrast (between voluntary and involuntary loss of blood).

This system of taboos erects a hierarchy of values that contradicts a hierarchy of powers. The power of female pollution is much greater than the value of men as warriors, hunters, and performers of rituals: "It is almost only as killers of humans that men can be dangerous to women as generators of humans" (Valeri 1990b: 248). This may also explain certain evidence that men admire the mysterious generative powers of women, even as they fear them. Headhunting in the past was connected with initiation and the practice of incising the penis. Young boys could only be incised by a headhunter, a man "who had seen blood" and would make them bleed so that they could become full men:

The "fake menstruation" of boys was effective precisely because it was both a menstruation and a "fake." In producing the bleeding voluntarily and artificially, and thus in a manner that demonstrated male control, [subincision] negated menstruation, and thus femaleness, by the very act of *representing* it. Boys were made men in the extreme act by which the epitome of undergoing was transformed—significantly by a headhunter's

knife—into the epitome of acting and controlling. . . . Thus by bleeding
once and for all as women, men became forever different from women.
(Valeri 1990b: 260)

Today, now that headhunting has come to an end, male initiation rites no longer include the incision of the penis. "This lack
of a sign on their penises is one of the signs, for the Huaulu,
that nowadays they are less manly, and thus less different from
women, than their ancestors were" (Valeri 1990b: 259).

Manliness and bloodshed are linked in the sexual politics of
many societies (see the papers of George, Metcalf, and Tsing), but
the sexual attractiveness of the headhunter is most visible in De
Raedt's account—the only eyewitness account we have of a headhunting feast. Paradoxically, his account includes very important
ritual roles for women—as spirit mediums and as the prophetess
who leads the whole ceremony. Female ritual specialists were possessed by male spirits, who asked to be propitiated with gifts of
wine, betel nuts, and cloth. The women then performed an erotic
dance with the headhunter, and sang songs about how a headhunter enjoys more sexual pleasure than any other man.

Female spirit possession is supposedly an involuntary act:
women's bodies are used as receptacles for spirits of male daring
and courage. But the prophetess as a ritual leader has a range of
powers that defies models of female passivity and male forceful-
ness. The specific guardians and "spirit dwarfs" who accompany
men on a headhunting raid speak through her, and she directs
both the attack and the commemorative feast.

De Raedt's account is ambiguous about just how much conscious control the prophetess has over her pronouncements. She
should accompany the raiders and cast the first spear when the enemy village is sighted, but she does not take part in the violence.
She leads the rites to dedicate the head at the village shrine, and
may finish them with words that incite others to kill. Though she
was supposed to speak only when possessed by male spirits, De
Raedt's account shows that she could also be held accountable for
her own actions. This prophetess had been criticized for not heed-
ing the new laws that suppressed headhunting. In the feast that
De Raedt observed, she responded to this criticism by asking participants to seek out outlaws who could be killed with impunity,
and later by telling the young men that they should not try to

refill the baskets where heads were stored since the time of killings was past.

The Buaya case suggests that a combination of male action and
female speech is needed for ritual efficacy. Although Buaya men
may come to a feast to boast of their earlier killings and enjoy ex-
aggerated female attentions, they also submit to female direction.
These Philippine headhunters do not use a social logic in which
taboos separate male and female domains, as in Huaulu; rather,
they require female mediation and spiritual guidance for masculine violence to be realized in actual raids. The power of the
prophetess to inspire further violence was much feared in the
community. The sacrificial efficacy of the Buaya festival to dedicate the head involves a miming of erotic excitement and the
merging of the two sexes when male headhunting spirits inhabit
women's bodies.

Despite their differences, the Buaya and the Huaulu share a dialectical view of the relation of gender to ritual violence. Valeri
suggests that "sometimes . . . male and female must be separated
in order to preserve their distinctiveness, but they always imply
each other" (1990b: 271). The contingent life that women bring
into the world cannot be replaced by the knife of action. Male and
female are mutually implicated in almost all Southeast Asian
feasts of release and renewal, as we can see by looking at the recent controversies over the "seed symbolism" of heads taken by
the Iban of Sarawak.

Derek Freeman has argued most forcefully that the indigenous
model of fertility and increase is a cult of phallic symbolism. For
him, "the primary evidence . . . for a trophy head having phallic
significance is the culturally accepted fantasy that such a head
contains seed" (1979: 237). In the course of the major festival to
commemorate headhunting (the *gawai amat*, which is still performed), aspiring headhunters split open a coconut in imitation of
Lang Sengalang Burong, the Iban god of war, who split a human
head and found it filled with rice seeds, which he sowed to grow a
human crop. Freeman notes that the Iban describe a head as a
"pointed red pepper, quick river fish and scalded pendant cu-
cumber," and sing about mythical serpents, cobras, or crocodiles
that help them in the hunt. Drawing on a wide psychoanalytic
literature that, he claims, confirms that the "symbolic equation

head = phallus . . . may be accepted as one of the basic symbolic identifications of many human cultures" (1979: 236), Freeman concludes that trophy heads "have a phallic significance as symbols of the regenerative power of nature" (1979: 237).

But why must this regenerative power be specifically phallic? Davison and Sutlive, recent ethnographers of the Iban who have reexamined this argument, note that nowhere do the Iban explicitly identify heads with penises (1991: 178–79). They do repeatedly identify heads as "fruit," especially the fruit of the mythical ranyai palm that grows in the Iban land of the dead. In the invocation recited at the head feast, taking heads is seen as gathering the fruit of this tree in the afterworld. Once the head arrives in the village, it begins to cry like a baby, is "nursed" by various female deities, and is finally presented to the wife of the festival sponsor, its "mother." The allegorical representation of headhunting as agriculture is followed by another allegory in which headhunting represents sexual reproduction, and warriors go to battle to get children for their wives.

Davison and Sutlive argue that the ritual significance of Iban headhunting is sustained by an "organic metaphor of frugiferous reproduction, rather than one of phallic procreation" (1991: 203). They note that women often enthusiastically urged men to go off to take heads, because it was ritually portrayed as a first step in enhancing the fertility both of their own bodies and of rice. Dyeing thread with mordants and weaving it into traditional textiles was described as the "war path of the women," and the designs of the *pua* cloth that received the head were explicitly said to compel men to seek new heads:

If women, through the fertility of their bodies and their identification with the soil which brings forth rice, can be seen as the physiological agents of reproduction, they nevertheless require men to go headhunting in order to provide them with seed; only then may they realize the potential fecundity of their bodies. In this respect, headhunting is identified, not only as supplying the raw material of reproduction, but also as its logical precursor or antecedent. . . . While both men and women alike may have an equal interest in seeing the success of the rice harvest and the birth of children, it is men, as headhunters, who are ritually identified as being ultimately responsible for setting this cycle of fertility in motion and who, accordingly, are granted the highest honors in Iban society. This potentially antagonistic situation . . . is countered by the ritual significance of weaving . . . portrayed not only as the female equivalent of headhunting, but . . . identified as a "cause" of men's headhunting. (Davison and Sutlive 1991: 212–13)

The "vegetative model" of reproduction and increase is given support by the wide prevalence of myths that link headhunting to rice planting, and cause modern versions of headhunting rites to be described as "harvest festivals." Women officiate at many of these rites, and are called on to nurture and sustain the life contained in the skulls. Illus. 4 from *Pagan Tribes of Borneo* (1912) depicts women dancing with dried heads, which they pretend to take from the enemy, and use in parallel harvest dances and victory dances (Hose and McDougall 1912, 1: 114). In highland Sulawesi, Sumba, and Timor, heads are described as "fruits" or "rice sheaves" and are harvested from "trees." Weaving is also important as the counterpart of headhunting on Sumba and Timor: severed heads are draped with textiles to "cool" them, or wrapped in a textile bundle when they are reunited with the victim's body and buried (Hoskins 1989a), and Belu women on Timor say that textile weaving is the "headhunting of the women." Parallel versions of the taboos headhunters and their wives observe during a raid may also apply to a woman giving birth or to indigo dyers preparing their secret herbal potions (Hoskins 1989b). Even where women are rigorously excluded from participation in headhunting (as in Huaulu), their power to affect the outcome through pollution is recognized.

It is naive to assume that female importance in headhunting rites necessarily upholds an "essentially egalitarian ethos" between the sexes (Davison and Sutlive 1991: 213), since gender is often the most prominent dimension of inequality in competitive warrior societies. Like women on Sumba and Timor, Iban women sing lullabies to their babies that urge them to seek revenge, goad their suitors to go out on the warpath, and mock the bloody head when it is first brought into the house (Masing 1981: 308–9; Mashman 1991: 263). But in all of these societies, the gender differentiation between weaving and warfare appears dialectical rather than hierarchical, establishing a mutual dependence as well as a mutual opposition.

Illus. 4. Iban women dancing with human heads. From Hose and Mc-Dougall 1912, plate 106.

Headhunting and Human Sacrifice

The sacrificial element of headhunting has long been observed, and it is clear that in many cases a victim could be either beheaded immediately or brought home and kept alive for a later sacrifice. De Raedt (this volume) argues most forcefully that "a headhunt is a human sacrifice to the highest of the spirits," and he documents this assertion with a detailed account of the *sagang* ceremony in which a prophetess and spirit medium dedicates the head to the invisible powers. His account, like the accounts from Sumba and Timor, suggests a flirting with the idea of cannibalism. The Buaya prophetess sucks blood from the head (or, in the case observed, the knife). The Sumbanese headhunters pretend to eat some of the flesh, then throw it away. Timorese warriors speak of the hunger of the "cat" (that is, the headhunter) and of themselves as hunters, but do not actually consume their prey.

Sacrifice is usually distinguished from headhunting by the ritual dedication of the victim before immolation. In several societies, such as those of the East Sumbanese and the Buaya, a living captive could be brought back and beheaded right at the village shrine. This was often considered the best form of sacrifice, but was hard to realize in practice. It is clear from the comparative evidence brought together here that human victims can be dedicated to the spirits after death, and in fact that was done in virtually all of the societies of Southeast Asia that practiced headhunting.

The most famous exception is the Ilongot, who do not bring the severed heads back to the village, but simply toss them into the air and leave them where they fall. A closer reading of the detailed ethnographies of Michelle and Renato Rosaldo, however, shows that great significance is attached to the tossing off of the head, which is said to "lift the heart," provide a release from feelings of grief, and qualify a boy for a new ritual status marked by special earrings. Although there is no festival to welcome the head into the village of the victors, the headtaking itself is commemorated in a song—the *buayat*. Several years after headhunting was ended, Ilongot informants were so deeply disturbed by the recorded sounds of a headhunting celebration that they began to cry. M. Rosaldo suggests that although headtaking was not heavily ritualized, it nonetheless represented an emotional catharsis that was irreplaceable. The buayat, which has no translatable "sense," is sung during an all-night sacrifice that celebrates a killing, and effects a series of strengthenings and purifications that remove the "angry" smell of blood from the house. As they sing, men drink cane wine and boast about earlier killings until someone finally challenges them and they finish with a drunken brawl (M. Rosaldo 1980: 55–56).

Despite its informal, improvised character, even the Ilongot be-heading has the marks of a ritual act. It is not the killer who gets credit for the killings, but the one who lifts up the head and tosses it, thereby "removing a weight from his own heart" and achieving release from sorrow. The killing of the chicken and the expecta-tion of a violent struggle at the celebration that follows reflect common Southeast Asian themes: the violent act is never finished when it is committed, but must be reenacted in new perfor-mances, which finally integrate it into a coherent vision. Almost all the contributors to this volume report a similar animal sacri-fice that follows the headtaking and serves to both consecrate and commemorate the human victim. Thus, I would argue that the practices of the Ilongot do fit our definition of headhunting as a form of ritual violence and even sacrifice.

Scholars of religion with an interest in the symbolism of rit-ual killings have often cited human sacrifice as the crucial ele-ment in the violent origins of society (Girard 1977; Burkert 1983; Hamerton-Kelly 1987). Renato Rosaldo conceded that Ilongot headtaking could be interpreted as "a kind of peculiar sacrifice" (Hamerton-Kelly 1987: 253). (His earlier discussions indicate that he may have meant that it was instead a *piacular* sacrifice, mean-ing an act performed to atone for a misdeed.) His key argument in response to these theorists, however, was that "headhunting has to be considered from the position of more than one subject" (Hamerton-Kelly 1987: 242). Girard's theories of mimesis and ri-valry could help explain a young man's desire to take a head, but not an older man's urge to do so out of grief and rage in loss. Not-ing that mourning prohibitions are lifted after a successful head-hunting raid in a large range of societies, Rosaldo argues that headhunting stems from a deep psychological need to conquer death, which, however, triggers different processes in young men and older men (Hamerton-Kelly 1987: 243).

Lincoln, working from texts concerning the sacrificial practices of "debreasting, disarming and beheading" among the Scyths and the Amazons, proposes that "sacrifice is most fundamentally a logic, language and practice of transformative negation, in which one entity—a plant or animal, a bodily part, some portion of a per-son's life, energy, property or even the life itself—is given up for the benefit of some other species, group, god or principle that is understood to be 'higher' or more deserving" (1991: 204). He includes beheadings in the same category as the Amazon woman's decision to cut off her breast to give greater strength to her arm, stressing how sacrifice is always part of hierarchy and the "radical asymmetry that exists between the sacrificer and sacrificed." This view reflects the highly stratified societies of antiquity (and their fertile imaginations—as Amazon debreasting may indeed be only imagined) but is more problematic in the shifting inequalities of Southeast Asia, where such radical asymmetries are subject to frequent historical reversals.

Maurice Bloch has recently formulated a theory of ritual as "rebounding violence" that explains the ritual aspect of headhunting as "a result of the attempt to create the transcendental in religion and politics" (1992: 7):

The basis of the symbolism is the need for establishing apparently immortal human structures on the necessarily mobile basis of human reproduction. This is done by creating an image of an inverted reproduction which ultimately requires the symbolic or actual presence of outsiders, who are there to have their vitality conquered, but who, unlike the main participants, do not then go on to conquer. This construction contains within itself the possibility of a further transformation into an imperialistic form. . . . When the actors of the ideology of rebounding violence are weak and in retreat, they will . . . develop the potential of the structure so that it is only concerned with reproduction. But . . . when expansionist aggression is a real possibility . . . the symbolism of the reconsumption of vitality is expanded and it becomes a legitimation of outwardly directed aggression. (Bloch 1992: 44–45)

Developed through a contrast of the peaceful Buid and the violent Ilongot that draws on Gibson's (1990) essay on the same theme, Bloch strives to construct a synthetic theory of ritual where violence is always at the core. In doing so, however, he must collapse and conflate many different historical experiences that do not reflect the same "irreducible structures" he purports to find.

Bloch defines headhunting as a form of sacrifice expressed as military aggression "directed fairly indiscriminately outside the basic social group" (1992: 44). Although he is supposed to be summarizing Ilongot practices here, detailed historical research (M. Rosaldo 1980; R. Rosaldo 1980) has shown that headhunting was only intermittent, with elaborate systems of alliances, peace covenants, and the suspension of hostilities. The Ilongot have a relatively underdeveloped symbolism of "inverted reproduction," and little concern for the "transcendental" or "immortal human structures." A great many other peoples in Southeast Asia, however, have elaborate mythologies of predatory spirits that hang upside down, invert proper forms of reciprocity, and show a much greater preoccupation with keeping heads and memories in order to turn them into something immortal.

In an earlier essay, "Death, Women and Power," Bloch argued on the basis of Jivaro and Iban material that "with headhunting the killer takes the substance of his enemies in order to increase himself by this notional means" (1982: 229). Headhunting was defined as a form of "positive predation" that recovers generative power by canalizing the pollution of death. But although the idea of stealing life from one's enemies is a common one, there is little evidence for either a "substance" captured or a "striving for immortality" among all headhunting peoples. Here, Bloch commits the same error of interposing an intermediate essence that Needham criticized in his essay, "Skulls and Causality": "The common premiss on the part of anthropological commentators on headhunting has been that in the clearly causal connexion between taking heads and securing prosperity there must subsist or intervene some forceful medium which brings about the effect. . . . The interpretation of headhunting . . . appears more a failure of European reason than a brutal misconception on the part of those who take heads in order to gain life" (1976: 79, 81). The idea that skulls might emanate or concentrate some substance was developed from the European interpretation of facts, like the assertion that a skull carried over growing rice makes the crop flourish, or a skull waved above the head of an old man restores his strength. When native informants failed to provide an explanation for the ritual efficacy of skulls, their ethnographers felt obliged to postulate a belief in a mystical force that, operating like electricity or magnetism, would produce these effects.

Bloch argues that all ritual systems, not just blood sacrifice or headhunting, are based on an idiom of "rebounding violence" in which the participants are symbolically sacrificed to become part of an immortal transcendent entity. Though this notion has the advantage of closing the conceptual gap between ourselves and

Illus. 5. Heads taken by Ibans. From Hose and McDougall 1912, plate 105.

headhunters, it also collapses all meaningful distinctions between real and symbolic violence. Violence is essentialized as the "irreducible core of the ritual process" (Bloch 1992: 1), rather than understood in its varying historical and cultural contexts. By generalizing the opposition between vitality and transcendence, Bloch loses sight of the specific social relations that link performers of these rites to the outside forces (neighboring peoples, the encroaching state, predatory traders or "developers") they represent. Most importantly, it fails to capture the most interesting tensions between real and imagined attacks.

Headless Headhunting Rites

Recent ethnographic reports collected in this volume indicate that headhunting ritual continues to thrive several generations after the suppression of headhunting as a practice. The elements that mark the rites as sacrifices remain: there is always a dedication of the victim, and usually some form of commemoration. There is often a second killing (most often, a decapitated chicken), and a re-enactment of the violent encounter. The Berawan use a bundle of *caang* leaves as an effigy that they carry in a procession (Metcalf, this volume), whereas the people of Pitu Ulunna Salu toss about a "stinking" coconut in a parade while sacred flutes are played (George, this volume). The violent taking of the leaves or coconut is then celebrated in song and storytelling long into the night.

What is striking about these rites is that no actual heads are taken, and the violence is all mimed, with the leaf bundle or coconut as a kind of stage prop to make the performance complete. What was once an effigy, a complement to the human skull, has become a surrogate, a replacement for the victim. In the somewhat more attentuated form that "headless headhunting rites" take on Sumba or Timor, verbal references to heads taken surface in alliance negotiations or land transfers, and the songs, dances, and costumes associated with predatory raids are performed for new audiences. Even when the rites are adapted to new contexts, however, they remain linked to a history of violence, and cast the long shadow of decapitation over the contemporary setting.

Bloch's analysis would encourage us to see this as a simple replaying of the old conquest of vitality theme without human blood shed. Commentators in this volume, however, propose different and varied interpretations. Metcalf (this volume) criticizes the psychological universalism of Rosaldo's famous linkage of grief and the headhunter's revenge (R. Rosaldo 1989) and argues for a social rather than a psychological reading of ritual meaning. George (this volume) contrasts one community in Sulawesi that reads its headhunting ritual as a representation of the historical past with another that sees it instead as an allegory about the battle between the sexes. In a related article, he argues that stories of heads taken from lowlanders by highlanders present a parable of violated reciprocity, evoking the new economic inequalities between two populations once linked as siblings (George 1991).

Animosities between domains in West Sumba that were once expressed through the exchange of heads have now been reformulated to permit the exchange of women, although marriage negotiations are still charged with the tensions of remembered violence (Hoskins 1989a, and this volume). The memory of the achievements of the Nabuasa clan has been translated into new forms of political prominence on Timor, although its relative position has suffered after pacification (McWilliam, this volume). Each of these transformations plays on the potential for violence to be transformed into alliance. Lévi-Strauss observed that waging war and exchanging wives could be understood as two sides of one opposition relation (1944: 122–39), and his observation holds as well for the ceremonial exchanges of Eastern Indonesia as it did for the endemic warfare of lowland South America.

But even when we accept the strong evidence for symbolic continuities between the violent past and the perhaps divisive but less bloody present, we must recognize that it is not merely the suppression of warfare that has had consequences for the world of hinterland Southeast Asian peoples. The transformations brought about by colonial conquest and the integration into a new nation-state have led to a new image given to the headhunter. Instead of demonizing the powers of predatory neighbors or ungenerous siblings, the headhunter is now seen as the servant of a more modern form of state terrorism.

Headhunting Scares and the Culture of State Terror

In many "out-of-the-way" parts of Southeast Asia (borrowing a phrase from Anna Tsing), the practice of headhunting expressed a group's marginal status in relation to traditional states, sultanates, or principalities. Any group that seemed primitive and isolated was at least suspected of raiding its wealthier and more "civilized" neighbors. As early as the nineteenth century, however, there were already reports that marginal peoples suspected the forces at the center of conducting their own raids on peripheral settlements. Tensions with the national government, foreign missionaries, and international business have been reflected in a new series of headhunting scares that focuses on what Metcalf calls "the unprecedented" in regional development: Pertamina oil drills standing off the shores of Borneo, huge stone cathedrals in Flores, dams in West Flores, bridges and irrigation projects constructed on Sumba or Timor.

Rumors about raids carried out by headhunters (*penyamun*) to provide human bodies to place in the cement foundations of new public-work construction projects have been reported on

Borneo since 1894 (Haddon 1901: 173–75) and have spread not only among peoples of the interior but also among Chinese and Malay coastal dwellers. In contemporary accounts, the headhunters themselves are often identified as Madurese or Buginese (Drake 1989: 270)—ethnic groups once heavily involved in the slave trade. But the logic of these reports is not simply a reflection of painful historical experiences; it also tells us about current political tensions, as Drake shows in his analysis:

The main motif of the rumor is "construction sacrifice" and the narrative elements repeatedly depict the Dayaks (or 'folk') as victims of state government needs. In fact the long history of Dayak relations with state societies is sufficient basis for this defensive, prejudicial stereotype. There has been a long-standing political context of brooding resentment about the loss of tribal sovereignty. . . . The tribe–state relationship is not just structural strain consisting of anxiety about prerogatives and confusion about intentions, but rather, injustice, distrust and suspicion as ideological representations of the state intrusions handed down through the generations, from the tributary economic exploitation by Malay rajadoms, through the sporadic suppressions by Dutch colonialism, to the nation-building efforts of modern states. (Drake 1989: 275–76)

In fact, rumors of heads taken for public-works projects can be found all over Southeast Asia, not just in Borneo. Erb (1991) and Forth (1991) present examples from Flores, Needham (1983) describes a headhunting scare on Sumba in the 1950s, and contributors to this volume report similar accounts from the other outer islands. While reporting to provincial authorities in Kupang, the Timorese capital, in 1979, I heard rumors that the new influx of long-haired European and Australian tourists signaled that heads would be taken and used to fortify the building of international hotels.

In its most attenuated form, the motif of construction sacrifice is found in Scandinavia, China, Russia, England, and Spain (Eliade 1970: 180, cited in Drake 1989: 274). However, the political meaning specific to many Southeast Asian societies is doubtless linked to its historical identification with a loss of political autonomy:

Colonial government found headhunting sufficiently repugnant to justify its forced suppression. Headhunting was . . . a predominant practice of hinterland political life . . . , the Dayak's particular form of interethnic (i.e. intertribal) relations . . . , a central tenet of the Dayak world view and a major principle of their traditional metaphysics. Their loss of political autonomy coincided with the loss of their traditional means of securing horticultural success, female fecundity, good health, and general prosperity by taking enemy heads for the gratification of their beneficent spirits. *The battle over tribal sovereignty was largely waged over the suppression of headhunting.* It is understandable that the forced suppression of this pivotal feature of their sociocultural order could take expression as public paranoia in headhunting scares. The simultaneous experiences with conscription into corvée labor projects or road-building and bridge-construction to consolidate colonial power further link headhunting, construction sacrifice, and state power intrusion. (Drake 1989: 277, my emphasis)

Not all peoples in the archipelago reacted to efforts to suppress headhunting with belief in government headhunters. In Kodi, West Sumba, a resistance movement lead by Wona Kaka, a prominent headhunter who raided Dutch forces in 1911, created a counter-image of headhunters as enemies of the state and defenders of local autonomy (Hoskins 1987). Since independence, Indonesian government officials have tried to reinterpret his legacy as part of a nationalist struggle against colonial rule, and named the local high school after him to signal his rehabilitated status. But questions remain about where the new boundaries of local autonomy should lie, and whether Sumbanese villagers really feel themselves part of the "imagined community" (Anderson 1983) of the new nation-state. Not all of Wona Kaka's descendants would agree that his resistance was only to the colonial administration. The ghost of this early "national hero" can also be summoned to encourage resistance to the imposition of centralized political control, evoking a somewhat different scenario of modern headhunters along the boundaries of state systems.

Sandra Pannel, describing a headhunting scare sparked by the presence of two Dutch engineers on the Moluccan island of Damar, argues that it may be more revealing to consider these stories as "political narratives which symbolically point to transformations in people's experiential world" (1992: 173). Before the beginning of this century, the Mayawo people expressed their opposition to outsiders by harnessing the power of their ancestors to go on headhunting raids:

Pacification of the region radically redefined notions of power obtaining between the different villages and groups in the region as well as between the local people and the Dutch colonizers. Up until this point in time, Mayawo were prevented from expressing and asserting their power in this way. The ascription of the headhunting practice to the Dutch, therefore, represents a recognition of the shift in the locus of power which pacification affected. The Dutch, in this context, are cast as the consumers of Mayawo vitality and, as such, are empowered to hunt heads in the way that the Mayawo once did. The cultural fragmentation and alienation that Mayawo experienced as a result of the Dutch colonialism is graphically reflected in these local beliefs. (1992: 173)

Pannel juxtaposes this local idea that the Dutch would need heads to strengthen the foundations of a quay they planned to construct with the fact that 29 heads from the Pacific, as well as numerous disembodied and decapitated masks, are currently on display in the South Australian Museum. Though Indonesian islanders were perhaps mistaken in believing that Western visitors were likely to abduct them and cut off their heads, they were not wrong to think that severed heads could be used by Western collectors as potent symbols of the power of the past:

In most cases, the skulls are presented against a highly pre-emptory background of bows, arrows, shields, spears, clubs and stone axes—the implements of warfare—which visually suggests to the public a cultural context of violence and barbarism. These icons of savagery are meticulously arranged in a fan-shaped configuration or aligned in linear fashion according to size. This spatial arrangement not only points to the classification of these items in terms of their perceived correspondence but also visually articulates the dominant taxonomic and metaphoric frames of evolutionism, the branching tree or the sequential line.

In some cases, the skulls are juxtaposed with photographs of various "native" individuals, giving observers the impression that they are looking at the actual person whose skull is exhibited. In one display case, entitled "New Britain," three elongated and distorted skulls are presented immediately below three separate photographs of "New Britain" men with the same cranial features of the skulls. What, indeed, is the visitor to make of this? (Pannel 1992: 173–74)

Western naturalists and museologists measured heads and classified them because heads were considered to be the repository of intelligence, knowledge, perception, and consciousness. Using heads collected from remote corners of the world, scientists quantified brain size, compared skull capacities, and ranked groups along an evolutionary scale in order to index cultural, racial, and mental characteristics. Displaying the remains of an individual apart from his or her social context, the naturalists turned him or her into a "specimen" and incorporated the person as an object of study in the comparative "science of man." Indonesian islanders who arranged skulls on a rack so that they could "look back into their past" and understand its meaning were not, in fact, acting on such different premises from Western scientists who sought skulls as evidence of the fact that all races had a common biological origin, and that these other societies simply represented a lower rung on the scale of human development.

A past tradition of headhunting is not necessary for rumors of head capture by government officials or missionaries to circulate (Erb 1991; Forth 1991), but it can contribute to the symbolic constitution of violence, often obliquely. Taussig (1987) argues that colonial officials in Colombia were terrified by accounts of native cannibalism and savagery and responded with their own "culture of terror"—torture, starvation, and executions justified with reference to the supposedly "savage" conditions of the New World. Perhaps the same logic can be found in documented instances of state terrorism in Indonesia: A 1992 news dispatch from the Indonesian government reported that the government paid a farmer in Irian Jaya four million rupiah ($1,965) when he gave government officials the head of a suspected guerrilla rebel who had sought shelter with him for the night. The "reward" was intended to encourage other members of the local community to do the same, and amounted to several times the average annual income in the province. Fretilin, the resistance force fighting Indonesian government troops in East Timor, has published many photographs of human heads severed by government soldiers and displayed on bayonets to local people (Retboll 1984: 51). Government soldiers who take the heads of rebellious guerrillas are not, in the terms of our definition, engaged in headhunting as a form of ritual warfare, but they are using the particularly gruesome imagery of a much older form of combat to dramatize their power.

Current news stories of Serbian heads shown as trophies to journalists by Muslim forces in Bosnia Herzegovina have a similar relationship to the history of headhunting in Europe. The Montenegro highlanders of the former Yugoslavia had a tradition of feuding and headtaking that was finally suppressed in the nineteenth cen-

Illus. 6. An enemy's head decorated by Kayans with various charms. From Hose and McDougall 1912, plate 162.

tury (Boehm 1984), but they certainly cannot be considered responsible for present atrocities that mime their actions for other purposes.

Headhunting as Practice and as Trope

We can take the idea of headhunting as an important symbolic medium a bit further if we distinguish between the *practice* of headhunting as a form of ritual violence once widespread (but by no means universal) in Southeast Asia, and the *trope* of taking heads, which is known throughout the region and used to imagine new historical conditions in which heads might be taken.

Most of the contributors to this volume have devoted their energies to the worthy project of contextualizing headhunting, treating it not as an exotic, essentialized attribute of the native as savage, but as a traditional practice with a concrete historical setting and specific local symbolism. However, headhunting is a phenomenon that struggles against the boundaries of local contexts and appears (or is believed to appear) in many of the "wrong places": in regions where heads were never systematically taken, attributed to agents who would not acknowledge it as a part of their ancestral traditions. The figurative extension of the term "headhunting," its movement from the domain of traditional practice to the modern mythology of external powers, is what I call its life as a trope.

Treating headhunting as a trope in the postcolonial world brings out ways in which the term is employed to speak metaphorically about other relationships, which might be characterized as ones of inequality, economic exploitation, and an unequal voice in political decision-making. The metaphoric imagery of headhunting treads the boundaries of the small-scale societies where it was once practiced to echo wider tensions in tribe-state relations, or in the relations of local communities to the Catholic mission or international business. To say that this is a metaphoric extension of headhunting is not to say that the violence suggested by these links is always metaphoric. Sometimes (as when Fretilin resistance leaders are beheaded) it is quite literal, but literal in a different way from the traditional raid.

Headhunting was an important part of the historical heritage of many people in Indonesia, Malaysia, Brunei, and the Philippines. Yet the imagery of headtaking is much more widespread than the actual practice, causing us to consider the differential globalness and localness of tropes. As part of local cultural traditions, head-hunting had a number of meanings, which varied with the historical circumstances. As a more global image of the illicit appropriation of vitality and the exploitative relations between state and subject peoples, it has acquired new meanings. The figurative use of headtaking images plays on some of the same themes as the literal severing of the victim's head: there is the idea, suggested by McKinley (1976), that the victim's humanity is taken away and made part of another group, and also the sense that heads can reinforce construction projects because these projects can only be built at a great cost in human life and labor.

The problem of the meaning of modern headhunters is explored by Maxwell, Metcalf, and Tsing in this volume. All agree that ideas of white headhunters are not the direct product of traditional practices, but neither are they unrelated to the historical past. Discourses that portray headhunters as the ultimate savages are answered by the "savages" with the argument that they feel terrorized by the many "civilizing" forces that were supposed to lift them out of primitivism—the Church, the nation-state, the frightening new buildings erected by international business.

Heads are taken—in the imagination as in traditional practice—to seize an emblem of power, to terrify one's opponents, and to transfer life from one group to another. Modern and traditional perceptions of headhunting stress its place within a model of sacrifice that plays on obligations to give to powerful forces that may claim their share in human flesh. Moving away from a narrowly contextualized notion of headhunting, we can also attempt a broader comparative perspective by looking at the kinship between headhunters and other famous images of the exotic savage.

Headhunting is not combined with cannibalism in any Southeast Asian group (although it does seem to occur in Melanesia), but the two are so closely associated in the popular imagination that most people who heard I was working on headhunting responded by asking questions about the consumption of human flesh. Practices like cannibalism, baby sacrifice, and headhunting are conceptual props used rhetorically to draw a line between civilized and savage forms of existence, to suggest a temporal separation between "our" world and "theirs" (Arens 1979: 145; Fabian 1983). These associations suggest a deeper relationship with ideas of "organic tribute" and the theft of body parts, which are much more widespread than either the practice or the trope of headhunting.

In the Andean highlands of South America, Gose (1986) describes the figure of the sacrificer (nakaq) who steals body fat from isolated villagers, taking the grease back to the city where it is used to lubricate machines, develop metallurgy, and produce pharmaceutical medicines. Like the white headhunter (penyamun putih), the sacrificer is an urban outsider who lurks around in the dark, stalking his victims to steal their vitality as he drains their bodies of an energy-producing substance. He is associated with foreign visitors—tourists, officials, even ethnographers. More recently, headlines in the Los Angeles Times (1994) reported a series of attacks on Western women travelers in rural Guatemala who were seen holding local children and were believed to have abducted them for illegal adoptions or organ transplants. Both of these countermythologies of Western predation can be understood as variations on the Southeast Asian idea that skulls are collected from a community to sap its vital forces, and through exploitation of local energies lend durability and permanence to new constructions.

The history of colonial conquest and imperial expansion contains many examples of magical uses of parts of the body—often first attributed to a "native" culture of "animism and fetishism" and later believed (perhaps rightly) to be practiced by the Europeans themselves. Pietz traces the history of the "fetish" (from the Portuguese fetisso, "manufactured object"), which emerged in the seventeenth and eighteenth centuries as part of the trading language used on West African slave routes. He notes that it quickly came to be used derogatively for charms containing bits of human hair and fingernails or spittle. The notion of fetishism was used to contrast primitive religions, which relied only on magic and the worship of idols, with Protestant Christianity (and also, in many cases, to criticize folk Catholicism). "The discourse of the fetish has always been a critical discourse about the false objective values of a culture from which the speaker is personally distanced," Pietz notes (1985: 14).

The various uses made of body parts by governments and medical professionals are understandably open to multiple interpretations. American Indians told to surrender scalps to French and British forces during what are called the "Indian Wars" queried whether these trophies of combat might have some ritual importance for Europeans. Western visitors to the Malay archipelago who showed an intense interest in skulls, stuffed animals, and ancestral bones were asked by local people if they were able to bring these "specimens" back to life on their return (Wallace 1869: 460). The strange habits of the scientist, explorer, and adventurer were quite likely to lead him to be perceived as a "conjurer" who manipulated strange and mysterious forces. Taussig (1980) cites similar beliefs about contemporary nurses, doctors, and health workers who brandish syringes and are able to both infuse strange substances into the body and suck them out.

Uniting all these various historical expressions is the phenomenon of projection, in which an aspect of one culture is imposed, with a distorted meaning, on the cultures with which it comes into dialogue through the colonial encounter. Foreign intruders can be demonized through the very idiom of Christian demonology that they have taught to local populations (Taussig 1980). Global structures of power are rephrased in terms of sacrificial tribute and the theft of vitality, since they are experienced at the local level as sapping people's resources to support a more powerful political force. Since foreigners do take away wealth, in the form of precious metals, lumber, petroleum, or agricultural crops, there is an idea that this wealth must be paid for in sacrificial fashion. Production, power, and riches often depend on the extraction of local labor and a loss of autonomy, which can be felt as a theft of vitality. But the metaphysics of political economy are not exactly the same as those of sacrifice, so we must be cautious in how far we merge the tropic force of headhunting and its separate life as a historical practice.

It is not possible to pull the many strands of this discussion into any single, essentialized "headhunting complex" that can be found all over hinterland Southeast Asia. There is no convenient list of "characteristic" beliefs and practices that are always associated with the taking of heads and their ritual consecration. In fact, this discussion has served to highlight some of the fuzziest boundaries between headhunting, sacrifice, and other forms of traditional warfare. It is possible, however, to argue that contemporary transformations of the image of the headhunter reflect tensions between indigenous groups and states and can be interpreted as a form of protest against the loss of political autonomy. The new meanings given to headtaking since colonial conquest must be analyzed in a historical context, where violence symbolized self-determination and self-renewal through ritual means. Discourses that portray headhunters as the ultimate savages are answered by the natives, who argue that they feel terrorized by forces meant to "civilize" them.

It is useful to look at this shift in meaning as the opposition between headhunting as a historical practice and headhunting as a trope. But the opposition cannot be fully sustained, since the figurative "tropic" use of headhunting images can also inspire anachronistic "repetitions" of headtaking in new contexts. A trope is itself a form of social practice, and has its own historical development.

The point of this critical essay is to highlight conceptual continuities in the significance given to the head and its relation to widespread notions of the appropriation and incorporation of vitality. These notions are not unique to Southeast Asia, and have been extensively documented in many other societies. However, the symbolic extension of headhunting motifs into an indigenous countermythology that forms a critique of colonial conquest and postcolonial development seems to be found only in Southeast Asia. The widespread indigenous religious beliefs that the taking of life is necessary to carry out large construction projects and that the "flow of life" (Fox 1980) must be ritually regulated through exchange forms the basis for this reversal of predator and prey in an indigenous critique of externally imposed power.

Participants in headhunts in relatively isolated hinterland societies before the turn of the century were most often members of small-scale societies defending their autonomy against peoples from "across the border." At first, the new agents believed to covet heads in reimaginings were Dutch colonial officials, German or Polish missionaries, and European visitors. Now, they might also include Japanese petroleum engineers, Batak doctors, Javanese civil servants—all of whom are also perceived as disturbers of boundaries, threats to local control, and usurpers of traditional territory.

The Malay-Indonesian term *pembangunan* means both "development" and "construction." The development-centered policies of the Indonesian New Order under Suharto have come to be identified primarily with constructing new edifices: dams, offices, oil riggers, airports, schools, factories. Local people are told they must "make sacrifices" for state development, using a phrase (*mengkorban diri*) that suggests a literal offering up of local lives to bring these projects to completion. The idea that local heads might be taken and planted in the concrete foundations is not a simple trick of language, however. It stems from an accurate perception of a double standard, wherein peripheral peoples must sacrifice their freedom and well-being to contribute to the economic prosperity of the majority populations of the inner islands.

With this form of "internal colonialism," the historical pattern of the reversal of predator and prey first documented during the colonial period has carried over into the postcolonial era of economic expansion and transmigration. The state monopoly on the legitimate use of force has been reconstrued as a license to serve as a predator on indigenous lives and resources. Many indigenous peoples who once roamed through rain forests now find themselves living on barren hillsides, where they are outnumbered by Javanese transmigrants. Unable to continue in their traditional subsistence of hunting or gardening, they are forced to become wet-rice farmers, traders, or timber workers. Once stigmatized as violent pagans, they now turn this stigma back on their oppressors to express their own resistance to victimization.

If the idea of "development" headhunters had been the invention of a single individual, a prophet of resistance, then it might be interpreted as a strikingly imaginative act of cultural subversion and re-presentation. Since it is a widespread pattern of responses, a full countermythology that has appeared in many different parts of the archipelago, it must be analyzed instead as part of the new consciousness of the colonized.

The colonial agenda included remaking native consciousness and bringing indigenous peoples into the realm of civilized discourse (Dirks 1992; Thomas 1994). The idea of violent savagery was part of the script that legitimated conquest, but that violence was then supposed to be tempered by a new Christian conscience and Protestant work ethic. Instead, indigenous people have stolen the script and rewritten it. The reversal of predator and prey in the countermythology of headhunting presents a critique of colonialism and state domination: the violence of the periphery is turned around and said to prey on the victims of political centralization. This reversal has continued into the age of independent nation-states, and has come to focus on predatory development and the continuing inequalities between the people who once controlled areas of rich natural resources and the people who now sell them.

The headhunter is a stubborn image of violence threatening from the outside. His bloody knife cuts through to the secret regions where power is transferred and vitality is stolen. Most Europeans thought he would vanish from the stage of history by the middle of this century, but his time has not passed, and indigenous peoples will not let us forget it.

References

Anderson, Benjamin
1983 *Imagined Communities*. London: Verso.
Arens, William
1979 *The Man-Eating Myth: Anthropology and Anthropophagy*. New York: Oxford University Press.
Atkinson, Jane M.
1989 *Art and Politics in Wana Shamanship*. Berkeley: University of California.
1990 "How Gender Makes a Difference in Wana Society." In J. Atkinson and S. Errington, eds., *Power and Difference: Gender in Island Southeast Asia*. Stanford: Stanford University Press.
Barton, R. F.
1919 *Ifugao Law*. Berkeley: University of California.
1938 *Philippine Pagans: The Autobiographies of Three Ifugaos*. London: Routledge.
1949 *The Kalingas: Their Institutions and Custom Law*. Chicago: University of Chicago Press.

Bennet Ross, Jane
1984 "Effects of Contact on Revenge Hostilities Among the Achuara Jivaro." In R. B. Ferson, ed., *War, Culture and Environment*. Orlando: Academic Press.

Bigalke, Terence
1981 "A Social History of Tana Toraja, 1870–1965." Ph.D. diss., University of Wisconsin-Madison.

Bloch, Maurice
1982 "Death, Women and Power." In M. Bloch and J. Parry, eds., *Death and the Regeneration of Life*. Cambridge: Cambridge University Press.

1992 *Prey into Hunter: The Politics of Religious Experience*. Cambridge: Cambridge University Press.

Bock, Carl
1881 *The Headhunters of Borneo*. London: Oxford University Press.

Boehm, Christopher
1984 *Blood Revenge: The Anthropology of Feuding in Montenegro and Other Tribal Societies*. Lawrence: University Press of Kansas.

Burkert, Walter
1983 *Homo Necans: The Anthropology of Ancient Greek Sacrificial Ritual and Myth*. Berkeley: University of California Press.

Cole, Fay-Cooper
1912 *Chinese Pottery in the Philippines*. Chicago: Field Museum of Natural History.

Davison, Julian, and Vinson H. Sutlive, Jr.
1991 "The Children of Nising: Images of Headhunting and Male Sexuality in Iban Ritual and Oral Literature." In V. Sutlive, ed., *Female and Male in Borneo: Contributions and Challenges to Gender Studies*. Shanghai, Va.: Borneo Research Council Monograph Series.

De Josselin de Jong, J. P. B.
1937 *Studies on Indonesian Culture*. Vol. 1, *Orata: A Timorese Settlement on Kisar*. Amsterdam: Foris.

Dirks, Nicholas B., ed.
1992 *Colonialism and Culture*. Ann Arbor: University of Michigan Press.

Downs, R. E.
1955 "Headhunting in Indonesia." *Bijdragen tot de Taal-, Land-, en Volkenkunde* 111: 40–70.

1956 *The Religion of the Bare'e Speaking Toradja of Central Celebes*. The Hague: Uitgiverij Excelsior.

Drake, Richard Allen
1989 "Construction Sacrifice and Kidnapping Rumor Panics in Borneo." *Oceania* 59: 269–79.

Endicott, Kirk
  1983 "Slavery and Slave Raids Against the Orang Asli of the Malay Peninsula." *Borneo Society Journal.*
Erb, Maribeth
  1991 "Construction Sacrifice, Rumors and Kidnapping Scares in Manggarai." *Oceania* 62 (2): 114–26.
Fabian, Johannes
  1983 *Time and the Other: How Anthropology Makes Its Object.* New York: Columbia University Press.
Ferguson, Brian
  1984 *War, Culture and Environment.* Orlando: Academic Press.
  1988 *The Anthropology of War: A Bibliography.* Occasional Paper no. 1. New York: The Harry Frank Guggenheim Foundation.
Ferguson, Brian, and Neil L. Whitehead
  1992 *War in the Tribal Zone: Expanding States and Indigenous Warfare.* Santa Fe: School of American Research Press.
Forth, Gregory
  1981 *Rindi: An Ethnographic Study of a Traditional Domain in Eastern Sumba.* The Hague: Martinus Nijhoff.
  1991 "Construction Sacrifice and Headhunting Rumors in Central Flores (Eastern Indonesia): A Comparative Note." *Oceania* 61: 257–66.
Foster, Mary LeCron, and Robert A. Rubenstein
  1986 *Peace and War: Cross-cultural Perspectives.* New Brunswick, N.J.: Transaction Books.
Fox, James J.
  1980 *The Flow of Life: Essays on Eastern Indonesia.* Cambridge, Mass.: Harvard University Press.
  1988 *To Speak in Pairs: Essays on the Ritual Languages of Eastern Indonesia.* Cambridge: Cambridge University Press.
Freeman, Derek
  1970 *Report on the Iban.* New York: Humanities Press.
  1979 "Severed Heads That Germinate." In R. H. Hook, ed., *Fantasy and Symbol: Studies in Anthropological Interpretation.* London: Academic Press.
  1981 "Some Reflections on the Nature of Iban Society." Occasional Paper, Research School of Pacific Studies, Australian National University, Canberra.
Friedman, Jonathan
  1979 *System, Structure, and Contradiction in the Evolution of "Asiatic" Social Formations.* Copenhagen: National Museum of Denmark.
  1985 "Post-Structuralism and the New Moon." *Ethnos* (1–2): 123–33.
Furness, William H.
  1902 *The Home Life of Borneo Headhunters.* Philadelphia: Lippincott.

Geddes, William
   1973 *Nine Dayak Nights*. Oxford University Press.
George, Kenneth
   1991 "Headhunting, History and Exchange in Upland Sulawesi." *Journal of Asian Studies* 50 (3): 536–64.
Gibson, Thomas
   1990 "Raiding, Trading and Tribal Autonomy in Insular Southeast Asia." In J. Haas, ed., *The Anthropology of War*. Cambridge: Cambridge University Press.
Girard, Rene
   1977 *Violence and the Sacred*. Baltimore: The Johns Hopkins University Press.
Gose, Peter
   1986 "Sacrifice and the Commodity Form in the Anes." *Man* 21 (2): 296–310.
Haas, Jonathan, ed.
   1990 *The Anthropology of War*. Cambridge: Cambridge University Press.
Haddon, Albert
   1901 *Headhunters Black, White and Brown*. London: Methuen.
Hall, Kenneth
   1985 *Maritime Trade and State Development in Early Southeast Asia*. Honolulu: University of Hawaii Press.
Hamerton-Kelly, Robert G., ed.
   1987 *Violent Origins: Ritual Killing and Cultural Formation*. Stanford: Stanford University Press.
Hose, Charles
   1927 *Fifty Years of Romance and Research: Or, a Jungle Wallah at Large*. London: Hutchinson.
Hose, Charles, and William McDougall
   1912 *The Pagan Tribes of Borneo*. 2 vols. London: Macmillan.
Hoskins, Janet
   1987 "The Headhunter as Hero: Local Traditions and Their Reinterpretation in National History." *American Ethnologist* 14 (4): 605–22.
   1989a "On Losing and Getting a Head: Warfare, Exchange and Alliance in a Changing Sumba, 1888–1988. *American Ethnologist* 16 (3): 419–40.
   1989b "Why Do Ladies Sing the Blues? Indigo, Cloth Production, and Gender Symbolism in Kodi." In A. Weiner and J. Schneider, eds., *Cloth and Human Experience*. Washington, D.C.: Smithsonian Institution.
   1993a "Violence, Sacrifice and Divination: Giving and Taking Life in Eastern Indonesia." *American Ethnologist* 20 (1): 159–78.

1993b *The Play of Time: Kodi Perspectives on Calendars, History and Exchange*. Berkeley: University of California Press.

Jones, William
1907–9 "The Diary of William Jones." Typescript. Field Museum of Natural History, Chicago.

Kapita, Oembu Hina
1976 *Sumba dalam Jangkauan Jaman*. Waingapu: Gereja Kristen Sumba.

Kruyt, Albert C.
1906 *Het Animisme in den Indischen Archipel*. The Hague: Martinus Nijhoff.
1922 "De Soembaneezen." *Bijdragen tot de Taal-, Land-, en Volkenkunde* 78: 466–608.

Lévi-Strauss, Claude
1944 "Guerre et commerce chez les Indians du l'Amerique du Sud." *Renaissance* 1: 122–39.

Lincoln, Bruce
1991 "Debreasting, Disarming, Beheading: Some Sacrificial Practices of the Scyths and Amazons." In B. Lincoln, ed., *Death, War and Sacrifice: Studies in Ideology and Practice*. Chicago: University of Chicago Press.

McKinley, Robert
1976 "Human and Proud of It! A Structural Treatment of Headhunting Rites and the Social Definition of Enemies." In G. Appell, ed., *Studies in Borneo Societies*. DeKalb, Ill.: Center for Southeast Asian Studies.

McKinnon, Susan
1991 *From a Shattered Sun: Hierarchy, Gender and Alliance in the Tanimbar Islands*. Madison: University of Wisconsin Press.

Mashman, Valerie
1991 "Warriors and Weavers: A Study of Gender Relations Among the Iban of Sarawak." In V. Sutlive, ed., *Female and Male in Borneo: Contributions and Challenges to Gender Studies*. Shanghai, Va.: Borneo Research Council Monograph Series.

Masing, J. J.
1981 "The Coming of the Gods." Ph.D. diss., Australian National University, Canberra.

Maxwell, Allen
1992 "Why Do People Take Heads?" Typescript.

Metcalf, Peter
1982 *A Borneo Journey into Death: Berawan Eschatology from Its Rituals*. Philadelphia: University of Pennsylvania Press.

Middelkoop, Peter
1960 *Curse, Retribution and Enmity*. Amsterdam: J. van Campen.

1963 *Headhunting in Timor and Its Historical Implications*. Oceanica Linguistic Monographs no. 8. Sydney: University of Sydney.

Needham, Rodney

1976 "Skulls and Causality." *Man* 11: 71–88.

1983 *Sumba and the Slave Trade*. Center of Southeast Asian Studies, Working Paper no. 31. Melbourne: Monash University.

Pannel, Sandra

1992 "Traveling to Other Worlds: Narratives of Headhunting, Appropriation and the Other in the Eastern Archipelago." *Oceania* 62: 162–78.

Pietz, William

1985 "The Problem of the Fetish I." *Res* (9): 5–17.

1987 "The Problem of the Fetish II: The Origin of the Fetish." *Res* (3): 23–46.

Reid, Anthony

1983 *Slavery, Bondage and Dependency in Southeast Asia*. New York: University of Queensland Press.

1988 *Southeast Asia in the Age of Commerce, 1450–1680*. Vol. 1, *The Lands Below the Winds*. New Haven: Yale University Press.

Retboll, Torben, ed.

1984 *East Timor: The Struggle Continues*. Document no. 50. Copenhagen: International Work Group for Indigenous Affairs.

Robarchek, Clayton

1990 "Motivations and Material Causes: On the Explanation of Conflict and War." In J. Haas, ed., *The Anthropology of War*. Cambridge: Cambridge University Press.

Rosaldo, Michelle Z.

1977 "Skulls and Causality: Comment." *Man* 12 (1): 168–70.

1980 *Knowledge and Passion: Ilongot Notions of Self and Social Life*. Cambridge: Cambridge University Press.

Rosaldo, Renato

1980 *Ilongot Headhunting, 1883–1974: A Study in Society and History*. Stanford: Stanford University Press.

1989 "Grief and the Headhunter's Rage." In R. Rosaldo, *Culture and Truth: The Remaking of Social Analysis*. Boston: Beacon Press.

Rousseau, Jerome

1990 *Central Borneo: Ethnic Identity and Social Life in a Stratified Society*. Oxford: Clarendon.

Siverts, Henning

1975 "Jivaro Headhunters in a Headless Time." In Sol Tax, ed., *World Anthropology*. Paris and The Hague: Mouton Publishers.

Taussig, Michael

    1980 "Folk Healing and the Structure of Conquest in Southwest Colombia." *Journal of Latin American Lore* 6 (2): 217–78.

    1987 *Shamanism, Colonialism and the Wild Man: A Study in Terror and Healing*. Chicago: University of Chicago Press.

Thomas, Nicholas

    1991 *Entangled Objects: Exchange, Material Culture and Colonialism in the Pacific*. Cambridge, Mass.: Harvard University Press.

    1994 *Colonialism's Culture: Anthropology, Travel and Government*. Princeton: Princeton University Press.

Turner, Paul, and David Pitts, eds.

    1989 *The Anthropology of War and Peace*. Granby, Mass.: Bergin and Garvey Publishers.

Valeri, Valerio

    1990a "Autonomy and Heteronomy in the Kahua Ritual: A Short Meditation on Huaulu Society." *Bijdragen tot de Taal-, Land-, en Volkenkunde* 146 (1): 56–73.

    1990b "Both Nature and Culture: Reflections on Menstrual and Parturitional Taboos in Huaulu (Seram)." In J. Atkinson and S. Errington, eds., *Power and Difference: Gender in Island Southeast Asia*. Stanford: Stanford University Press.

Van der Kroef, Justus M.

    1969 "Some Headhunting Traditions of Southern New Guinea." *American Anthropologist* 54: 221–35.

Van Wouden, F. A. E.

    [1935] 1968 *Types of Social Structure in Eastern Indonesia*. The Hague: Martinus Nijhoff.

Vayda, Andrew

    1969 "The Study of the Causes of War, with Special Reference to Headhunting Raids on Borneo." *Ethnohistory* 16: 211–24.

Wallace, Alfred Russell

    1869 *The Malay Archipelago: A Narrative of Travel, with Studies of Man and Nature*. London: Macmillan. Reprinted New York: Dover, 1962.

Warren, James F.

    1981 *The Sulu Zone, 1768–1898*. Singapore: Singapore University Press.

Watson, J. L., ed.

    1980 *Asian and African Systems of Slavery*. Berkeley: University of California Press.

Kenneth M. George

Lyric, History, and Allegory, or the End of Headhunting Ritual in Upland Sulawesi

This essay is about the end of a ritual headhunt—in two senses. On the one hand, I am interested in exploring the commemorative and aesthetic practices that almost always follow an act of ritual violence. Ritual violence is seldom recognizable as such unless it leads to a commemorative act of some kind, be it song, drama, or narrative; thus a headhunt needs both a victim and a time of commemorative play and reflection. On the other hand, I am interested in exploring the significance of ritual head-hunts at a time when they may no longer take place except as simulacra of former practices. With these interests in mind, I am going to discuss two communities that today stage ritual about the headhunting rituals of the past. The central problem concerns divergent interpretations of a single headhunting song. A singer from one village had a decidedly historical understanding of the song lyrics, thinking of them as a commentary on the interethnic tensions of the past. A singer from a different village, however, heard in the same lyrics an allegory about the sexual politics of marriage. Taking a comparative look at the communities in question, I will show how the historical perspective makes sense in a socially homogeneous and cohesive village, while the allegoristic one works meaningfully in a community strained by internal differentiation and status tensions. In the end, I believe these two hermeneutic perspectives can be related to the strategic use of tradition in shaping a village polity and maintaining ideological control of the past.

Why Song?

Along with instrumental music and oratory, song stands out as a widely reported art in headhunting traditions throughout island Southeast Asia. Yet with the exception of Michelle Rosaldo's (1980a) brief but insightful commentary on the Ilongot *buayat*, most anthropological analyses of headhunting have overlooked the ways in which singing shapes the local understanding and experience of ritual violence. The neglect of headhunting songs may stem in part from a tendency to mistake singing for an aesthetic frill on practices more "serious," more violent, and more deadly. This neglect suggests, too, that many commentators are inclined to think of headhunting as a relatively transparent cultural practice in no need of aesthetic mediation. In their failure to treat song as a crucial form of native discourse about headhunting, such commentators leave us with a limited understanding of how traditions of ritual violence work.

Without wishing to claim vocal music as *the* privileged entry point into the study of headhunting, I would like to sketch an argument for making song a focal concern. To begin, song lyrics may voice some of the most crucial ideas, representations, and interpretations of ritual violence. Of course, a ritual headhunt may let loose a vast traffic in meanings and commentaries—some of them implicit, others explicit—and indeed, the very act of felling a victim in a headhunt can be a powerful sign or representation. It may render, for example, a bold act of terror and domination, a transformation in the social and cosmological relations of exchange (McKinley 1976), the interplay of grief and desire (M. Rosaldo 1977, 1980a; R. Rosaldo 1980, 1984), a youth's passage into maturity, or a community's moral vitality. Yet I suspect that communities rarely, if ever, bring headhunting ritual to a close without first commenting on such basic, presumed symbols and representations. A headhunt always ends in song (or some other commemorative or celebratory genre). Some of the songs may foreground or make explicit the stable, "assumed" meanings that surround and inform ritual violence. Others may lead to new insights, mysteries, and attitudes. Still others may challenge, parody, or collapse prevailing representations of the headhunt. In short, song gives singers and listeners a chance to reflect on headhunts real and imagined. It is in these reflexive moments that people can grasp the tensions and ironies lying between an ideal vision of the headhunt and those headhunts that take place amid the historical contingencies and constraints of a lived-in world (cf. Smith 1978, 1982).

The meaning and effectiveness of song lyrics, of course, emerge through performance (cf. Atkinson 1987, 1989; Brenneis 1987; Kapferer 1979a, 1979b; Schieffelin 1985). Lyrics alone do not determine the meaning of a song or the response it engenders. Rather, the ideology and practice of vocal music compel certain attitudes, experiences, and understandings in the production and reception of lyrics. Any number of factors my come into play: ludic (or agonistic) performance strategies, the social organization of singers and listeners, rhythm, pitch, melody, antiphony, and bodily motion, to mention but a few possibilities. By way of performance, lyrics not only mean something but also help fuel emotional responses; they may inflame desire, stir pride and anger, amuse, or bring on a wave of nostalgia.

Performance may also constrain understanding and response. In a suggestive essay on ritual speech and song, Maurice Bloch (1974) argues that the highly formal conventions of ceremonial language limit the semantic range of sacred genres. As "impoverished languages," ritual speech and song oblige speakers and listeners to forsake interpretive choice for authorized understandings. As Bloch puts it—somewhat ambiguously—"One does not argue with a song" (1974: 71). Bloch, I believe, points helpfully to the constraints of genre and to their importance in shaping the social practice of language as such. Nonetheless, his argument suggests both an idolatry of form and a mismeasure of its various manifestations and consequences (cf. Becker 1979; Irvine 1979; Schieffelin 1985). Failing to remember that "authority comes to language from the outside" (Bourdieu 1991: 109), Bloch mistakenly looks for determinant power in the syntactic and prosodic features of ritual discourse itself. As I will show in this article, people can indeed argue *about* a song, even if they do not argue *with* it in the narrow sense, or argue *using* it. Interpretive differences concerning the most formulaic of lyrics are possible. In fact, some kinds of ritual song clearly entail interpretive choice, perhaps interpretive conflict, and show a significant degree of semantic instability and ambiguity. I will argue, then, that the motivations and constraints shaping interpretation have less to do with form than with the social, political, and cultural interests that surround performance (cf. Bourdieu 1991; Fish 1989). In this light, the problem of ritual language makes better sense if formulated with regard not to semantic closure and stability, but rather to efforts at authorizing and stabilizing a text for repeated and continuous interpretive work.

The study of ritual singing can also deepen our understanding of tradition. I point here not to remnant texts, tunes, and customs that "survive" from the past, but to the historical process of reinterpretation with which a community links the past to the present (Smith 1978). As Raymond Williams makes clear, tradition is an active modifying force that brings about a "selective version of a shaping past and a reshaped present" (1977: 115; cf. Handler and Linnekin 1984; Vansina 1985). Traditions of ritual singing hold enormous potential for representing, negotiating, reworking, affirming, and at times denying the historical forces that shape a community. The songs of headhunting ceremony are no exception. Through them we can discover process, change, and difference in local tradition as a community confronts a world with the acts, arts, and simulacra of ritual violence.

Ethnographic and Historical Background

The specific problem I wish to explore has roots in my ongoing study of *ada' mappurondo*, the ancestral ritual tradition of Pitu Ulunna Salu, a religiously plural ethnic region located in the rugged hinterlands of Sulawesi's southwest coast (see George 1996 and 1989). Irrespective of religious orientation, the highlanders in this region think of themselves as neither Toraja nor Mandar but rather as *Todiulunnasalu*, "the people of the headwaters." Language further distinguishes "the people of the headwaters" from their Toraja and Mandar neighbors. Without center or fixed standard, the family of Todiulunnasalu languages takes in a number of related village dialects. Upstream and to the east along the Salu Mambi and Salu Hau, village dialects show syntactic and lexical kinship with the so-called Southern Toraja languages. Downstream and to the west, village dialects have more in common with Mandar.

Those who make up the mappurondo community are much like their Christian and Muslim kin. Most of them are farmers who tend swidden gardens, rice terraces, and coffee groves. Everyday activity revolves around the household, the exogamous household cluster (or hamlet), and the *hapu,* the group of relatives that makes up a person's bilateral kindred. Uxorilocal residence strategies are prevalent and have promoted the formation of mother-sister-daughter "cores" within the household and hamlet. Owing to hamlet exogamy, a preference for village endogamy, and perceived advantages in marrying second or third cousins, the mappurondo households in each village form a relatively close-knit group of kin with shared politico-religious interests and anxieties. In my experience, these persons show a deep sense of belonging to their birthplace and homestead, of being tied not only to other people born in the village but to its paths, to the shadows from surrounding hills, and to the sound of the rivers running below it. The village and its lands thus conjure up a comforting image through which people recall a common history and a common way of life.

Since the arrival of Islam in the eighteenth and nineteenth centuries and of Christianity in the twentieth, village society has fractured along religious lines (see George 1993a). Muslims and Christians have turned their backs on ada' mappurondo, refusing to take part in what they view as pagan custom and even prohibiting marriage with anyone in the mappurondo fold. To date, the Indonesian government has not recognized ada' mappurondo as a legitimate religion; instead, state policy has been to insist on monotheistic religion as a keystone of solid, progress-oriented citizenship. As a result, the bureaucratic state effectively denies the mappurondo community any ideological or institutional support and fuels the censorious attitudes of Muslims and Christians toward the ritual practices of their pagan ancestors and contemporaries. The dominant modern order not only debases ada' mappurondo but aggressively supports the alternative ideologies and socioeconomic formations that have lured villagers away from the path of their ancestors.[1]

[1] For discussion of the politics of religion in Sulawesi and in Indonesia more generally, see Atkinson 1983 and Kipp and Rodgers 1987.

Having dwindled to about a tenth of the region's population, followers of ada' mappurondo today make up a minority religious
community with a distinct ideological focus and identity. I want
to emphasize, however, that "pagan" identity has an anchor in
traditional ritual practice. The mappurondo community exists
only insofar as it remains committed to a tradition of ritual performance. That is to say, being mappurondo entails a commitment
not only to ancestral teachings and tabus but also to ritual performances as such (cf. Hymes 1981). Struggling to remain the authoritative voice of local tradition, the mappurondo community appears anxious, confused, and at times divided over what to draw
from the past and how to sustain it. In light of the region's religious pluralism and the state's civil policies, ritual tradition has
become a cultural problem even as it is the basis of mappurondo
identity and polity. In this context, ritual performance is arguably
the most crucial political act the mappurondo community can undertake, especially in its effort to retain ideological control of tradition and, thus, its past (cf. Hoskins 1987).

When I took residence in the area in 1983, I was surprised to
find that followers of ada' mappurondo staged annual, postharvest
headhunting rituals, called *pangngae*. What makes pangngae so
striking these days is its artifice. No enemy actually is slain, no
actual head is taken. In place of a head, villagers use a coconut or
some other skull-shaped surrogate. Sometimes no "head" is used
at all. Further, the cohort of headhunters to be honored by a village is most often no more than a weaponless group of youths, led
by one or two elders. Villagers often left me wondering about their
understanding of this violence in the "subjunctive mood" (cf.
Schechner 1985; Turner 1982). I recall one moonless night when a
cohort of warriors returned home from their journey in a soaking
rain and startled sleeping villagers with shouts, cries, and eerie
blasts from their *tambola*, a mammoth bamboo flute. Villagers
spilled down from the hamlets to the terraces to greet the headhunters. As the leader of the cohort held up the bag containing the
surrogate head, people cried out, "*Bossi'! Bossi'!*" ("It stinks! It
stinks!") and then broke into gales of laughter. Villagers knew a
stage prop when they saw (or smelled) one, and took delight in it.
These headhunters were self-conscious dramatists who appeared
to savor (and on other occasions, to fret over) the ironic disconti-

nuities between ritual theater and reality. Yet they also knew moments when the illusion and artifice of ritual, by way of their illocutionary entailments and performative force (Tambiah 1985), supplanted or augmented reality.

What happens during pangngae, then, is not a headhunt but something staged to look and work like one. The collective purposes of pangngae are relatively easy to characterize and have much in common with those of other headhunting traditions in island Southeast Asia. First, the mappurondo community in each village is obliged to hold pangngae after every rice harvest. Men, women, and children all take part, although it falls to men to organize and run the ritual. The chief idea behind the rite is to bring an end to *public* mourning for those who have died during the year (George 1995).[2] As the community emerges from the debilitating atmosphere of grief, it goes on to celebrate the general fertility and prosperity of the village. The villagers give offerings and praise to the *debata* (spirits) for the harvest just past, and seek further blessings for the rice crop to be planted in the coming year. Villagers also view pangngae as a crucial rite of passage for mappurondo boys. By joining the cohort of headhunters, youths take on the trappings of manhood. Last, pangngae is a rite upon which all others, save mortuary ceremonies, are contingent. In particular, pangngae is said to "open the hamlet" (*untungka'i botto*) to a season of household rituals held under the authority of women.

Consensus on the collective purposes of headhunting rites should not blind us to the personal interests, experiences, emotions, and understandings of different villagers as they stage pangngae (cf. R. Rosaldo 1984). For example, the different status interests of elders and young headhunters can come into play quite prominently. Hosting the ritual does a great deal for the reputation of a man and his household. A youth, on the other hand, may join the cohort of warriors to earn the acclaim of the village and perhaps impress the young and marriageable. Women and girls, meanwhile, have a smaller stake in the ritual when it comes to status. Their interests may revolve around their expertise as songleaders, or around having a son, a brother, or a father

---

[2]A term commonly used to describe the tenor of pangngae is *maringngangi'*, "to lighten [or ease] a burden." The term is also used as a name for a specific version of the rite.

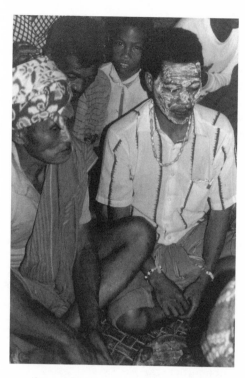

Illus. 1. Elder men honor the surrogate head—here placed on a makeshift centerpost and swathed in cloth (lower right)—with a gift of betel and tobacco. The man on the right is the ritual specialist who directs headhunting ceremonies. He sports a headhunter's bracelets and necklace, and has caked his face with rice paste to refine his complexion for the final celebrations of pangngae. Photograph by Kenneth M. George, 1984.

serve as one of the heroic warriors. By and large, the atmosphere during pangngae is one of exuberance. Yet even as the headhunter swells with pride, others may look upon him with envy or desire. One person may leap into the singing and drumming. Yet another—like a friend of mine who had lost a daughter-in-law a month before the ritual—may sit immune to the festivity, unable to do anything but grieve. And many elders see pangngae as an occasion to speak nostalgically of their youth, to voice a longing for the friends and rituals of their past.

These collective ends, personal interests, and subjective experiences do not come together coincidentally, but emerge through and gain moral cogency from an overriding concern with sustaining mappurondo tradition and village polity (that is, the mappurondo community in a specific village). Pangngae not only promotes the material prosperity of the village, its people, and its land but also invigorates village tradition. This concern comes into focus most sharply at the close of pangngae, when each headhunter and any man so moved makes an impassioned speech dedicating himself to the village, to the words and deeds of his ancestors, and to ada' mappurondo. Pangngae goes farther than other mappurondo rituals in calling attention to local tradition as such and in shaping historical consciousness. As with most ritual, performance itself puts the continuity of tradition on show. But in the case of pangngae, ritual performance commemorates the headhunts of the precolonial era. When the warriors begin their journey, they step into the social and political terrain of the past, a terrain depicted in ritual drama and, above all, in ritual song. They find their victim back in time, before the coming of the Dutch and the birth of the Indonesian order. Thus, contemporary headhunts conflate the present with an imagined or remembered past, permitting today's headhunters to become consubstantial with the heroic figures of another era.

By fusing past and present in the performance of headhunting rites, villagers can "stage" history around sacred acts of violence and, in so doing, can shape a positive, authoritative, and memorable past for village society (cf. Vance 1979). Insofar as this is true, the moral and political vitality of every mappurondo community has its roots in the headhunters' recreation of history. Were the community to neglect pangngae, it would lose control of its past and surrender its life in the present. At the same time, the commemorative process creates a context in which personal experience and reflection attach to the reproduction of the community. On the one hand, villagers are able to discover and celebrate moral value and heroic virtue in commemoration of the headhunt. On the other, the performance of this commemorative rite elicits sentiments and attitudes that help sustain the village polity. For example, the envy a youth may feel toward a headhunter may fuel his desire to become a ceremonial warrior him-

Illus. 2. Men reenact the headhunters' assault in dance and song. Photograph by Kenneth M. George, 1984.

self. In this way, subjective states that might be threatening in other contexts can enter usefully into the reproduction of village polity, village history, and village ritual tradition.

It is difficult to write confidently about the headhunts of the past (see George 1996 and 1991). Villagers insist that their tradition of headhunting ritual is unbroken, dating back almost sixteen generations. At the same time, they insist that they had stopped taking real heads long before the arrival of the Dutch (in 1906) and their pacification campaigns. Published records of the colonial administration and mission for this particular region are sketchy and few, and make no mention of headhunting. Their surprising silence would seem to support local claims. Without wishing to exclude the possibility of colonial intervention in this headhunting tradition, I believe it is analytically useful—and ethically proper—to privilege local accounts in reconstructing the history of headhunting. Not to do so would be to deny the mappurondo community *its own* history—yet another act of pacification—and to lose sight of the complexity of local ritual practice.

Judging from the chanted or sung discourse of the ritual itself, and from the informal commentaries of elders, the headhunts of the past played into exchange relations between this highland region and the coastal settlements of the Mandar and Bugis.[3] In general, the highland and lowland communities were interdependent, with the mountain settlements markedly subordinate in terms of prestige, material wealth, and political power. Pangngae momentarily reversed the hierarchical relations of interdependence: headhunters would ambush a person in a coastal hamlet, take the victim's head back to the mountains, and ritually offer it to the debata to assure the prosperity and power of the upstream region. Headhunting practices thus served as a dramatic expression of upland resistance to a powerful and often threatening coast. By the late nineteenth century, however, political and economic realities appear to have led uplanders to use a skull-shaped surrogate in place of a severed head (George 1996). If the use of a surrogate marked a crucial shift in the politics and polemics of regional exchange, it also ushered in an era of bloodless resistance to forces that threatened the highlands.

Equally difficult is the question of how the commemorative headhunt, with its specific vision of history, mediates current relations between the mappurondo community and the outside world. The vantage point of the present is critical, for history and ritual tradition are themselves products of contemporary sociohistorical forces. In fact, it is doubly critical in that mappurondo villagers have staked the reproduction of community, polity, and tradition on ritual performance. I suggest, then, that the historical work of pangngae be considered a collective response to the ideological and institutional pressures brought to bear on the mappurondo community by the state order. At times, I have been tempted to find in the historical discourse of pangngae an allegory of resistance to the modern order. But such a view strikes me as mistaken. If it is true that pangngae tries to recapture a bygone era in which the uplands had opportunity to resist encompassment and domination by external forces, then today's ritual constitutes not so much an allegorical discourse of struggle against the contemporary order as a practical discourse of retreat into the past. Since the state denies mappurondo practices any ideological or

---

[3] I explore headhunting and regional exchange relations more deeply elsewhere (George 1996, 1991). For comparative materials, see Hoskins (1989, and this volume), who shows how Sumbanese headhunting practices factored into eras of exchange, alliance, and trade between rival groups.

institutional legitimacy in the present, it seems realistic for this minority religious community to seek legitimacy in its past. The mappurondo concern for controlling local tradition and history thus appears well founded. In particular, the ritualized commemoration of the past found in pangngae stands out as a strategy for stabilizing and maintaining cultural continuity with the community's historical foundations.

Even if the social, political, and cultural need for village history proves to be the determining force behind contemporary headhunting, it is worth recalling that this ritual connects manhood to the reproduction of polity. In the theater of headhunting ritual, historical consciousness takes shape in a discourse of masculine interests, interests that necessarily conflate village politics with local sexual politics (George 1996, 1993b). Multiple (socio-) logics are at work in pangngae (cf. R. Rosaldo 1984). It should come as no surprise, then, if different villages place different thematic emphases on their ritual endeavors.

Interpreting a Song from a Headhunt

Having sketched some of the basic tensions in mappurondo ceremonial life, I can now come back to the question of ritual singing and its place in the discourse of headhunting tradition. The principal genre of song in pangngae is the *sumengo* (literally, "the singing"). Though liturgy and oratory do figure significantly in these rites, the sumengo is so prominent that it would not be far off the mark to call the headhunt a kind of sumengo-fest. To an American ear shaped by very different music traditions, the sumengo melody can be haunting, somber, and slow. The first time I heard these very brief songs, I imagined worlds of sadness, pain, and longing. This was during the early months of my fieldwork, when I didn't know the language very well and couldn't follow the lyrics. In time I learned that the songs had little to do with sadness. Often the performances were occasions for exuberant play, nostalgic reflection, and festive commemoration. And as I worked on translations of the lyrics, I learned that sumengo performances comprised a running commentary on the drama of the ritual headhunt. For me, they became an obvious place from which to fathom the complexity of pangngae and mappurondo tradition.

Villagers say that sumengo performance gives them a chance to *ma'kada senga'*, "to speak other [that is, sublime] words." Nevertheless, the language of the sumengo largely shares the syntax, vocabulary, and metaphors of everyday speech. Sung by groups of women or men (and sometimes both together), sumengo lyrics commonly consist of three octosyllabic phrases performed to a set tune.[4] The first phrase is always performed by a *tomantokko*, or songleader, as a strained, high-pitched solo. The two following phrases are choral, sung by the tomantokko and his or her chorus. In most instances, the phrase triads show semantic and rhetorical integrity and are recollected and performed as "set pieces." At the same time, singers enjoy weaving the songs into a ludic dialogue of choruses. As mentioned above, all the lyrics concern a headhunt in some way. I have found it helpful to think of the sumengo as a corpus of tableaux and commentaries from pangngae.

Like most of the verbal and musical arts in the mappurondo community, the sumengo fall under a rigid set of tabus. Villagers may not sing, rehearse, or even discuss them except during the annual headhunt—a period lasting between three days and two weeks. I should add that it is perfectly all right for someone to sing a sumengo outside a formal ceremonial gathering, but in my experience, that is seldom done. The tabus that confine sumengo performance to the ritual period associated with the headhunt also shaped my work with singers, lyrics, and performance. In particular, they framed the contexts in which performers and I could comfortably engage in a give-and-take with one another. By placing my inquiry within the sphere of local traditional practices, I put a partial check on my impulse to control ethnographic dialogue. At the same time, the "performance period" gave me a chance to raise questions about the sumengo and to ask villagers to reflect on the meaning of the songs.[5]

Just a few months before I was to leave the uplands, discussion of the sumengo turned up an illuminating problem in interpreta-

[4]A very basic linguistic and musicological analysis emphasizing some of the formal patterns in sumengo text and tune is available in George 1989. A transcription of a sumengo melody, using Western music notation, can be found in George 1990.

[5]Fabian (1990) has explored the theoretical and practical implications of linking performance, power, and ethnographic dialogue to cultural knowledge. I would count his monograph as a key project in dialogical anthropology. See, too, the pioneering work of Tedlock (1983).

tion. It began with my first and only visit to the village of Saludengen, during the postharvest ritual season. Unlike mappurondo
followers elsewhere, the villagers at Saludengen had put sumengo
lyrics into written form, crafting them into a "narrative" song
cycle that depicts a ritual headhunt from start to finish (George
1996 and 1990). On the eve of the final ceremony of pangngae, villagers gather into two large semichoruses—one male, the other female—and sing the cycle three times. Their nightlong performance is devoted wholly to the sumengo. By way of contrast, the
other ceremonies that make up a headhunting ritual in this village include only a few of the songs.

While listening to the cycle, I heard more than twenty songs I
had never before come across in two years of work. One song sung
by the male semichorus stood out because it was so different in
tone from the sumengo familiar to me. It was about the humiliation and failure of the upland headhunters, rather than their valor
and power. Here are the words to the song:

Made workers for the Bugis	*Naposarokam Bugi'*
we're fed handouts by the Mandar	*natenakan ToMinanga*
it falls down into the water.	*loe tama ri uai.*

A key term in the song is *saro*, which denotes a common form
of labor exchange between highland households.[6] In a saro arrangement, a person works at the request of a relative or friend,
generally getting a meal and a token share of the harvest (or wage)
in the course of the task. The friend or relative then works in return, and he or she, too, will receive a meal and shares. Failure to
reciprocate does not indebt the friend or relative but implies that
his or her status is too high to permit work for another. In certain
situations, the lack of reciprocity would offend those who once
lent aid. On the other hand, to work for someone without being
able to call for labor in return marks a person as a social inferior.
Those who find themselves in such a situation—because they
have only meager landholdings, for example—are not affronted,
but humiliated by their own circumstances.

The song underscores the humiliation the uplanders might feel
when working for coastal patrons without hope of calling them to

[6] See Volkman 1985 for a good discussion of the saro relationship in the
Sa'dan Toraja region.

the hills to reciprocate under saro arrangements. The uplanders get handouts of food (*tena*) for their work but do not have the chance to give food to the Mandar or Bugis in their own fields back home in the mountains. These humiliating conditions provoke the stereotypic expression of futility heard in the last line of the song. The uplanders' chance to maintain prestige and honor "falls down into the [river] water" and is washed away.

The following evening I had a chance to discuss this song with my host, Ambe Siama', and a few of his friends and family. For them, the song recalled a history of subordination to coastal patrons and voiced resignation to the humbling realities of regional exchange. The lyrics acknowledged that headhunting could end in disappointment, that the upland headhunters might fail in striking back at the exogenous powers that denied them honor, prestige, and prosperity. For me, this unique and arrestingly frank appraisal of the upland past demanded a rethinking of my views on pangngae. Indeed, the theme of failure never emerged in the songs from other villages, nor did the women's sumengo performed in Saludengen carry a hint of a headhunter's shame.

Some days later, I made my way upriver to Salutabang to join in another headhunting ritual. The harvest had been an especially good one, and pangngae promised to be a long, festive event. I settled in the home of Ambe and Indo Teppu, two people who had often guided me in exploring ada' mappurondo. One evening, I pulled out the tape cassettes that I had recorded at Saludengen and played them for Ambe Teppu. The skilled voices of the tomantokko and the narrative arrangement of the songs pleased him very much: "Straight and in place. I think our ancestors once sang [the sumengo] just that way. "Like me, Ambe Teppu was unfamiliar with the song about the saro. He called to Indo Teppu to listen to the tape, and she, too, could not recall having heard the song before.

I ventured that the song was about the failed headhunts of the past. Ambe Teppu countered with a different understanding: "That song is about husbands and their wives." I clearly didn't get it, so Ambe Teppu took me through the lyrics. As he saw it, the Bugis and Mandar mentioned in the song were wives to whom husbands devoted their labor. "We [men] work for them and we get a little bit of rice, maybe some fish. But we are poor, there is so little, what can we give back?"

Ambe Teppu's interpretation puzzled and troubled me for a long time. I had difficulty in making sense of it, in following the cultural (or intertextual) paths that would allow me to connect enmity, dependence, history, and a husband's humiliation before his wife. And I also found it hard to grasp why a person from one village would give the song a straightforward historical interpretation while another, from a different village, would insist on an allegorical "reading." My first instinct was to privilege the "historical" at the expense of the allegorical, a move that favored the seeming straightforwardness (or literalness) of the former and looked with suspicion upon the contemporaneity of the latter. The same outlook also privileged the lyrics' singers and authors as interpretive authorities at the expense of listeners who were encountering the song for the first time.[7] Since then I have come to feel that both the historical and the allegorical have to be treated as figured speech, as turns of expression and understanding, as countermovements that happen in each other's shadow.

These two versions of understanding invite an exploration of the "prior texts" (Becker 1979) and "intertextual webs" (Ramanujan 1988) that surround and shape song lyrics, song performance, and song interpretation. We should begin such an exploration, it seems to me, not with the biographical particulars of Ambe Siama' and Ambe Teppu, but rather with the communities in question. Here I borrow from Stanley Fish (1980), who argues that the "interpretive community" is the source not just of texts and performances but of all acts of interpretation. In his view, members of an interpretive community have common purposes and goals, and thus have common ground in the making of texts and commentaries. As a cautionary note, let me emphasize that we should expect such communities to encompass diverse perspectives or strategies and to be shaped by potential clashes of ideological outlook. In short, there are real dangers in presuming a homogeneity of interpretive practice in a given community (cf. Bakhtin 1981; Vološinov 1973). At the same time, interpretive differences within a community should not lead us to overlook com-

---

[7]I leave aside the problem of chronological or temporal privileging. That is, I tended to favor the interpretation I had heard first as the authoritative and conditioning one.

monalities. In fact, the virtue of a coherent system of interpretive strategies and perspectives is that it gives a community a common and therefore contestable culture.

I want to suggest, then, that in addition to forming socially and spatially distinct settlements, the mappurondo households of Saludengen and Salutabang form different, if related, interpretive communities. The different views of Ambe Siama' and Ambe Teppu, I would argue, result from communal differences. Further, I believe the different interpretive strategies that the two men brought to bear on the sumengo in question were but different responses to a general concern with preserving mappurondo tradition and polity—a concern that lies at the heart of the ritual headhunt.

There are, of course, theoretical problems in taking differences between specific "readings" of song lyrics and projecting them as differences between interpretive communities (cf. Culler 1982). The tacit danger is to mistake the idiosyncratic for the commonplace. Yet my claims are not so reckless. A song does not carry a single, fixed meaning. Nor does a community of singer-listeners have but a single, fixed interpretive strategy for understanding song. But song interpretation is constrained nonetheless. As Fish writes, interpretation "is not an abstract or contextless process, but one that elaborates itself in the service of a specific enterprise" (1989: 135). To sing a sumengo and to reflect on it is to be "deeply inside a context . . . to be already and always thinking (and perceiving) with and within" the standards, purposes, and traditions that shape and are shaped by that context (Fish 1989: 127).

The challenge, then, is to find those contextual features that have the most relevance for the politics of interpretive practice. Such a contextual framework would not only stabilize and authorize specific understandings of song but also allow both idiosyncratic and commonplace interpretations to make sense. I focus, therefore, on grasping how the views of Ambe Siama' and Ambe Teppu become intelligible, convincing, and "right" within their respective communities. In making sense of the ways Ambe Siama' and Ambe Teppu make sense of a song, I am trying to discover something about the sumengo and the intertextual field that informs it. Whether the song interpretation in question is commonplace or singular is probably beside the point. Nevertheless, I think each man offered a "reading" both consonant with and indicative of others in his respective community. Each "read with the polity." Just as important, Ambe Siama' and Ambe Teppu enjoy reputations as elders well versed in ritual tradition, and thus enjoy an edge of authority in saying what songs are all about.

The interpretive paths that these two men followed in telling me about the sumengo do not exhaust its semantic potential. Yet what they had to say remains significant, for their efforts were projects that made sense in a context. Without wishing to slight the biographic particulars of Ambe Siama' and Ambe Teppu, or my positioned involvement as an ethnographer, I find it most reasonable to begin an exploration of context by looking at the communities in question. As I have argued, to interpret at all is to interpret with the polity.[8] Further, the commentaries of Ambe Siama' and Ambe Teppu, however partial and positioned, called attention to some of the domestic and intercultural tensions that concern the mappurondo communities.

In the discussion that follows, I briefly look at several social patterns and practices that shape communal life in Saludengen and Salutabang. With them, I hope to take measure of mappurondo identity and polity in each locale. I should point out that these features of mappurondo village life are not the "sociopolitical correlates" of sumengo performance and interpretation. Rather, they are traces of the "intertextual web" that surrounds the sumengo and that marks the lines along which meaning may be spun.

Saludengen

The roots of the mappurondo community at Saludengen are deep and firmly planted. All people living in the village—whether mappurondo or Christian—call themselves *ToIssilita'* (people from the land; that is, original inhabitants).[9] The settlement dates back sixteen or more generations and has long been a center of resistance to exogenous forces that have threatened

---

[8] Interpreting "with the polity" nonetheless allows for the production of oppositional discourse, a condition Ross Chambers (1991) would call "room for maneuver."

[9] There are no Muslim households in Saludengen or Salutabang.

mappurondo tradition. For example, it refused to accommodate Dutch-sanctioned leadership in the district (Smit 1937), and it served as the headquarters of local resistance during the island-wide rebellions of the late 1950s. Protestant Christianity, however, has gained a significant foothold in the village. By 1985, roughly 58 percent of the households in Saludengen (70 of 120) were Christian. The followers of ada' mappurondo responded by sequestering their community topographically. After several years of bitter dispute with Christian residents over ritual and ritual-ized planting practices, they exchanged and consolidated terraces and moved upstream along the banks of the Salu Dengen, leaving Christians to occupy contiguous sites downstream. Of the five hamlets that make up Saludengen today, two "belong" to the mappurondo community and three to the Christian congregation.

The community is determinedly endogamous, admitting no males from other villages as sons-in-law and letting no daughters move off in wedlock. (According to figures maintained by the district administration for the period 1971–84, no marriage in the mappurondo community involved a partner from outside Saluden-gen.) In effect, each hamlet is home to a number of related mother-sister-daughter "household cores," who in principle, if not in practice, exchange brothers and sons with the women of the other hamlet. Village endogamy, combined with a preference for hamlet exogamy, uxorilocal residence, and second- or third-cousin mar-riage, has fostered a closely knit community. The social and spa-tial consolidation of the mappurondo hamlets is further strength-ened by the distribution and location of terrace holdings. The average terrace holding for a household amounts to 1.0 hectare, whereas the household with the most rice land owns no more than 1.5 hectares. And unlike other households in the district, the mappurondo families in Saludengen neither own nor rent rice fields outside village territory.

In light of the above, it is hardly surprising that the mappurondo community has done well in maintaining a hierarchy of political and ritual authority within its ranks. Since the beginning of the century, succession to the position of *tomatuatonda'* (the elder of the village; that is, the village head) has been undisputed. No rit-ual office goes vacant, and the community has a full complement of male and female specialists to conduct ceremonial life. Indeed, the mappurondo community at Saludengen is one of the few places where a full ceremonial calendar thrives. Further, the status interests of men are kept in check—and indeed, assured—by hamlet exogamy and village endogamy. Marriage is key to gaining a political voice, even if it requires a man to subordinate himself to his wife's father.[10] Yet in the context of hamlet exogamy, a husband's father-in-law is but an elder from the same hamlet and a person who has similar obligations and interests vis-à-vis natal and affinal hamlets. Generally speaking, then, the status differential among men in Saludengen rests upon age or generation.

Salutabang

Compared with Saludengen, Salutabang is something of a "frontier" settlement. Once the site of a ToIssilita' village, the area fell into the hands of the *ToSalu* (people of the river), who came as a group of intruders from the Salu Mokanan watershed lying roughly ten kilometers to the south. The first ToSalu to settle Salutabang did so around 1870. In the view of contemporary To-Salu, village history dates back to those first settlers—five or six generations back, roughly speaking. Thus, the community is historically and genealogically shallower than Saludengen. Further complicating the picture are several households that continue to trace their ancestry back to the ToIssilita'.

Christianization began in Salutabang the same time that it did in Saludengen, and the church has been able to claim a similar proportion of followers. In 1985 about 58 percent of the households (74 of 128) embraced this religion. Tensions between Christians and the mappurondo community arise from time to time. When relations are calm, the village is *kalebu tellu*, "round like an egg" (that is, characterized by external and internal unity). When they are strained, the village is *kalebu lemo*, "round like an orange" (characterized by a surface unity masking internal divisiveness). No steps have been taken to sequester the mappurondo community and its landholdings topographically. As a result, there are mappurondo and Christian households in each of the

[10] See M. Rosaldo 1980b and Collier and Rosaldo 1981 for discussion of how sexual asymmetry in simple societies may be thought of as a concomitant to male status hierarchies.

eight hamlets that make up Salutabang. Further, members of a single household sometimes follow different paths of belief. At the time of my fieldwork, there were also a few individuals (all men) who shifted back and forth between being mappurondo and being Christian.

Marriage patterns and landholding figures are revealing. Like the people at Saludengen, those at Salutabang prefer village endogamy and hamlet exogamy and consistently pursue uxorilocal residence strategies. Yet the mappurondo community at Salutabang shows a strikingly high rate of village exogamy. For the period 1971–84, 48 percent of all mappurondo marriages involved in-marrying males born in another village—almost always ToSalu youths, and quite frequently second or third cousins.[11] The average terrace holding for a single household amounted to about 0.6 hectare. The most prosperous household in the community owned roughly 1.5 hectares of terrace land. Overall, then, there is evidence of a greater disparity in the distribution of land and material wealth in Salutabang than in Saludengen. Moreover, roughly 17 percent of mappurondo terrace holdings lie outside Salutabang, mostly in the ToSalu villages lying downstream and in the Salu Mokanan valley. In principle, these holdings fall under the ritual jurisdiction of the other villages. As a result, several ToSalu households have material and ritual ties to other villages, in addition to those forged by kinship and marital alliance.

Political and ritual authority in Salutabang is seriously eroded. During the past 75 years, the position of tomatuatonda' has often been in dispute, and in 1985 at least four ritual offices went vacant. In principle, persons born and raised outside the village may not hold such prestigious positions. Sadly, many local specialists have converted to Christianity without passing on their knowledge and authority to stage various household rites. In fact, for rituals other than pangngae, the mappurondo community at Salutabang often has to "borrow" ritual specialists from other ToSalu villages. Even then, some mappurondo households are reluctant to host the more elaborate women's ceremonies for fear of mak-

[11] Factionalism within the Salutabang mappurondo community may have sparked interest in welcoming young men born outside the village. No males native to Salutabang married out of the village during this period.

ing liturgical errors that would invite the wrath of the debata. The grand ritual known as *malangngi'*, for example, has not taken place in Salutabang since 1950. By comparison, Saludengen has staged malangngi' as recently as 1982, the year before I began my fieldwork.

In sum, the mappurondo community at Salutabang appears far less cohesive than the one at Saludengen. The community's shallow history probably does little to strengthen collective bonds. But in my mind, the most significant factors at work against the strengthening of collective identity and tradition are the political consequences of village exogamy. The numerous in-marrying males do not have the political voice of "native sons." Their prestige and authority depend critically upon the status of their local-born wives, their ability to expand material resources, and demonstrable proof of achievement. At the same time, in-marrying males have material and ritual commitments to their natal villages. The bonds of communal tradition and polity at Salutabang are hence much looser and allow far more latitude for individualism and status competition than those in Saludengen.

Differences in Headhunting Rites

Differences in the village-based polities come to the fore in pangngae. The community at Saludengen practices but one version of pangngae, called *maringngangi'* (to ease; to lighten a burden; to relieve). Although the scale and the enthusiasm with which the ritual is run may vary, the villagers conduct their headhunt with the idea of bringing public mourning to an end. In contrast, the community at Salutabang has seven ways of running pangngae. Of these, three are fully collective in character: *untungka'i botto* (opening the hamlet), which shares the emphases of maringngangi'; *untauam bahata* (being persons who mourn), which takes place after the death of the tomatuatonda'; and *mahhaha banne* (putting blood on the seed), which follows a poor harvest.

But it is not unusual for a Salutabang man to put his own mark on pangngae by staging the ritual for the benefit of the village, thereby advancing his personal status and reputation. Basically, a villager has the prerogative of holding the settlement's annual ritual at his home in order to make good on a personal vow to the spirits.[12] Vows connected to the restoration of personal health culminate in *undantai kalena* (striking [making a thudding noise on] one's image). Those made in order to seek the strength and resources to build a new house or rice terrace end in *ulleppa'i samajanna* (releasing one's vow). But it is also possible for a man to combine sacred vows with a desire for personal aggrandizement. One way is to stage *umpokasalle kalena* (enlarging one's image; also called *malampa sali-sali* [making and loading the offering rack]), a version of pangngae in which one displays one's good fortune, devout moral character, and stature in the community by giving substantial offerings to the debata. The most elaborate of such "signature" rites is *ma'patuhhu'i botto* (having the hamlets follow). Here a villager makes a vow of unusual breadth or sincerity; in return for providential blessings, he pledges to lead most of the able-bodied men and youths out of the village on a headhunt and host an enormous feast in their honor.

The headhunters' and elders' speeches at the close of pangngae give further measure of the strength of communal tradition and polity. Known as *mamose* (to stomp [in rage]), these oratorical performances call for the headhunter or elder to leap to center floor, being sure to make a loud thudding noise with his feet when landing. Holding a cloth or palm frond aloft in his right hand, he struts and stomps before the crowd and delivers an impassioned speech dedicating himself to the village and ada' mappurondo. When I visited Saludengen in 1985, every headhunter—fifteen in all—and two elders made mamose speeches. By way of contrast, there was but one (rather inchoate) speech at Salutabang in the course of two pangngae seasons (1984 and 1985; mahhaha banne and ma'patuhhu'i botto, respectively). Assuming the "enraged" look befitting a headhunter, the man rushed his words, got tongue-tied, clenched the handle of his machete for a moment, and then sat down. The speech fell into the water, as the saying goes.

[12] I think the literature on Southeast Asian headhunting ritual has overlooked the potential importance of vows or pledges. It seems to me that when viewed as a particular kind of speech act with specific moral entailments, vows create a moral logic that connects violence, communal polity, and well-being (George 1996). And as a line of inquiry into the question of why headhunting should have something to do with fertility and vitality, a moral logic

In short, the polities at Salutabang and Saludengen are constructed and experienced in different ways. The men at Salutabang
are less inclined to subordinate their interests and moral passions
to the community and village tradition than are their counter-
parts at Saludengen. This does not mean that the Salutabang male
is pitted against the communal body. In fact, village ritual tradition here offers a means for individuals to undertake communal
tasks for personal ends. At the same time, it provides a context in
which narrowly personal or selfish concerns can advance community interests. What is celebrated at Salutabang, then, is a loose
collectivity of status-conscious moral agents. In contrast, the rites
of pangngae at Saludengen end in a leveling (and, in the mamose
speeches, an outright denial) of status differences among villagers—if only momentarily. The community is as one.

Differences in Sumengo Performance

Before returning to the readings of Ambe Siama' and Ambe
Teppu, we may find a final set of comparisons helpful in establishing interpretive differences between the men's respective communities. Here I wish to look at some features of sumengo performance, for performance itself is a form of interpretation (Fabian
1990; Tedlock 1983).

Basically, sumengo performance at Salutabang emerges as a ludic and oftentimes agonistic polylogue between small choruses of
men and women. The choruses try to outperform one another in
what might be termed song duels. The idea is to get the better of
another chorus by coming up with a lyric rejoinder, sung loudly
and in a manner that "steps on" an ongoing performance. Thus, it
is not unusual to hear two or three sumengo being performed simultaneously. In the song play between men and women, no effort
is made to sing the songs in any particular order. The tomantokko
use their skills and memories in the tactics of play. For instance, I

---

sketched through speech act theory seems to me more promising than the
symbolic logic propounded in structuralism (cf. Needham 1976; M. Rosaldo
1977). Consider, too, the emotional force of casting off or being released from a
vow. Can casting off a vow be compared or analytically linked to casting off
grief? See M. Rosaldo (1980a) and R. Rosaldo (1980, 1984, and 1987) on casting
off grief.

once listened to a chorus of Salutabang men sing about the an-
guish caused by the headhunters' raid:

One homestead the place of widows	*Sambanuami tobalu*
one hamlet the place of orphans	*satondo'mi ana' bium*
one mountain the place of the graves.	*santanetemi u'bu'na.*

Meanwhile, a chorus of women sang in praise of the headhunters.
Its song likened the warriors to ripening sugarcane, and the warriors' wives or lovers to excited parrots:

Striped colored cane just coming up	*Ta'bu sure' mane dadi*
just starting to reach for the sun	*mane lulangam allona*
the parrots' dance along the branch.	*paneteanna kaloe'.*

Before these singers had finished, yet another group of women
started up with a song about the felling of a victim:

Black sugar palm on the wide plain	*Indu' ajangan di rante*
its fronds hewn by the cockerel	*lao natotoi london*
carried by the kulu-kulu [an omen bird].	*nababa ma'kulu-kulu.*

While that song continued, the chorus of men performed a flatter-
ing rejoinder to the first group of women. Picking up the reference
to parrots, the men invited the women to keep singing:

Parrots over there on the Manda'	*Kaloe' sambali' Manda'*
fly long and far on the way here	*pentia' lambe'ko mai*
we're going to take up your song.	*lakiperapi onimmu.*

A song exchange such as this creates a swirl of images from a
headhunt. The story of the headhunt is absent—or, more precisely, dismembered and strewn through different sumengo verses.
At best, the sequence of songs may show some thematic order.

The sumengo lyrics at Saludengen, it will be recalled, have been
written down in a narrative cycle that recounts a ritual headhunt
from beginning to end. As a story, the cycle has no plot, no development of character, no moral tension, no foreshadowing of
events. Rather, the narrative consists of lyric episodes that tell of
the headhunters' departure, their predatory raid on the Mandar

Illus. 3. *Striped colored cane just coming up, just starting to reach for the sun.* A young headhunter in his finery listens to songs of praise during pangngae. Photograph by Kenneth M. George, 1984.

coast, their trek homeward, and their ritual welcome in the celebrations of pangngae. For example:[13]

The hawk blackened with mortar stain	*Langkam borim panuntungan*
goes to scratch circles on the coast his talon marks spiral and coil.	*lao mengkaroi bonde' malepom pengkaroanna.*
Do not shroud us like that the hawk blackened with mortar stain	*Samboaki' tole langkam borim panuntungan*
goes to scratch circles on the coast.	*lao mengkaroi bonde'.*

[13]Elsewhere (George 1989) I provide a complete transcription of the su-mengo cycle.

Two songs later:

Fine and daring that cockerel bird	*Mapianna mane' londong*
hiding in a place of ambush	*lembun tama pangngabungan*
his tail feathers cascading down.	*tisoja' ula-ulanna.*

A bit further along in the cycle:

Wide and low-boughed banyan	*Barane' rumape*
whose shade darkens the river mouth	*umbalumbunni minanga*
felled down there by the cockerel.	*sau' natotoi london.*

The narrative goes on to include a long conversation between the headhunters and their wives: the men tell of their exploits, and the women respond with songs of adulation. Thereafter, the narrative finds the men and women engaged in a riddling session. The story closes with a melancholy coda: the song and music of head-hunting ritual must be put away for another year.

The narrative has displaced the memories of the tomantokko and the play of singers as the source of pattern and authority. At the same time, singers form but two choruses, one male, the other female. In performance, the semichoruses take turns, and so the sumengo narrative unfolds in an alternating dialogue between men and women. As a result, specific songs take on a gendered voice and perspective. Interestingly, this song dialogue not only structures the performance of the cycle but also enters into its narrative constitution (see George 1996 and 1990). Men and women sing about men and women conversing. In a sense, the dialogue that narrates is also the dialogue that is narrated.

We see, then, different sets of contextual constraints at play in sumengo performance in these two villages. At Saludengen, the interpretation of song (in performance or its aftermath) presupposes a narrative that powerfully shapes the meaning and direction of lyrics. A story is being told with the sumengo, and interpretation will tend toward (or derive from) its reconstruction or retelling. The dialogue of husbands and wives—if I may so transfigure the dialogue of the semichoruses—is constitutive of (and thus subordinate to) the same narrative. Gendered dialogue serves the story. At Salutabang, on the other hand, no such narrative constraints come into play. Song interpretation relies on thematic associations and the experience of playfulness between men and women trying to best one another. In that village, the meaning of lyrics (as a dismembered and unremembered story) excites the playful combat of spouses.

History and Allegory: Reading with the Village Polity

It strikes me that Saludengen's effort to forge (or reclaim) a headhunting narrative reflects a strategy of cultural reproduction wholly consistent with the community's self-consciousness about identity and polity. Secluding themselves socially, spatially, and ideologically, people in the mappurondo fold here have shaped a powerful, deeply rooted communal identity. Their ethos is one of control, and it extends not only to people and material resources, but to the past as well. The ritualized and inscribed narrative of headhunting helps moor the community morally and ideologically even while it provides a coherent vision of the past.

Looking back to when I asked Ambe Siama' to reflect on the sumengo, I see that he was "reading" the lyrics in line with local political experience. Although no doubt skilled at weaving allegory from the threads of song lyric, Ambe Siama' was inclined to remain within the orbit of history and the story of upland versus coast, of an ethnic "us" versus "them." By the same token, his interpretation was in line with the path of cultural reproduction at Saludengen. Pangngae provides a ritual mechanism allowing Saludengen to internalize—and momentarily overcome—its subordination to exogenous forces, one of the central tensions in local political life.

I would argue, too, that for villagers at Saludengen, "reading with the village polity" through the narrative cycle precludes, or makes unlikely, any connection between the domestic relations of wife and husband and the song in question. It should be obvious that domestic relations and the interests of wives and husbands do factor into local political life at Saludengen. A wife's political interests, status, and participation are crucial to social life, but they do not go much beyond the household and hamlet. Insofar as a husband's political interests span both natal and affinal hamlets, his "sphere" is coextensive with the village as a whole; men thus assume guardianship of the collective good.[14] Marriage, of course, is an important factor in a man's entry into the role of community guardian. He must obtain a wife, just as he must obtain an enemy "head," if he is to become an equal among men. Several sumengo at Saludengen *do* concern husband-wife relations, and all involve an "I-Thou" dialogue in which a husband seeks flattery and reassurance and a wife obliges. But the lyrics that Ambe Siama' explored for me appear very early in the sumengo narrative cycle, when the headhunters (of the "story") are preparing to depart on their journey. Sung by men, the lyrics are ambiguous as to who the listener might be: the semichorus of wives, the debata, the coastal victims, or all three. However, the song comes right before one that warns the coast of an impending attack:

Watch out you on the horizon	*Malallengko toibirin*
you low on the foot of our land	*tomatilampe bambana*
the blackened hawk is heading there.	*lembum matil langkam borin.*

Thus, the Bugis and the Mandar mentioned in the lyrics in question can be linked straightforwardly to the victims lying beyond the horizon of the community.

Reading with the polity at Saludengen means reading with the written narrative cycle, not against it or away from it. Equally, it means reading with the experience of a homogeneous community that is fearful of exogenous forces and untroubled by the status competitions of native sons. The narrative cycle itself mediates and enters into the production of social homogeneity and solidarity and stands out as an explicit effort to hold on to village tradition as a basis of communal identity.

Ambe Teppu shaped his interpretation of the sumengo with a different set of textual constraints and emphases and a different understanding of political experience. Reading with the polity at Salutabang means seeing all sumengo as weapons in a ludic contest between choruses of husbands and wives. It also means being familiar with the status competitions between men and with the way such competitions are played out through wives, the persons through whom men gain prestige.

[14]Relations between men and women appear particularly asymmetric when viewed from the vantage point of village-oriented political life.

Ambe Teppu was not alone in interpreting songs as metaphorical or allegorical commentaries on the relations between husbands and wives. A song about the felling of a banyan tree offers a case in point:

You, you banyan trees over there	*Iko barane'-barane'*
if you are called to be cut down	*keditambako dilellen*
fall here into our village lands.	*loe maiko bambaki.*

From a perspective that looks toward the intercultural relations between mountain and coast, the song is about felling a Mandar victim. It expresses hope that the victim's head will "fall into the village" and bring prosperity to the uplanders. But several of my male friends at Salutabang felt that the lyrics of this song alluded to a marriage proposal. In their view, a woman does not pass from youth to maturity until she is "felled" by a marriage proposal and, like the timber of a properly felled tree, made usable.

The mappurondo community at Salutabang, in contrast to the one at Saludengen, emphasizes sexual tensions rather than intercultural ones. For a community with a significant number of in-marrying men, the village polity is more clearly an arena for status achievement and competition than a tightly organized and controlled body politic with a tradition compelling one's commitment or allegiance. If one is to judge by the remarks of elders, sexual tension and status competition were even more fierce in the past. Many elderly men and women recalled an era of wife-stealing, a powerful means of upstaging status rivals. Felling a wife—or someone else's wife—is more strongly emphasized here than in Saludengen. If committing oneself to village tradition and polity is the key political act for a Saludengen man, felling a woman is the key achievement for his Salutabang counterpart.

It is not surprising, then, that the themes of eroticism, seduction, and envy are so pronounced in the sumengo sung at Salutabang. Many songs exalt a headhunter's splendor or a woman's golden voice. Others suggest a tryst. And many express envy of a headhunter's achievement and erotic appeal. Further, the erotic play of headhunter-husband and wife or lover also has an analogue in performance style. Whereas the narrative song cycle at Saludengen produces a history capable of uniting native sons in communal solidarity, the playful song duels at Salutabang promote an erotic tension that allows a man to fell a woman, and thereby advance, or assure, his position in the theater of prestige politics.

Let us return briefly to Ambe Teppu's understanding of the sumengo from Saludengen. The humiliation a husband might experience in household life probably has little to do with an inability to call for services from his wife. In fact, he can reasonably expect a wife to help him as long as she is well disposed toward him. But a husband must be anxious at times insofar as he must serve not only his wife but his wife's kin as well. Thus, I would argue that a man's sense of failure and resignation in his interdependency with a spouse necessarily involves a prolonged and humiliating subordination to some of his key status rivals: his in-laws. In an uxorilocal context, to depend upon a wife for both hearth and political platform is to depend upon that wife's parents and siblings, persons who inevitably view an in-marrying youth as an inferior outsider. A man must give his wife and in-laws the gift of labor. Their favor is critical to his sexual privileges and political status as a married man, and it is never assured.

Ambe Teppu's interpretation of the lyrics makes an allegorical shift away from intercultural politics to the politics of marriage and male status competition. Still, it presumes and develops through a historical understanding of upland-lowland tensions and political-economic patterns that obtained in the past. In other words, the allegorical supplement, precisely because it is allegory and supplement, requires the cover of a "straightforward" historical reading in which it can hide (cf. Chambers 1991: 237–38, 251–52). In this instance, the tactics of an upland headhunter can perhaps tell us something about how to interpret a song, inviting us to think of allegory as an ambush, a reading that bursts out from the brush of a text to dismember an innocent but no less figured understanding. For the song in question, it is history that is ambushed and allegorized so as to clarify gender politics. Alert to other possibilities, I have been unable to find any counterallegories lurking in the songs about husbands and wives. That is, I have yet to meet the singer or listener who would use song lyrics that are ostensibly about local sexual politics to discover and understand the conditions of the uplands' historical subordination to exogenous forces.[15]

[15] The discourse of contemporary headhunting ritual thus fails to illuminate the past with the imagery of husband and wife. Interestingly, this is pre-

To use a musical metaphor, Ambe Teppu transposed tension, conflict, and rivalry from the key of historical intercultural politics to the key of gender relations. The headhunters' fleeting subordination of a social and historical "other" is, in Ambe Teppu's reckoning, analogous to a confrontation with a domestic other—a wife and the wife's kin. The headhunters' victim had to be subdued by violence. Yet a woman, too, is a kind of "prey," who must be momentarily subordinated in the agonistic play of courtship, sex, and marriage (see George 1993b). In neither case, however, can the headhunters shake loose the bonds of interdependency that position them as status inferiors to lowlanders and wives.

The mappurondo community at Salutabang, then, cooperates less as a village than as an aggregate of households. In these circumstances, the moral traditions and concerns of the village are diffuse and less powerful in shaping the political interests of men. At the same time, village men at Salutabang are quite anxious about their sociopolitical status vis-à-vis other men. A man's political participation and prestige hang on his ability to marry and to maintain a household. For the in-marrying husband, the path to sociopolitical parity or prominence always runs through his wife and her kin. Thus, domestic gender relations move to the foreground in the political life of this village, while communal concerns (especially with regard to exogenous threats) recede in importance or relevance. It comes as no surprise that the interpretation of headhunting songs in Salutabang should share the same emphasis.

So far I have stressed the differences between the mappurondo polities at Saludengen and Salutabang. It should be kept in mind, however, that these two communities have in common, among other things, a headhunting tradition. That tradition is politically crucial for both communities in that being mappurondo demands a commitment to ancestral ritual practice. In both instances, the village polity is the overriding concern of pangngae. More specifically, pangngae is a key means of linking the community to the past (and thus controlling the latter) and of reproducing the collective body as such. The communities at Saludengen and Saluta-

cisely the imagery used in local myth to explain the social and political origins of the highland region.

bang are basically similar in their organizational tensions and logic. They differ in the way those tensions and logics are played out, and in the villagers' strategic use of tradition (that is, the historical processes of reinterpretation) for making sense of their sociohistorical circumstances.

The sexual politics so prominent in Salutabang are hardly absent in Saludengen. Nor is the coherent historical vision that typifies Saludengen wholly lacking in Salutabang. The different emphases placed on sexual politics and communal history issue from the sociohistorical trajectories of the two villages. In the arena of headhunting ritual, these themes undergo constant change as the communities adjust to exogenous pressures and the stresses of communal reproduction.

The sumengo, as constitutive of ritual practice, modulate changes of understanding in this tradition. Singer, listener, song performance, and postperformance reflection assume a place amid local circumstances and historical contingencies (cf. Fish 1980; Said 1979). How people interpret the singing is both constrained and motivated by this web of circumstances and prior texts. When I visited with Ambe Siama' and Ambe Teppu, a historical stance appeared to be a stable and fitting hermeneutic strategy for one, whereas an allegoristic stance proved to be a key tactic for the other. The inscribed narrativity and textual fundamentalism of sumengo practice at Saludengen compelled Ambe Siama' to read with communal history. The song duels and textual play at Salutabang, on the other hand, coaxed Ambe Teppu to read away from history to discover allusions to local sexual politics.

Having sketched the effective forces that encouraged different responses to a single set of lyrics, I can return to a claim I made earlier about the historical discourse of pangngae. The problem, as I see it, is to determine whether current headhunting practices comprise an allegory of resistance to the modern order or a practical retreat into the past. Generally speaking, the headhunters of today are eager to prove themselves good citizens. Yet they remain isolated and perplexed by the ideological demands of the Indonesian state. They must make a painful choice: give up the headhunt and, with it, mappurondo history and polity, or remain headhunters and suffer the epithets *yang terbelakang, yang terasing, orang kafir, tomalillin*—the backward, the remote, the godless, the persons of the dark—all euphemisms for those thought to resist the dominant order. What is at stake, then, is the making of social relations and social meanings. Staging a ritual headhunt, in this sense, is a gambit in the asymmetrical play of conflicting social and cultural spheres.

Looking to pangngae for an allegory of this contemporary struggle is not unwarranted. After all, subordination and resistance to exogenous forces are key themes in the headhunt. Nevertheless, I am hesitant to read the ritualized past as a transfiguration of current social and ideological tensions without taking into account the ways mappurondo villagers choose to interpret and allegorize their history. The lesson Ambe Teppu gave me in interpreting the sumengo shows that a history of intercultural relations can allude to the sexual politics so basic to village order. If anything, his interpretation suggests that the central political tensions at Salutabang have shifted inward, that the fate of mappurondo tradition there has already been conceded to encroaching ideologies and the heat of individual interests. Ambe Siama' has provided a different picture with his historical understanding of song lyrics. At Saludengen, having an autonomous history at all is a way to resist the modern order and requires no allegorical supplement. To put it somewhat differently, the present struggle to maintain mappurondo identity and ideology at Saludengen, although inevitably fought *in* history, is also fought *with* history.

Is the discourse of pangngae closed to the asymmetrical relations that currently link the Sulawesi uplands with the outer world? By no means. The making of pangngae necessarily takes place amid the social, political, and ideological pressures bearing on the mappurondo communities. I want to suggest, however, that these asymmetries and pressures are so clearly present, so readily grasped, that villagers have little need of allegory to frame understanding or response. In fact, the upland headhunters occasionally have stepped out of the past to challenge the present directly. In 1958, for example, warriors from a village not mentioned here took a head from the separatist rebel force occupying the market town of Mambi. At another headhunting celebration, in yet another village, in 1985, I heard villagers sing the *ma'denna*, a long antiphonal song praising the virtuous exploits of the headhunters. Along with mentioning Bugis and Mandar figures from the past, the lyrics explicitly listed the titles of contemporary civil administrative officers who would have to meet the upland warriors in battle. The headhunter does not need allegories drawn from the past to discover a threatening opponent in the present, save perhaps at Salutabang, where he looks to history to find images of domestic tension and worry.

The theater of headhunting ritual, with its imagery of violence, manhood, and valor, its explicit concern for tradition, history, and polity, its discourse of opposition and dependency, represents a struggle for meaning. As Hans Medick reminds us, that struggle "is formed in the context of the social relations of individuals, groups, classes, and cultures, which are at the same time constituted by the struggle. Reciprocity, dependency, and resistance— and their mingling—are therefore not 'structurally given'; in reality they come into being only in the struggle for meaning" (1987: 98). Sumengo performance and the reflections of Ambe Siama' and Ambe Teppu are part of this struggle for meaning-at-a-moment-in-history. As such, performance and reflection are practices motivated by the spinning and tearing of intertextual webs between ritual violence, prestige, marriage, communal identity, relations with the outer world, and the past. In this context, historicizing and allegorizing are tactical modes of understanding, of reading with the sociopolitical interests and strains of the mappurondo communities. By the same token, making histories and making allegories are tactical modes of constructing the internal and external dimensions of village polity. The specific understandings and constructions reached will differ from community to community according to sociohistorical circumstance, but they will have in common the need to link past with present. This is the work of mappurondo headhunting tradition. In the face of changing social and political realities, the arts and simulacra of ritual violence assure the construction of meaning, history, and the village polity.

Acknowledgments

This essay first appeared in 1993, dedicated to the memory of A. K. Ramanujan. It is reprinted in slightly revised form from *American Ethnologist* 20 (4): 696–716 (copyright 1993, American Anthropological Association). I gratefully acknowledge support from the Social Science Research Council; the Fulbright-Hays Doctoral Dissertation Abroad Program (Project no. Goo-82-00543); the Wenner-Gren Foundation for Anthropological Research (Grant no. 4144); the University of Michigan Institute for the Humanities; and the National Endowment for the Humanities. My thanks also go to Lembaga Ilmu Pengetahuan Indonesia, Pusat Latihan Penelitian Ilmu-Ilmu Sosial at Universitas Hasanuddin, and to the people of Desa Bambang (Kecamatan Mambi, Kabupaten Polmas) for their cooperation during the 30 months of research (1982–85) that led to this paper. I am obliged as well to the following colleagues for their helpful comments: A. L. Becker, Judith Becker, Donald Brenneis, Karl Heider, Michael Herzfeld, Janet Hoskins, Webb Keane, Joel Kuipers, Vida Mazulis, Gregory Nagy, Kirin Narayan, Sherry Ortner, Mary Steedly, Nur Yalman, Aram Yengoyan, and members of the National Endowment for the Humanities seminar, "Poetics and Social Life" (Indiana University, 1990).

References

Atkinson, Jane Monnig
   1983 "Religions in Dialogue: The Construction of an Indonesian Minority Religion." *American Ethnologist* 10: 684–96.
   1987 "The Effectiveness of Shamans in an Indonesian Ritual." *American Anthropologist* 89: 342–55.
   1989 *The Art and Politics of Wana Shamanship.* Berkeley: University of California Press.
Bakhtin, Mikhail M.
   1981 *The Dialogical Imagination.* Edited by M. Holquist. Austin: University of Texas Press.
Becker, Alton L.
   1979 "Text-Building, Epistemology, and Aesthetics in Javanese Shadow Theatre." In A. L. Becker and A. A. Yengoyan, eds., *The Imagination of Reality: Essays in Southeast Asian Coherence Systems,* pp. 211–43. Norwood, N.J.: Ablex.
Bloch, Maurice
   1974 "Symbols, Song, Dance, and Features of Articulation: Is Religion an Extreme Form of Traditional Authority?" *European Journal of Sociology* 15: 55–81.

Bourdieu, Pierre
  1991 *Language and Symbolic Power.* Edited by J. B. Thompson, trans-
    lated by G. Raymond and M. Adamson. Cambridge, Mass.: Harvard
    University Press.
Brenneis, Donald
  1987 "Performing Passions: Aesthetics and Politics in an Occasionally
    Egalitarian Community." *American Ethnologist* 14: 236–50.
Chambers, Ross
  1991 *Room for Maneuver: Reading Oppositional Narrative.* Chicago:
    University of Chicago Press.
Collier, Jane F., and Michelle Z. Rosaldo
  1981 "Politics and Gender in Simple Societies." In S. B. Ortner and
    H. Whitehead, eds., *Sexual Meanings: The Cultural Construction of
    Gender and Sexuality*, pp. 275–329. Cambridge: Cambridge Univer-
    sity Press.
Culler, Jonathan
  1982 *On Deconstruction: Theory and Criticism After Structuralism.*
    Ithaca, N.Y.: Cornell University Press.
Fabian, Johannes
  1990 *Power and Performance: Ethnographic Explorations Through Pro-
    verbial Wisdom and Theater in Shaba, Zaire.* Madison: University of
    Wisconsin Press.
Fish, Stanley
  1980 *Is There a Text in This Class? The Authority of Interpretive Com-
    munities.* Cambridge, Mass.: Harvard University Press.
  1989 *Doing What Comes Naturally: Change, Rhetoric, and the Prac-
    tice of Theory in Literary and Legal Studies.* Durham, N.C.: Duke
    University Press.
George, Kenneth M.
  1989 "The Singing from the Headwaters: Song and Tradition in the
    Headhunting Rituals of an Upland Sulawesi Community." Ph.D.
    diss., Department of Anthropology, University of Michigan.
  1990 "Felling a Song with a New Ax: Writing and the Reshaping of Rit-
    ual Song Performance in Upland Sulawesi." *Journal of American
    Folklore* 103 (407): 3–23.
  1991 "Headhunting, History, and Exchange in Upland Sulawesi." *Jour-
    nal of Asian Studies* 50 (3): 536–64.
  1993a "Dark Trembling: Ethnographic Notes on Secrecy and Con-
    cealment in Highland Sulawesi." *Anthropological Quarterly* 66 (4):
    230–39.
  1993b "Music-Making, Ritual, and Gender in a Southeast Asian Hill
    Society." *Ethnomusicology* 37 (1): 1–26.

1995 "Violence, Solace, and Ritual: A Case Study from Island Southeast Asia." *Culture, Medicine and Psychiatry* 19 (2): 225–60.

1996 *Showing Signs of Violence: The Cultural Politics of a Twentieth-Century Headhunting Ritual.* Berkeley: University of California Press.

Handler, Richard, and Jocelyn Linnekin

1984 "Tradition, Genuine or Spurious." *Journal of American Folklore* 97 (385): 273–90.

Hoskins, Janet

1987 "The Headhunter as Hero: Local Traditions and Their Reinterpretation in National History." *American Ethnologist* 14: 605–22.

1989 "On Losing and Getting a Head: Warfare, Exchange, and Alliance in a Changing Sumba, 1888–1988." *American Ethnologist* 16: 419–40.

Hymes, Dell

1981 *"In Vain I Tried to Tell You": Essays in Native American Ethnopoetics.* Philadelphia: University of Pennsylvania Press.

Irvine, Judith

1979 "Formality and Informality in Communicative Events." *American Anthropologist* 81: 773–90.

Kapferer, Bruce

1979a "Introduction: Ritual Process and the Transformation of Context." *Social Analysis* 1: 13–19.

1979b "Entertaining Demons: Comedy, Interaction, and Meaning in a Sinhalese Healing Ritual." *Social Analysis* 1: 108–52.

Kipp, Rita Smith, and Susan Rodgers, eds.

1987 *Indonesian Religions in Transition.* Tucson: University of Arizona Press.

McKinley, Robert

1976 "Human and Proud of It! A Structural Treatment of Headhunting Rites and the Social Definition of Enemies." In G. N. Appell, ed., *Studies in Borneo Societies: Social Process and Anthropological Explanation,* pp. 92–126. DeKalb, Ill.: Center for Southeast Asian Studies, Northern Illinois University.

Medick, Hans

1987 " 'Missionaries in a Row Boat'? Ethnological Ways of Knowing as a Challenge to Social History." *Comparative Studies in Society and History* 29: 76–98.

Needham, Rodney

1976 "Skulls and Causality." *Man,* n.s. 11 (1): 71–88.

Ramanujan, A. K.

1988 "On Translating a Tamil Poem." Unpublished manuscript.

Rosaldo, Michelle Z.
  1977 "Skulls and Causality." *Man* n.s. 12 (1): 168–70.
  1980a *Knowledge and Passion: Ilongot Notions of Self and Social Life.* Cambridge: Cambridge University Press.
  1980b "The Use and Abuse of Anthropology: Reflections on Feminism and Cross-cultural Understanding." *Signs* 5 (3): 389–417.
Rosaldo, Renato
  1980 *Ilongot Headhunting, 1883–1974: A Study in Society and History.* Stanford: Stanford University Press.
  1984 "Grief and a Headhunter's Rage: On the Cultural Force of Emotions." In E. M. Bruner, ed., *Text, Play, and Story: The Construction and Reconstruction of Self and Society,* pp. 178–95. Washington, D.C.: American Ethnological Society.
  1987 "Anthropological Commentary." In R. G. Hammerton-Kelly, ed., *Violent Origins: Walter Burkert, René Girard, and Jonathan Z. Smith on Ritual Killing and Cultural Formation,* pp. 239–56. Stanford: Stanford University Press.
Said, Edward
  1979 "The Text, the World, the Critic." In J. V. Harari, ed., *Textual Strategies: Perspectives in Post-Structuralist Criticism,* pp. 161–88. Ithaca, N.Y.: Cornell University Press.
Schechner, Richard
  1985 *Between Theater and Anthropology.* Philadelphia: University of Pennsylvania Press.
Schieffelin, Edward L.
  1985 "Performance and the Cultural Construction of Reality." *American Ethnologist* 12: 707–24.
Smit, P. C.
  1937 *Gegevens over Bambang (1936). Adatrechtbundels XXXIX: Gemengd.* The Hague: Martinus Nijhoff.
Smith, Jonathan Z.
  1978 *Map Is Not Territory: Studies in the History of Religions.* Leiden: E. J. Brill.
  1982 *Imagining Religion: From Babylon to Jonestown.* Chicago: University of Chicago Press.
Tambiah, Stanley
  1985 *Culture, Thought, and Social Action: An Anthropological Perspective.* Cambridge, Mass.: Harvard University Press.
Tedlock, Dennis
  1983 *The Spoken Word and the Work of Interpretation.* Philadelphia: University of Pennsylvania Press.

Turner, Victor
    1982 *From Ritual to Theatre: The Human Seriousness of Play.* New York: Performing Arts Journal Publications.
Vance, Eugene
    1979 "Roland and the Poetics of Memory." In J. V. Harari, ed., *Textual Strategies: Perspectives in Post-Structuralist Criticism*, pp. 374–403. Ithaca, N.Y.: Cornell University Press.
Vansina, Jan
    1985 *Oral Tradition as History.* Madison: University of Wisconsin Press.
Volkman, Toby Alice
    1985 *Feasts of Honor: Ritual and Change in the Toraja Highlands.* Urbana: University of Illinois Press.
Vološinov, V. N.
    1973 *Marxism and the Philosophy of Language.* Translated by L. Matejka and I. R. Titunik. Cambridge, Mass.: Harvard University Press.
Williams, Raymond
    1977 *Marxism and Literature.* Oxford: Oxford University Press.

Allen R. Maxwell

Headtaking and the Consolidation of Political Power in the Early Brunei State

Over the last two thousand years, a traditional head-hunting society centered on the southern shores of Brunei Bay has evolved into the Islamic Malay Sultanate of Brunei Darussalam. The ancestors of modern Brunei probably live in a complex, wealth-financed, individualizing chiefdom (Earle 1991: 3) containing differences of both rank and social class (Fried 1967: 109–10; Rousseau 1990: 164–80), and are likely to have actively taken human heads. Midway through the first millennium, elements of an Indianized Hindu or Hindu-Buddhist culture probably began to change traditional Brunei society.[1] The introduction of Islam sometime in the second millennium triggered yet further changes in Brunei life.[2] State organization was well developed by

[1] The source and first date of Indian influence on Borneo are unknown. The A.D. 1365 Old Javanese poem *Nagara-Kertagama* claims that Brunei was then under Hindu-Buddhist Javanese hegemony from Majapahit (Pigeaud 1960, 1: 11; 3: 16–17; 1962, 4: 31–32). Late-seventh-century Old Malay inscriptions of the Musi and Hari river valleys of southeast Sumatra and Bangka Island show clear evidence of Indian influence in neighboring areas (see Maxwell 1984).

[2] Experts differ about when Islam first arrived in Brunei. A leading Brunei historian argues that Islam had arrived by the early fifteenth (Mohd. Jamil 1977: 40–42) or late fourteenth century (Mohd. Jamil 1990b: 86ff.). Younger Brunei scholars argue from Chinese dynastic sources and tombstone inscriptions in Brunei for a much earlier date than that suggested by Western scholars, claiming that the 977 A.D. mission of the ruler of Brunei to China was guided by three Arabs, P'u Ya-li (Abu Ali), Kadi Kasim, and Syekh Noh (Abdul Karim 1988: 57; Fatimah 1990: 27; Muhammad bin Abdul Latif 1988: 13; Muhammad Hadi 1988: 19; Mohd. Jamil 1990c: 24). European historians have suggested that Islam did not arrive in Brunei until the late fifteenth century or the early sixteenth. D. G. E. Hall claims that Brunei accepted Islam as a result of trading relationships with Malacca (1981: 229, 265). Meilink-Roelofsz expresses a similar view (1962: 100). Exactly when Islam first came to Brunei is a

1521 A.D., when the first European, Pigafetta, visited Brunei. Post-1521 contact with Europeans brought new and powerful influences, accelerating in the nineteenth century and continuing to the present day. The practice of headhunting, an important feature of ancient Brunei life, survived these transformations and persisted as an instrument of Brunei political policy until the late nineteenth century.

The only information concerning headhunting in ancient Brunei is contained in a traditional unpublished Brunei Malay epic poem, the *Sya'ir Awang Simawn*, which presents a Bruneian view of the origin and development of the Sultanate in highly poetic and metaphorical language.[3] Though silent about the ideology (Needham 1976; Rosaldo 1977; Metcalf 1982: 130) and symbolism (Freeman 1979; Davison and Sutlive 1991) of headhunting, it is nonetheless an "indigenous account of violent deeds" (Rosaldo 1977: 168).[4] Headtaking is confined to Part 2 of the poem, which depicts the expansion of Brunei power from the original homeland located on Brunei Bay and contains events that cannot be dated (though they take place well before 977 A.D.; see below). Here, the taking of the heads of people defeated in battle, from one con-

---

very sensitive issue. One Brunei scholar, for example, refers to the opinions of Western historians on this subject as "slanders" or "calumnies"—*hujah-hujah* (Muhammad bin Abdul Latif 1988: 14). Bowen notes a similar case of tension between Western and local ideas about the coming of Islam to Aceh and northern Sumatra (1991: 247ff.).

[3] Though mentioned by numerous writers (e.g., Harrisson 1949: 97–98; 1960: 44–45; Abdul Latif 1970: 39–40, 44; D. E. Brown 1970: 134–35; Mohd. Jamil 1971: 1–17; 1973: 1–8; 1990b: 38, 43, 53; Muhammad Abd. Latiff 1980: 12–13; Abdullah and Muslim 1984: viii–ix; Maxwell 1987: 9–10; Awang 1989: 17, 30–32; Md. Yussop 1989: 20), the only discussions of the *Sya'ir Awang Simawn* are two brief outlines of its contents by Kimball (1979: 36–43) and Brown (1984: 11–13). Damit (1986) gives a short account of one of the early episodes. Brief excerpts have been published by Harrisson (1949: 97–98); Abdul Latif (1970: 44, 39); Ismail (1982: 105–6); Awang (1989: 30–32); and Mohd. Jamil (1990a: 3; 1990b: 53 n. 3). I have collated six different versions of the text (Maxwell 1988), phonemicized the one tape-recorded (Maxwell 1989c) and five romanized versions (Maxwell 1989d, 1989e, 1990, 1991, 1992a), and drafted an outline of the episode contents (Maxwell 1992b). The collated six versions contain approximately 3,300 four-line rhymed verses.

[4] The only other indigenous account of Borneo headhunting appears to be the brief description of the paraphernalia of a headhunter of the Upper Kapuas and Melawi valleys of West Kalimantan by Wan Masyuhur, a *jaksa* (judicial official) of Sintang (Kater 1876).

quered territory after another, is steeped in connotative and symbolic meaning.

Within the ethos of Malay kingship, it is entirely reasonable and proper for a divine ruler to demand submission from all about him. To oppose a request of a Raja can be blasphemous, or worse, constitute treason (*durhaka*—see Milner 1982: 60–61, 68; Kratz 1993). Milner describes the Malay state as "a state where treason is unthinkable, where social life, the past, and the outside world are comprehended only through the prism of the Raja, where every person has a fixed position understood only in relation to the Raja, provid[ing] us with a picture . . . of a singularly absolute society" (1982: 104). In the *Sya'ir Awang Simawn*, the Brunei leader, Raja Awang Halak Batatar, dispatches his heroes and their troops to crush any opposition, to obtain submission to his authority and person. The taking of heads by the representatives of the Brunei Raja simply illustrates how battles were fought and how the values and sentiments of the kingship were upheld. The taking of heads in the symbolic framework of the Malay *Kerajaan* (the monarchical government based on a Raja)—transforming conquered people into loyal subjects—is what makes Brunei unique in the Malay world.

Curiously, Awang Halak Batatar twice declines to accept for himself any of the heads his forces have brought home to Brunei. In the pre-Islamic Borneo context of this portion of the tale, in which possessing heads is good in and of itself, this refusal seems incongruous. (In the text, heads are important items of bridewealth [*barian*], necessary if a youth is to marry.) But if Awang Halak's activities are seen as politically foundational, as part of a long process through which Brunei leaves the old pagan world of Borneo to join the more cosmopolitan and international world of protohistoric and later historic Southeast Asia, his actions take on wider and more worldly significance.

Brunei's Early Days

Local traditions place Brunei's origin in the descent of its royal line from a group of culture heroes[5] fathered by a man (or his son)

---

[5] The "heroes" are not so designated in Brunei (Standard Malay *pahlawan*, Brunei Malay *palawan* [hero, which is bookish]). Kadayan commonly refer to

who emerged from an egg that had fallen from the sky, landing in
the upper Limbang Valley of modern Malaysian Sarawak (Maxwell 1989b: 235–36).[6] These fourteen heroes flew up into the sky
to meet the King of Heaven, Raja Kayangan, and then returned
to earth to different areas around Brunei Bay. These men, through
their fantastic and miraculous deeds, founded the nation of Brunei. In Nicholl's periodization of Brunei historiography, these
events occur in the first era of Brunei's history, which ended
around 1000 A.D. (Nicholl 1980b: 222–25).

Few dates in early Brunei history are well established. Brunei
rulers sent missions to the Emperor of China in 977, 1082, 1371,
1405, 1407, 1408, and 1412 A.D. (Brown 1972). The 1408 mission
received Chinese support for severing the Javanese state of Majapahit's hegemony over Brunei. The first Western-language account
of early Brunei is the glowing description of the Brunei court by
Antonio Pigafetta, chronicler of the Magellan voyage (Pigafetta
1969: 88–100). A satisfactory account of the origins of the use
of writing, the elaborate court ceremony, and the rich material
culture Pigafetta saw in 1521 remains to be written. Despite Hall's
(1981: 229) and Meilink-Roelofsz's (1962: 100) claims of early-
sixteenth-century Malaccan influence on Brunei, no adequate explanation exists of how or why an elaborate Malay court society
developed on the northwest coast of Borneo.

The sixteenth century saw the zenith of the Brunei empire
(Brown 1970: 140), which then encompassed the northern coasts
of the island of Borneo and stretched into the southern Philippines. At various times Sulu, the Calamines, and other Philippine
islands sent tribute to Brunei (Mohd. Jamil 1990a: 25–26). Late in
the sixteenth century, Brunei's Borneo domains stretched from
Sambas and Tanjung Datu in the west to Tanjung Kinungan and
Bulungan in the east (Mohd. Jamil 1990a: 25). At this time, a
series of conflicts developed with the Spanish, based in the Philippines (Nicholl 1975). In the seventeenth and eighteenth cen-

---

them as *urang kuat* (literally, strong person or persons), a lexeme denoting
one who is enormously strong, often invulnerable (*kabal*), with preternatural
abilities. Kayan *lakin* (war leader, hero) also refers to ancestral Kayan culture
heroes.

[6] An origin from an egg or an object fallen from the sky is found in several
Bornean groups (see Maxwell 1989b; cf. Brown 1980). A similar idea is also
known from ancient Mesopotamia (Hyginus 1975: 125).

turies, Brunei had only sporadic contact with Europeans. By the early nineteenth century, the Sultan of Brunei's Borneo territories stretched from Tanjung Datu to Kanukungan Point (now Tanjung Mangkalihat) in the Makassar Strait, in the east (Hunt 1846 [1812], 2: xx). Finally, in 1839, a relationship began with the British that continues to the present (Brown 1970; Ranjit Singh 1984).

The practice of headtaking in nineteenth-century Borneo was very different from that in the first phase, more than a millennium before. At least two historical processes led to the nadir of Brunei's political fortunes in the nineteenth century. Malay control of seaborne commerce slowly declined following the Portuguese conquest of Malacca in 1511; and after securing economic footholds in Indian ports, Europeans began to dominate maritime trade in Southeast Asia (Wolters 1967; 1970: 171–80). By the nineteenth century, Brunei rulers were reduced to utilizing the threat of marauding Kayan headhunters from the Baram Valley of Sarawak to attempt to control recalcitrant Lun Bawang (Murut) populations in valleys close to the capital (St. John 1974 [1862], 1: 90–92, 2: 54–57; Hall 1955: 164).[7]

Headhunting in the *Sya'ir Awang Simawn*

In the mythological past of the *Sya'ir Awang Simawn*, headtaking involves one group of people expressing power and dominance over another with a victory in armed conflict. The matter-of-fact, almost boastful recitation of the large number of heads taken by the warriors suggests that George's hypothesis that headhunting originates as sacred violence in ritual (1991: 545–46) is inapplicable in this case. The distance of the headtaking attacks from the Brunei homeland also seems to rule out Vayda's suggestion that headhunting is inextricably connected to warfare (Vayda 1969, for the Iban). Headtaking in the *Sya'ir* is part of a mythological charter explaining how the Brunei empire came to be, and how out-

[7] The history of Brunei relations with the Baram Kayan is unknown. In 1837, Dickenson (1838: 178–80) saw three Baram boats with 70 men at the Brunei capital, and recorded words from Lokiput (Lakiput, or "Long Kiput") and two other unidentified languages. In the nineteenth century, the Kayan dominated the Lakiput area politically. In 1868, James Brooke received a letter from Raja Tamal, a Baram Kayan claiming to be responsible for Kayan relations with Brunei (Keppel 1853, 2: 100–101).

siders could be fitted not into a scheme of "joy about being human beings" (McKinley 1976: 126), but into the structure of the traditional Brunei sociopolitical system (Brown 1970: 76–85).

The main protagonists of the *Sya'ir Awang Simawn* are Awang Halak Batatar, the all-powerful ruler who eventually becomes the first Muslim ruler of Brunei, Sultan Muhammad Shah; Awang Simawn, the text's eponymous hero; his constant companion, Damang Sari; and Awang Jarambak.[8] Though the poem is silent about their ethnicity, they are commonly said in Brunei to have been Murut, probably Lun Bawang (see Mohd. Jamil 1973, 2: 2–3; 1990b: 40, for discussion of Murut or possible Iban origins). Others claim they were Bisaya (Mjöberg 1929: 47; Sandin 1971: 1–6).

Just what does the *Sya'ir Awang Simawn* say about headhunting? Taking heads is mentioned in 51 verses of the collation (22–27 verses in five of the six versions collated). These verses all occur in Part 2 of the poem, "Brunei Conquests."[9] Part 2 (41 episodes, 726 collation verses) depicts the many conquests of the Brunei heroes in Borneo, the southern Philippines, and unidentified areas (in Borneo or neighboring islands, to the east). Part 1, "The Origins and Beginnings of Brunei" (10 episodes, 527 collation verses), tells of the origins of Brunei in the sky, introduces the cast of characters, describes the move to the historical location of the Brunei capital, and explains the extraordinary powers of the heroes.

Parts 3–16 are concerned with events within Brunei itself (relations with Johor, Java, China, and the Spanish; the arrival of Islam in Brunei; Brunei ceremonial ritual; and the adventures of later Brunei Sultans) and do not mention the taking of heads. Parts 1 and 2 comprise slightly more than one-third of the text in the six versions examined. This discussion focuses primarily on Part 2 of the *Sya'ir Awang Simawn*.

---

[8] The other heroes who play lesser parts in the drama are Patih Barbay (or Marbay), Patih Sandayung (or Sindayung), Damang Libar Dawn, Patih Malakay, Patih Tuba (or Tawba), Hapu Awang, Layla Langgung, Patih Payt, Patih Manggarun, Patih Sangkuna, and Patih Mambang. Si-Nuay, son of Awang Jarambak, plays an important role in two incidents. Numerous other figures from Borneo, China, and the Philippines appear in particular episodes in the text.

[9] I tentatively divide the *Sya'ir Awang Simawn* into sixteen parts, of from one to 41 episodes, primarily based on content. Lexical clues sometimes support these divisions. The text itself is entirely seamless, without headings or internal divisions.

Illus. 1. Murut head feast. From Shelford 1916, plate XXII.

Though the dates of the events depicted in the epic are un-known,[10] the arrival of Islam in Brunei occurs in Part 10 of the text, consisting of only one episode of ten verses. In other words, Islam arrives after more than four-fifths of the tale of the *Sya'ir* has been told. China is first mentioned in Part 7, more than two-thirds of the way through the text. Whatever the date, therefore, the epic depicts these events as occurring *long before* Islam ar-rives in Brunei, and also predates the first Brunei mission to China in 977 A.D. (Brown 1972; Wolters 1967: 175–76, 314 n. 104, 321–22 n. 21).

All references to headtaking in the text revolve around the adventures of the three main warrior-heroes—Awang Simawn, Awang Jarambak, and Damang Sari—who, with their troops, de-

[10] The recent discovery of a tombstone inscribed "Roqiah binte Sultan Ab-dul Majid ibni Muhammad Shah Al-Sultan" led Jaafar to conclude that Sultan Abdul Majid was the son of the first Sultan of Brunei, Muhammad Shah (Awang Halak Batatar), living in the early fifteenth century (Jaafar 1988: 31; Mohd. Jamil 1990a: 9–11). No ruler of this name appears on Brunei's official royal genealogy (Brunei 1988: 109).

feat one local leader after another, laying waste to their countries, wealth, and citizens. The conquests can be conveniently grouped into two phases, separated by a brief direction-changing episode. The initial attacks occurred southwest of the capital of Brunei, in the lands of modern Sarawak and western Indonesian Kalimantan (see map). Once these territories have been conquered, the forces return to Brunei to bring the news to the ruler, Awang Halak Batatar. In a brief interlude, Ilanun and Bajaw forces from the Kinabatangan and Tungku areas of eastern Sabah, led by Datu Barambun, attack Brunei. The Brunei heroes, as expected, defeat the invaders. The second series of conquests occurs northeast of Brunei, in Sabah, the southern Philippines, the east coast of Kalimantan, and an unidentified area, possibly on the west coast of Sulawesi (Celebes).[11] The main groups defeated by the Brunei heroes in this phase of their conquests are the Ilanun, the Suluk, and the Bugis.

The Brunei Expansion to the South and North

In Part 1 of the *Sya'ir Awang Simawn*, the heroes meet to pay homage to the ruler, Awang Halak Batatar. (Only two text versions contain this episode.) Patih Barbay (who in some traditions becomes the second Sultan of Brunei, Sultan Ahmad) advises the ruler that it would be a good idea to ask countries whether they will follow his authority or oppose it. Next follows a long list of territories lying to the south and west of Brunei. Tutong and Belait lie within modern Brunei.[12] Twenty areas between the Baram and Sarawak Rivers fall within the borders of Malaysian Sarawak (see map). Two other places, Sambas and Puntianak, now lie in Indonesian Kalimantan, further to the south.[13]

[11] Identification of possible locations in Sulawesi is uncertain. The phrase "Pulaw Bugis" could refer to "The Island(s) of the Bugis" (Sulawesi); an unidentified island inhabited by Bugis; a group of settlements somewhere on the island of Borneo inhabited by Bugis; or an island in the southern Philippines. The text does, however, plainly indicate that the Brunei heroes defeated a large number of Bugis somewhere.

[12] See map for locations. An identification of a place name on the island of Borneo on the map refers to the river of that name, except when (mainly in Sabah) it is clear that a settlement is intended.

[13] Only identified places are listed. Unidentified place names are Anih, Suman, Batak, Bayanan, Tanjung Puraga at Batu Mandi, Balayangan, and Lubuk Paringgi, which may refer to locations in Sarawak. Balintung and Batu Gadung are possibly in Patani, southern Thailand, and Trengganu, in the northeast of the Malay Peninsula.

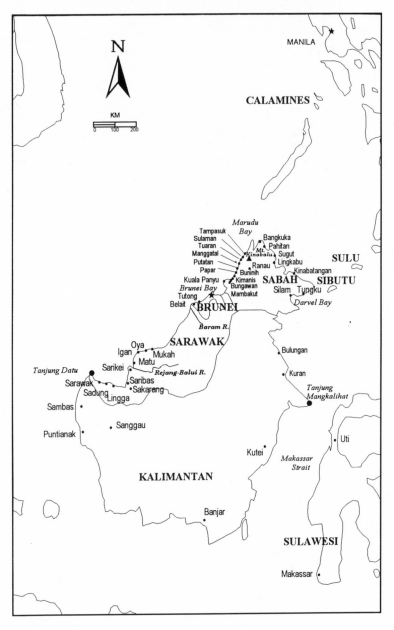

Conquests of ancient Brunei.

The Raja's forces first visit Tutong, twenty miles to the west-southwest. Pambakal Bangis leads the delegation and requests that Mawangga, the Tutong leader, present himself at the capital.[14] Mawangga replies that he and his followers are not free to do so because they are only *hamba jarahan*, or conquered slaves. Tutong was then under the overlordship of the great Melanau leader Basiung (Andreini 1931; Anonymous 1907; Lawrence 1909, 1911) and his in-law Tugaw, living at Igan about 300 miles to the southwest.[15] Mawangga directs Awang Halak's men to Igan. If the Melanau leader will submit to the Brunei Raja's authority, Tutong will do likewise. At the end of Part 1, the troops and Mawangga leave for Igan to meet Basiung.

The leader of the Brunei forces tells Basiung that Awang Halak Batatar wants him and his men to come to Brunei to submit to his authority at Junjungan. The Igan leader is perplexed and uncertain, indicating that he is the recipient, not the giver, of homage, just taking women and children without bothering to ask. The Brunei Raja should come on his knees to pay *him* homage, Basiung replies, and should Awang Halak be slow in coming, Igan will attack. Bangis, the Brunei emissary, says that he has no power to alter a request of the Raja, and that the Igan leader would do well to assemble his troops, because the Brunei forces are not inconsiderable. Bangis gives Basiung nine days to make up his mind. Basiung says he will wait, and he tells Pambakal Bangis to bring his troops by the thousands, and also gifts, saying that if the Brunei leader appears in a timely fashion, without delay, and in earnest, he will not be killed. Bangis replies with some agitation that Basiung should wait for the return of all the Brunei forces in

[14] Identifications of parties and places differ in some versions and are important to the multiform character of the *Sya'ir*. Variants designate persons of secondary importance to what is primary, the history of Brunei as told through the exploits of its most illustrious culture heroes, Awang Halak Batatar, Awang Simawn, Awang Jarambak, and Damang Sari. Their names are virtually never confused. Lower-ranking individuals in the Brunei forces and leaders of opposing forces are of lesser concern.

[15] All versions agree that Tugaw was Basiung's in-law, but not whether he was Basiung's father-in-law, *bapa minantu*, or his son-in-law, *anak minantu*, simply identifying him as "*minantu*." The ethnicity of the Igan people is never identified. Elsewhere Basiung and Tugaw are legendary Melanau leaders (Hang Tuah 1971; Anonymous 1907; Lawrence 1909, 1911; Andreini 1931). Mohd. Jamil records a Brunei tradition that Simawn was Tugaw's father (1973, 2: 3).

nine days, and then either acknowledge Brunei's supremacy or be killed himself. The Brunei mission then returns home with Basiung's reply.

On hearing the news, Awang Halak Batatar is both in despair and offended. One of his ministers advises that they should attack. Drums are sounded to call all the followers together. Patih Barbay tells Awang Simawn, Damang Sari, Awang Jarambak, Layla Langgung, and the others assembled that this Basiung must be put in his place. They all shout that they will attack: Jarambak with his *mangaris* spears, Simawn with his blowpipe, and Damang Sari with his mattock.

The Igan Valley of Sarawak, just north of the great Rejang-Balui river delta, thus became the very first region of Borneo conquered by Brunei. The Igan is a short river located in the traditional territories of the Melanau-speaking peoples. The Melanau were traditionally sago cultivators, heavily influenced in recent centuries by Islam and the sociopolitical system of Malay-speaking Brunei (Morris 1953: 4–6; 1978: 39–40). In the text, Igan's subjugation is described in two quite different ways.

The first (in only one text version) involves the three main battle heroes, Simawn, Jarambak, and Damang Sari, in a fight with a mythological being, the *gihin* Bilantapura. Upon arriving on the scene, Bilantapura, threatens to split Jarambak's head open. After fighting for nine months, Simawn and Damang Sari grow weary. Simawn further challenges Bilantapura, saying they are prepared to fight for 100 months. Meanwhile, while wandering around at Pulaw Marindang, Jarambak, who is none too bright, finally hears the sounds of battle. He meets a *gargasi*, a tusked cannibal-ogre-demon, from whom he obtains a magically endowed fish skin.[16] He promptly climbs on and flies off for nine months, finally arriving at the Plain of Igan. He slashes Bilantapura's head from the air. Bilantapura flies away, but Jarambak pursues the demon, finally catching and beheading him. Jarambak soars back to Igan, where Simawn and Damang Sari are astonished to see him fly in. He announces that Bilantapura is dead, his head split off at Biduk

---

[16] Wilkinson identifies *gargasi* as a forest ogre, associated—along with *raksasa* and *bota*—with the aboriginal inhabitants of an area conquered by intruding newcomers (1959 [1932]: 357–58).

Tanah. Jarambak stores the magical skin in his loincloth, and all pile up corpses, and steam and torch the heads taken.[17]

In the second description of this conquest (four versions), Simawn, Damang Sari, and Jarambak present themselves to Awang Halak Batatar. He advises them not to fall asleep, wishes them good fortune, and admonishes them to stay away from misfortune and surprises. The forces leave in a great tumult. This time their foes are the human Basiung and his Igan followers. The Melanau call in their allies, from Sambas and Sarawak, from Matu, Sadung, and Sarikei; all 9,000 assemble at Igan. When the Brunei forces reach Igan, the stupendous power of the Brunei heroes' weapons frighten Basiung and his lieutenants.

Early one morning, the Brunei forces attack by the hundreds, thousands, and tens of thousands, with missiles raining down on both sides. The troops are protected by Awang Halak Batatar's kingly supernatural influence (*dawlat*). Thousands die, and many flee. Basiung and Tugaw are in tears, realizing that all is lost. Simawn's forces are fierce, and by the ten thousands, the Murut bachelors make the special *garanjang* baskets (still used today for transporting fruit from the forest) to carry the heads they have taken, which will become their betrothal gifts.[18] With a thousand heads each in their possession, some warriors burn all the houses, while others smash all the pottery and raid the jars of *burak* (rice wine). Thousands of slaves (*hulun*) are taken, and the booty seems endless. Jarambak climbs up into Basiung's house and bellows out that the Igan people are too haughty. He orders Basiung to make obeisance to the conquering forces, which he does straightaway. Basiung and Igan now acknowledge the overlordship of Awang Halak Batatar. the Brunei forces should feel free to take whatever

[17] References to "steaming and torching" heads probably relate to traditional methods of preserving skulls. Sellato reports that "even the severed heads could be decorated, although in most cases they were simply boiled and skinned or smoked" (1989: 35). Rutter notes that Sabah Murut boiled, skinned, and smoked their skulls (1985 [1929]: 192–93), and Hoskins reports the boiling of heads in Sumba (1987: 605, 607).

[18] A *garanjang* is a large basket made on the spot in the forest, from a length of bamboo (four to six inches in diameter), split several times from the top. The strakes, interwoven with rattan or vines, spread outward from the bottom to the top in an ever-widening diameter. The basket is two to three feet wide at the top, and is carried on the back with shoulder straps. The top can extend over a man's head, and the narrow bottom to the small of his back or below.

they wish; the Melanau no longer dare to resist. The victorious troops continue their plundering of the historically Melanau areas of Oya, Matu, and Mukah, all the way to Sambas.

So ends the first of many conquests by Awang Halak Batatar's followers, seeking respect for and submission to the sovereignty of the Brunei ruler. The conquest of Igan is the only major battle in modern Sarawak in the text. Other Sarawak territories plundered and defeated by the Brunei heroes during the Igan campaign are allies of Igan.[19]

After subjugating these areas southwest of Brunei, the heroes return home to Garang to bring Awang Halak the booty and news of their conquests.[20] Meanwhile, a force of Ilanun and Bajaw sails from the east coast of modern-day Sabah to attack Brunei. The Ilanun and their allies are vanquished in a furious battle. Patih Barbay advises Awang Halak Batatar of the evil character of the Sabah countries (*Nagri Saba jahat katara*, "The Saba countries are clearly evil"). Troops are called to assembly, and Awang Halak Batatar directs his followers to proceed north and lay waste to the upstarts. Thus begins the second phase of the Brunei conquests.

The account of the northern conquests (31 episodes) is longer and more complex that the account of the southern expansion. Some 32 different locations are mentioned, either as being attacked and defeated or as giving obeisance and tribute to Brunei authority (see table below; map). These territories are located

[19] Sarikei and Rajang are no longer inhabited primarily by Melanau, but possibly were in the past. Two other valleys of Sarawak, Sadung and Sarawak, and the regions lying to the east of Tanjung Datu, have been peopled in recent times by the "Land Dayak." "Land Dayak" labels an ethnic and linguistic congeries, well established in the anthropological literature. "Bidayuh," the current Sarawak term, is but one of a number of mutually unintelligible "Land Dayak" speech forms. Others include Puruh, Lara', Jagoi, Lundu, Bukar-Sadung, and Selako (Nais 1989: 369); Bekati, Benyadu', Jongkang, Sanggau, Kembayan, Pandu, Ribun, and Semandang (Hudson 1970). Unlike the other "Land Dayak" isolects, Selako is very closely related to Malay, and is classified by Hudson as "Malayic-Dayak." A final area, Lingga, has been an Iban territory for over a century. Three other areas, Sambas, Puntianak, and Sanggau (on the upper Kapuas River), all now lie in western Kalimantan.
[20] This reference to Garang, located on Brunei's swampy Temburong coast (Mohd. Jamil 1973, 2: 6; 1990b: 14) and the original home of the heroes, appears to be an anachronism. By this time, the heroes had already moved to the Brunei River (located of the modern capital), after it was discovered by Patih Barbay. Other traditions place the origin a bit further east, in modern Sarawak.

along the west coast of Sabah, across the north coast, and down the east coast of this modern-day Malaysian state. The Brunei warriors also defeated a number of territories on the east coast of Indonesian Kalimantan, as far south as Banjar (the modern Banjarmasin). In the Philippines, Suluk (Sulu or Jolo) was defeated, and Manila acknowledged Brunei hegemony and sent tribute.[21]

Headtaking by Brunei Forces

The plunder and booty taken by the heroes in the attacks north of Brunei are described in greater detail than are the spoils of conquests to the south. Heads taken in the encounters are specifically mentioned for only one place to the south, Igan. In Episode 12, two verses say of Igan:[22]

Simawn's people, are oh so fierce,
   tens of thousands, make head
  baskets;
all the Murut, whoever is unmarried,
   take heads, to bring betrothal
  gifts.

Ra'yat Simawn, tarlalu garang,
   baribu laksa, barbuat garan-
  jang;
sakalian Murut, barang yang
bujang,
   mangambil kapala, mambari
  tunang.

A thousand a person, the heads
their gains,
   half of them torch, all the
  houses;

Saribu saurang, kapala ulihnya,

   satangah manunu, sakalian
  rumahnya;

[21] The territories to the north, either conquered or acknowledging Brunei hegemony, included Kuala Panyu, Mambakut, Bungawan, Kimanis, Binunih, Papar, Putatan, Manggatal, Tuaran, Sulaman, Ranau, and Tampasuk along Sabah's west coast; Bangkuka and Marudu in the north; Pahitan, Sugut, the island of Lingkabu, Kinabatangan, Tungku, and Silam on the east coast; and Bulungan, at the mouth of the great Kayan River, which flows northeast through East Kalimantan, Kuran (a Brunei Malay term for Berau, just south of Bulungan [Hunt 1846 (1812), 2: lxiii]), Sandungan, Mutu, and Banjar along the east and south coasts of Kalimantan. (Sandungan and Mutu are not yet identified, but lie close to Bulangan.) In addition to Suluk and Manila, Simbatu, or Sambatu, may be the Philippine island of Sibutu, lying about 30 miles east-southeast of Tungku, at the mouth of Darvel Bay. Three sites remain unidentified: Papan, Rantungan, and Lantay. Another site, variously rendered in the text as Uti, Uni, Utay, Warti, or Wati, may be the settlement of Oti, located on the northwest coast of Sulawesi, just above the mouth of the bay leading out of the Palu river.

[22] The comma breaking each line of the Malay text marks a caesura. The grammatical subject of a sentence may be omitted in Brunei Malay. See the introductory note to the appendix, below.

there are those who plunder, the *lutu* jars,	*ada yang marampas, pasu lu-tunya,*
others plunder, the jars of rice wine.	*layn marampas, tajaw bu-raknya.*

Other versions have 10,000 heads a person, or 10 heads a person, instead of 1,000. Later, in Episode 17, while the heroes are still at Igan and about to return to Brunei, the heroes have thousands of *garanjang* baskets, full of heads to take back with them. When the spoils are being divided, Awang Halak Batatar makes it clear to his followers that he wishes to have none of the heads.

"Wait just a bit, all you Awangku,[23]	"*Nanti dahulu, Awangku sagala,*
and all your people, along with you;	*sakalian ra'yat, basarta pula;*
don't let me, be given any heads, if there are any, just some jewels."	*jangan lah aku, dibari kapala, jikalaw pun barulih, intan kumala.*"

Later in the text, Awang Halak Batatar rejects both heads and "bales of cloth" (*kayn bandala*)—or, in other versions, "boxes and bales [presumably filled with something]" (*kaban bandala*)—and indicates that he will accept "half the *ambin* baskets." [24]

Other kinds of plunder obtained in the Igan compaign include the contents of houses (*isi rumah*), various kinds of jar (*gusi, pasu, tajaw*), and thousands of slaves (*ulun*). The items taken from Igan, Oya, Mukah, and Sambas are fewer in number and less frequently mentioned than those from the northern conquests. The heroes further demand that the conquered leaders send tribute to Awang Halak Batatar in Brunei once a year. The defeated, of course, agree to send the children, riches, slaves, and thousands of *gusi* demanded.

With the defeat of Igan, Sarawak falls to Brunei, implying that the whole of the northwest coast of Borneo south of Brunei Bay was then under the overlordship of Melanau Igan. Other evidence supports the existence of a very early center of trade and politi-

---

[23] *Awangku* are male nobles (females: *Dayangku*). Nobles, male or female, can also be designated *Pangiran* or *Raja*, which are also commonly used as second- and third-person pronouns, and as name-prefixes—much as the English Mr., Ms., Miss, Mrs.—for Barunay nobles (see Brown 1970: 171–74).

[24] An *ambin* is an all-purpose back basket woven from split rattan.

cal power, somewhere near the modern center of Melanau territory. Brown refers to Vijayapura, a contemporary of Srivijaya, as
located by Wolters "somewhere in western Borneo," and by
Moens as "connected with the Melanau peoples . . . on the Rejang
River of Sarawak" (Brown 1970: 132; Wolters 1967: 204, 212, 354–
55; Moens 1939: 32–38). Nicholl reviews the early western cartography on Borneo and concludes that Melanau has been located
in the same area for more than six centuries (1980a, 1976).[25] Thus,
by conquering only Igan, Brunei became heir to the rest of the
modern-day Sarawak territories.

A quite different picture emerges from the Brunei conquests to
the north. Rather than launch a single major attack on one location, the Brunei forces engage in some twenty attacks on at least
fifteen different sites, suggesting that to the north of Brunei, unlike in Sarawak to the south, there was no single dominant political center that controlled the many smaller centers scattered
along the coasts. In these northern battles, heads are taken in at
least ten different locations. This information is summarized in
the accompanying table.[26]

Awang Halak Batatar repeats that he wishes to have none of the
heads taken in the northern victories.

Awang Halak spoke, in a pleasant voice,	*Awang Halak barsabda, manis suara,*
"Hail younger brothers, and relatives;	*"Ayuhay adinda, sanak saw-dara;*
thanks to be free, from peril, the booty of plunder, take it immediately.	*sukur tarlapas, daripada mara,* *ulih marampas, ambil lah sigara.*
"The goods gotten, and all the heads,	*"Barang barulih, sakalian kapala,*
or the gains, of *bandala* boxes; the booty of plunder, all of it, don't let me, be given heads."	*ataw barulih, kaban bandala;* *ulih marampas, itu sagala,* *jangan lah aku, dibari kapala."*

[25] Nicholl shows the location of Melanau at or just north of the Rejang
River, from 1375–1622, under various names: Malao, Mallao, melang, belanos,
r demalano, demalano, Rio d'maluno, mallano, Malano, and Millano (1976,
1980a).

[26] Regarding hands, Sellato notes, "The Dusun and Murut also used to sever
their victims' hands and feet to display as offerings, and the Kayan offered
pieces of human flesh to the hawks, often considered embodiments of one of
the principal gods" (1989: 34).

Incidents of Headhunting During Brunei's Northern Conquests

Location	Episode no.	Details of headtaking incidents
Kuran	21	Bugis heads taken from dawn to dusk
	23	Tons (*barkuyan-kuyan*) of Bugis heads taken
Banjar	22	A number of (*babarapa*) Bugis heads taken
	25	Thousands of heads taken
Uti	26	1,000 heads per warrior taken, OR
		10 heads per warrior taken, OR
		1,000 warriors took heads
Papan	27	Tons of heads taken
Bulungun	28	Heads taken from dawn to dusk
Sandungan	29	Heads taken every day
		Brunei troops cut off all the heads
		Severed heads all stacked up and packed together, OR severed heads resembling a hill
		Severed heads piled upstream and downstream
		Severed heads piled up like Mt. Kinabalu
Mutu	30	The booty of heads was not a few
		All the forces made *garanjang* baskets
		1,000 heads per warrior were counted
Tungku	33	Severed heads piled up resembling a hill
		1,000 heads per person piled up like nutmegs
Pulaw Bugis	39	Thousands of heads are damaged running aground
		The forces slash, taking heads
		Raja Tawaju, the Bugis leader, threatens to split Jarambak's head open
		Severed heads piled up resembling a hill
		Each warrior has his own garanjang basket
Rantungan	42	Brunei forces cut off thousands OR hundreds of Kalangan Dusun heads and hands
All countries	45	1,000 heads per person taken
		Nine fathoms wide the garanjang baskets
Not given	46	Balut had 1,000 heads
		Simawn and Jarambak brought their heads and wealth
		Basiung packed his heads and *lampit* mats
		Basiung had a pile of heads like a hill on his raft
Bulungan, Simbatu	47	1,000 heads were offered as prestations
Not given	48	Basiung and Lilit had heads piled up
Tungku	49	Some tens of thousands cut off heads
Silam	49	Heads of drowned victims were cut off
Nagri Bugis	50	Newly wed men and fathers no longer had their heads
Tungku	50	Tens of thousands had had their heads cut off
Silam	50	Heads of drowned victims were cut off

NOTE: "OR" indicates variations between versions.

If his warriors were all so keen to take heads, why does the great Brunei leader not wish to have any of them for himself? The text gives no answer. Headtaking appears to have been a common enough practice in recent historical times; Dalton reports that in one raid, a great chief of the Kutai River, Selgie, received 250 of 700 heads for himself and his sons, and all of the women taken (1968 [1831]: 49). One could suppose that Awang Halak was engaging in a well-known political stratagem—that of not concerning himself too much with the activities of his followers (Barker 1992: 68–69).

The amounts and types of plunder and tribute obtained by the Brunei forces in the north stagger the imagination: "the goods of the afraid," "the contents of houses," "everything," all the "nice things," things "beyond description." Included are four different kinds of spear, four kinds of cloth, three kinds of knife, three kinds of jar, two kinds of mat, shields, jewels, birds, rattans, coconuts, oil, wax, camphor, tinder, and tobacco, all in great quantity. Human booty included two different kinds of slave by the thousands, hundreds of children, and a huge number of women. The number of heads, captives, and goods obtained for Brunei by the heroes— either as booty or as tribute yet to be sent—is of truly epic proportion. Specific amounts mentioned are hundreds, thousands, and tens of thousands, of various measures.

The large numbers might appear to be exaggerations, but such a presumption ignores the special place the *Sya'ir Awang Simawn* occupies in Brunei's ritual and ceremonial life. Until fairly recently, entertainment during wedding rituals frequently included performances of the poem (Brown 1988: 78; cf. St. John 1974 [1862], 2: 260). Oral texts are typically characterized by repetition (Renoir 1987: 534–35, 537) and "thrift" (Parry 1930: 266), a device that minimizes the kind of variation typically found in "creatively" written works. The huge amounts of heads, captives, and goods need not represent accurate numbers, but may constitute an affective device, intended to impress upon the audience the power and majesty of Brunei, announcing that any resistance to its claim of sovereignty would be folly.

The poem makes little mention of the ethnicity of the foes to the south, in Sarawak and West Kalimantan, but is much more specific for enemies to the north: the Bajaw (two episodes), Ilanun

Illus. 2. Start of a 1900s head-recovering expedition. From Shelford 1916, plate XVII.

(four), Suluk (three), Bugis (nine), and Dusun (two). Only the Dusun are indigenous to Borneo. The first three groups are native to the Philippines, and the Bugis to Sulawesi. All three groups exogenous to Borneo have at various times had major settlements on the island of Borneo.

The Bajaw are part of the battle force that attacked Brunei from the north. Other references are only to the Bajaw country(-ies) (Nagri Bajaw) and are not tied to any specific location.[27] The Bajaw were traditionally boat people pursuing a nomadic hunting and foraging life-style, shifting locations frequently. The Bugis are located at Kuran, Banjar, Saba (which could include any of the locations to the north of Brunei), and Uti. There are also references to the Bugis country(-ies) and the Bugis island(s) (Pulaw Bugis).

---

[27] Malay has no obligatory grammatical category of number. Nagri Bajaw is singular or plural. Since the distinction does not exist in Malay, there is no way to determine whether the phrase is intended to be singular or plural.

The Ilanun, who with the Bajaw comprised the main battle force that attacked Brunei, are located at Tungku and the Ilanun country(-ies). The Suluk are placed at Manila, Marudu, Kinabatangan, and Lingkabu, as well as the Suluk country(-ies). The Dusun of modern Sabah are mentioned as having 1,000 of their number killed in Rantungan.[28] The Ranau Dusun supply Jarambak with "piles of women" (parampuan bartimbun). Just three verses later, Awang Simawn obtains 1,000 Kalangan or Galangan Dusun slaves (ulun).[29]

Patih Barbay, in his recommendation that Awang Halak Batatar determine which of the many countries would submit to his authority, mentions no locations to the north of Brunei, only territories to the south. It was the Ilanun and Bajaw attack on Brunei that redirected the flow of events in Brunei's history northward. The greater detail in the record of battles and severity of fighting to the north, and the naming of only southern territories in the request for submission to Awang Halak Batatar's overlordship, suggests a traditional Brunei orientation to the south, rather than to the north.

This conclusion is supported by the qualifications that define citizenship in modern Brunei. The rights of citizenship follow a modified principle of *jus sanguinis*. To qualify as a citizen in modern Brunei, one must be born in the country of parents of one of the country's five Malay ethnic groups (Barunay, Kadayan, Bisaya, Dusun, or Murut); or, if born outside the country, one must be of a father born in Brunei and Malay, or of parents born in Brunei who were members of one of the fifteen "other" non-Malay ethnic groups. Citizenship is determined by the citizenship of one's parents. Thus, in order to qualify for citizenship in Brunei, one must be a member of one of the ethnic groups scheduled in the Brunei

[28] These Dusun are the "Kalangan Dusun." The modern settlement of Kalangan is located on a tributary of Sabah's Papar River, flowing westward into the South China Sea; it is unclear if this is the location intended. The incident is embedded in discussion of battles that occur on Sabah's east coast.

[29] Phonological differences—Ratu/Ranu/Ranau, Galangan/Kalangan—are not problematic. The t/n and k/g alternations vary according to how *jawi* consonants are "dotted." Jawi "wau" can be u, au (aw), or w. Though phonologically unproblematic, the variations are nonetheless significant, underscoring the oral traditional nature of the *Sya'ir Awang Simawn* (Foley 1990: 5–19). Modern Ranau lies about 30 miles to the east-northeast of Kalangan.

Constitution of 1959 (see Brunei n.d.). All of these groups are currently located in either modern Brunei or Sarawak. Most of the "other" ethnic groups now live in Sarawak; none is in Sabah.[30]

Though the origins of the *Sya'ir Awang Simawn* lie lost in the past, the deeds of Brunei's ancient heroes live on, both in the poem and in oral folkloric traditions. When did these events take place? If the position taken here—that the *Sya'ir Awang Simawn* is a multiform work of oral traditional literature—is substantially correct, then any question of when the work was "composed" is misplaced. Traditional singers "compose" a work anew each time they perform it, yielding a myriad of "compositions" (Lord 1960: 4–5, 13–29). More germane is the question of when the *tradition* began, to which there is currently no answer. In the six versions examined, the tale exhibits a temporal trajectory congruent with the relative chronology of historical events in the region known through other sources. In other words, the diachronic flow of the work does not violate the sequence of known historical events.[31] I earlier inferred that the tale begins long before the coming of Islam, but this inference does not speak to the question of when the tradition of presenting this story of Brunei in *sya'ir* format began. The *information* in the tale, like that in the ancient Sanskrit Vedic hymns, may well have been passed down orally from one generation to the next long before the four-line rhymed *sya'ir* literary form was introduced to Brunei. It is well known that an *a-a-a-a* rhyme, such as that of the *Sya'ir Awang Simawn*, antedated the first appearance of the *sya'ir* literary form in Southeast Asia (Sweeney 1971: 63).[32]

[30] Today, there are Barunay and Kadayan communities in Sabah and Sarawak, the result of population movements beginning in the nineteenth century, or earlier.

[31] There is no independently known chronology of many of the events in the *Sya'ir Awang Simawn*. Future research may modify this claim, but for the present it is substantially correct.

[32] One of the earliest—if not the earliest—Malay *sya'ir* known is the eight-verse, silver-inlaid inscription on a bronze cannon, now located on the grounds of Chealsea Hospital, with a cartouche dated Dhul'l-qa'dah 4, 1063 A.H. (26 Sept. A.D. 1653). The mark of the engraver, Abu Mandus, indicates he was from Singgora (the modern town of Songkhla) on the far southeast coast of Thailand, just north of the modern peninsular Malaysian border (Sweeney 1971: 52–56). This date, however, is probably not relevant to the dating of the *Sya'ir Awang*

The significance of headtaking in the *Sya'ir Awang Simawn* is threefold: it constitutes a link between Brunei's ancient, pre-Muslim Bornean past and the present; it symbolizes successful conquest and defeat of enemies and foes; and it signals that the Brunei heroes and their king have established their will over those Bornean groups mentioned in the text.

Awang Halak Batatar is not the only leader in Borneo history to refuse heads from his victorious forces. The Sarawak Iban of Saribas and Sakarang, who frequently attacked Sambas and Puntianak in West Kalimantan, utilized Malay pilots "who always show the way; the spoil is the property of the pilots, the women and children and the skulls are the property of the Dayaks [i.e., Iban]" (Boudriot 1854–55, quoted in Pringle 1970: 49–50). During the expansion of Sarawak power in the period 1841–49, Raja James Brooke used Iban troops to put down rebellious Malay and Arab satraps loyal to Brunei (whom Brooke was quick to label "pi-

---

Simawn, because although the Arabic word *shi'r*, covering "poetry in general" (Teeuw 1966: 433), or "all genres of Islamic poetry" (Sweeney 1971: 63), is certainly the source of the Malay word *sya'ir*, the existence of the Brunei poem probably predates the arrival of this literary tradition, which Teeuw suggests was "probably not earlier that 1600" (1966: 445). Though three of the leading scholars of the Malay *sya'ir*, Andreas Teeuw, Syed Muhammad Naguib al-Attas, and Amin Sweeney, generally agree that this poetic form in Malay literature originated in the work of the late-sixteenth-century Sufi mystic of Barus (northern Sumatra), Hamzah Fansuri (see Teeuw 1966; al-Attas 1968; 1970: 3–30; Sweeney 1971: 68), there also existed an earlier form of Malay verse having an *a-a-a-a* rhyme. This is one of the two different types of four-line verse form of the *nyanyi*, found in the *Sejarah Melayu*, or "Malay Annals" (Sweeney 1971: 63; Shellabear 1967 [1896]: 95, 173; Brown 1952: 69, 115), manuscripts of which are believed to date from at least as early as 1536 and 1612, and possibly as early as the late fifteenth century (Josselin de Jong 1961: 1–5; Windstedt 1969 [1961]: 158–62). (The other form of the *nyanyi* has the same *a-b-a-b* rhyme as the *pantun* [Shellabear 1967 (1896): 67, 201, 208, 233, 245, 273; Sweeney 1971: 63].) However, evidence of the *nyanyi* in the *Sejarah Melayu* suggests that there existed a form of Malay poetry of *a-a-a-a* rhyme—predating the literary form of the *sya'ir* developed by Hamzah Fansuri, from the Arabic *shi'r*—but later labeled by a more widely used term, namely *sya'ir*, with which form it shared the same rhyme. I suggest this latter view for the Brunei Malay *Sya'ir Awang Simawn*, that it represents a very early, currently undatable form of oral epic, which, at some point in time after it became widely popular, picked up the name *sya'ir*. The widespread distribution of oral epics among other indigenous Bornean groups, such as the Lun Bawang, Kenyah, Kayan, Iban, Kelabit, Kajaman and Sekapan, Lahanan, and Sebop, I suggest, supports this view (see Maxwell 1989a: 171, Table 2, and passim).

rates") all along the southern reaches of modern Sarawak's coast (Pringle 1970: 49–55).[33] Though heads were taken on both sides of these conflicts, Malay and Arab leaders received only shares of the booty and plunder; heads were left to the Iban (St. John 1974 [1862], 1: 67).

The conquests detailed in the *Sya'ir Awang Simawn* form a kind of folk historical—narrowly, an "ethnohistorical" (Sturtevant 1968: 462–64)—account of the origins of the Brunei empire. Europeans described the splendor of the Brunei court at the height of its power during the sixteenth century (Pigafetta 1969: 88–100). By the mid-nineteenth century, when the first continuous European reportage on Brunei began, the court and empire were only pale shadows of their former selves.

How did the early Brunei state arise? The analysis of the poem's account of the conquests suggests that early Brunei society was a chiefdom (Sahlins 1968: 20–27; Service 1971: 133–69) that expanded from an earlier homeland centered on Brunei Bay. Through conquest, this polity was transformed into a hegemonic system in which conquered territories were held in a subordinate, tributary relationship to the ruler at the captial of Brunei. Evidence from the last few centuries suggests that the dominance exercised by the center was probably never very great, and was perhaps even primarily ritual in nature. In addition, this control probably waxed and waned, depending on internal fissures and disputes within the royal court. Ancient Brunei seems to have then grown into a maritime state with a highly developed ritual system of central administration, which is what it appears to have been in protohistoric times.

In ancient Brunei, heads were significant not for exchange (George 1991), alliance (Hoskins 1989), or symbolic fertility (Freeman 1979), but for separating winners from losers, lords from subjects, those who receive obeisance from those who give it. In other words, taken heads, whatever their significance in the ancestral

[33] Controversy in Britain over his use of Iban troops to attack his rivals, the Iban of Sakarang and Saribas, at the 1849 Battle of Beting Marau forced James Brooke to appear before a Royal Commission of Inquiry in Singapore in 1854, which investigated charges that he had "butchered" innocent native peoples to enhance his own power and influence (see Mills 1960: 283–310, esp. 298–310; Irwin 1955: 127–50; Pringle 1970: 81–83, 350–53). The taking of heads by Brooke's auxiliaries no doubt stimulated the ire of some of his critics.

cultures of pre-Brunei times, were at some point incorporated into the Malay *Kerajaan* of Brunei as a symbolic expression of subjugation and submission to the Raja.[34] The fact that there was no *Kerajaan* in the mythological time of the heroes' conquests is not a problem. Hoskins skillfully shows for Sumba (1987) that historical formations can project backward, and can incorporate earlier historical elements to serve the purposes of more recent times. By a device of anachronistic compression, the *Sya'ir Awang Simawn* is able to blend pre-Malay and Malay elements to produce a unique history of an Islamic state in Southeast Asia.

Appendix: A Selected Passage from the *Sya'ir Awang Simawn*

The selection given here is a phonemicized transcription of a tape-recorded version of the *Sya'ir Awang Simawn* chanted by a man who sang from a written jawi manuscript, not of an "actual performance" of the text. Brunei Malay differs from the standard language primarily in having only three phonemic vowels: /i, a, u/.

The *Sya'ir Awang Simawn* is an oral traditional text, with many of the characteristics of oral traditional composition (Foley 1990: 5–19). One of these is the "adding style" so often seen in oral poetry, typified by the frequent use of nonperiodic enjambment (see Lord 1960: 131, 217) and the presence of a caesura (",") in a line of verse. In a pro-drop language (Chomsky 1986: 28, 240, 253–54) such as Brunei Malay, the grammatical subject of a verb may be omitted. The translation (Version A, verses 544–60) reflects both the adding style and the missing grammatical subject characteristic of the Brunei Malay original.

No two of the six versions of the *Sya'ir Awang Simawn* examined are exactly alike. For the selected passage, five versions lack a number of verses.

While traveling, all together,	*Saraya barjalan, kasamuanya,*
with the cheers, and the shouts;	*basarta surak, kukuynya;*

[34] There is no contradiction between this conclusion and the earlier reference to the importance of heads for the warriors' bridewealth. Awang Halak Batatar rejected the trophy heads; he left them to his followers. The combination of a Malay Raja leading pagan, non-Muslim troops in campaigns is, according to any evidence we know, anachronistic. There is no factual informa-

the din reached, to the country,
   Simawn blowpiped, the forts
flew.

While hurling, Awang Jarambak,
   all the houses, were completely
   peeled away;
the forts and mountains, completely scraped away,
   thousands died, the citizens[a]
   many.

The forces[a] plundered, to the right
and left,
   so many thousands, of vassals[b]
   fled;
the plunder, was much it is told,
   cutting off heads, every day.

Thunder crashed, rain drummed in
bright sunshine,
   the Kitar lightning, forked and
   branched out;
the mountains were teased, the
fields were spread out,
   the powerful signs, of the war
   to come.

Aid arrived, from the Bugis of
Makassar,
   nine thousand, officers and
   soldiers;
Damang Sari struck, and the
ground moved in a circle,

datang bahana, kapada nagrinya,
   Simawn manyumpit, tarbang
kutanya.

Saraya manabak, Awang Jarabak,
   sakalian rumah, abis tarkubak;

kutanya gunung, habis barambak,

   baribu mati, ra'yatnya[a] banyak.

*Ra'yat[a] marampas, kanan dan
kairi,*
   barapa ribu, hamba[b] yang lari;

rampasan itu, banyak tarpari,
   mamutung kapala, sahari-ari.

*Barbungi guruh, lalam maram-
bang,*
   *Kilat Si Kitar, barcabang-
   cabang;*
*gunung barusik, padang bargum-
bang,*
   *alamat basar, parangnya
   datang.*

*Datang lah bantu, Bugis
Mangkasar,*
   *sambilan ribu, hulubalang
   lasgar;*
*Damang mangampas, bumi barga-
gar,*

---

tion indicating that these two social entities ever coexisted. During World War
II, some Malay Kadayan may have taken the heads of individual Japanese soldiers during the occupation, but, as everyone—including the Japanese—surely
knew, "Malays never take heads." Whether combined in an oral tradition or in
the real world, headtaking and monarchical government based on a Raja (*Kerajaan*) simply do not go together.

  [a]*Rayat*, ultimately a borrowing from Arabic, can refer to the subjects of a
country, but also to conscript troops (versus "professional troops," *hulubalang*
or "soldiers, infantrymen," *lasgar*). It is not possible to reflect these semantic
differences easily in an English translation.

  [b]Etymologically, the term *hamba* means "slave, unpaid servant," but it also
can indicate one performing humble service without connotation of slavery.

the dead piled up, the corpses were scattered all about.	*bartimbun mati, bangkay barkampar.*
Simawn blowpiped, with both hands,	*Simawn manyumpit, dua balah tan[g]an,*
the Makassar forces,[a] flew off all about;	*ra'yat[a] Mangkasar, baratarabangan;*
Jarambak hurled, one need say no more,	*Si Jarambak manabak, dikata jangan,*
the conscripts[a] flew off, to the middle of the channel.	*tarbang ra'yat,[a] ka tangah harungan.*
The troops[a] cut off, all the heads, hither and thither, in a great tumult;	*Ra'yat[a] mamutung, sagala kapala, ka sana ka mari, barhiru-hila;*
the country of Sandungan, was struck by the force,	*Nagri Sandungan, tarkana bala,*
tens of thousands died, uncontrollably.	*barlaksa mati, tiada bargala.*
The subjects[a] died, not a few, lying one on another, tight one against another;	*Ra'yatnya[a] mati, bukan sadikit, bartindih-tindih, barpindit-pindit;*
as far as the eye can see, corpses packed together,	*saluas mamandang, bangkay barpipit,*
the severed heads, like a hill.	*kapala tarputung, saparti bukit.*
Heads floated, upstream and downstream,	*Kapala bartimbun, ka saba ka hulu,*
each, of the heaps passing by;	*masing-masing, tumpuknya lalu;*
many tens of thousands, of widows,	*babarapa laksa, parampuan balu,*
the pile of heads, a Mt. Kinabalu.[c]	*timbunan kapala, Gunung Cinabalu.[c]*
The thunder and rain with sunshine, were terrifying,	*Guruh dan lalam, targarun-garun,*
the Kitra lightning, scattered all about;	*Kilat Si Kitra, bartampiaran;*
it is the cheers and shouts, that were heard,	*surak dan kukuy, yang kadangaran,*
the din reached, to Indra's Heaven.	*bahananya datang, ka Ka'indarahan.*

[c]Mt. Kinabalu, in Sabah, is the highest mountain in Southeast Asia, about 4101 meters.

Hukacu looked out on, his country all desolate,
  excited by anger, towns sparsely populated;
descending to the ground, carrying a sword,
  while chopping, in the front and behind.

His slashing was not, questioned, the subjects[a] retreated, all of them;
oh so, very swiftly,
  completely flown away, the mountains and fields.

Then he was slashed, by Awang Simawn,
  struck in the body, smoking and fogging;
mountains in rain and sunshine,
piled up in a column,
  the thunder sounded, in terrifying fashion.

Hukacu had been hacked, by Jarambak already,
  Damang Sari chopped, and responded further;
struck in the head, but not split,
  turned into a tiger, this Hukacu.

The three of them, he caught,
  the tiger [caught them/was caught], silently;
dashed down, flat against the rocks,
  the body of Hu, [as] big as a complete hill.

Simawn, made himself enlarge,
  [like] Mt. Kinabalu,[c] that's the size;
while even Hu, caught by him,
  out into the sea, hurled by him.

Hukacu mamandang, nagrinya ladang,
  hatinya garam, banda[r] barlingang;
turun ka ta[n]ah, mambawa padang,
  saraya manatak, hadapan balakang.

Tataknya tiada, bartanya-tanya,
  ra'yat[a] pun undur, kasamuanya;

tarlalu sakali, sangat darasnya,
  abis tarabang, gunung padangnya.

Lalu ditataknya, Awang Simawn,

  tarkana di tubuh, barasap barambun;
gunung barlalam, bartimbun tabun,
  guruh barbungi, targarun-garun.

Hukacu ditabak, Si Jarambak sudah,
  Damang mamangkur, lagi maningkah;
kana di kapala, tiada dibalah,
  manjadi harimaw, Hukacu itu lah.

Katiga urang, ia manangkap,
  harimaw pun dapat, tarsingap-singap;
dihampaskan, di batu pun lakap,
  tubuhnya Hu, basar bukit mangginap.

Simawn, mambasarakan dirinya,
  Gunung Cinabalu,[c] itu basarnya;
saraya Hu pun, ditangkapnya,
  ka dalam lawt, ditabakannya.

Landing in the sea, in the waters blue,	*Runduk di lawt, ayr yang biru,*
sulking to Gubi, at Garu Reef;	*marajuk ka Gubi, di Takat Garu;*
his head was smashed, at Barliru Reef,	*kapalanya pacah, di Takat Bar-liru,*
straight away died, Husaluru.	*salajur mati, Husaluru.*

Acknowledgments

Research in Brunei from 1968 to 1971 was funded by a National Institute of Health grant and a Wenner-Gren Foundation for Anthropological Research predoctoral fellowship. Local support by the Dewan Bahasa dan Pustaka, Brunei, and its then-director, Yang Dimuliakan Pehin Orang Kaya Amar Diraja Dato Seri Utama (Dr.) Awang Haji Mohd. Jamil Al-Sufri, greatly aided my efforts. The Brunei Museum curator, P. M. Shariffuddin, and assistant curator, Lim Jock-Seng, were very supportive. Several people commented on an earlier draft of this paper: George N. Appell, J. Peter Brosius, Donald E. Brown, Janet Hoskins, Richard A. Krause, Michael D. Murphy, and Vinson H. Sutlive, Jr. The N.E.H. Summer Seminar in 1991, "The Oral Tradition in Literature," led by John Miles Foley at the Center for Studies in Oral Tradition, University of Missouri, Columbia, was very helpful to my understanding and appreciation of the *Sya'ir Awang Simawn*. Delana Robinson assisted greatly in preparing the map.

Appreciation is also due ancient Brunei's singers (*panambang*; verb *tambang* [*sayr*], "chant [a *sya'ir*]"), whose understandings and artistic creativity are embodied in surviving versions of the *Sya'ir Awang Simawn*, and who therein recorded the achievements of their ancestors, the founders of the Sultanate of Brunei, and inscribed a set of cultural values in an oral tradition for posterity. (Havelock [1963: 61–84] suggests that an epic functions as a "social encyclopedia," preserving the *nomos* ["custom-laws"] and *ethos* ["folk-ways"] of a culture.)

References

Abdul Karim bin Haji Abdul Rahman
    1988 "P'u-Kung Chih-Mu." *Pustaka* 2: 57–58.

Abdul Latif Haji Ibrahim
   1970 "Padian—Its Market and the Women Vendors." *Brunei Museum Journal* 2 (1): 39–51.
Abdullah Hussain and Muslim Burmat
   1984 *Bunga Rampai Sastera Melayu Brunei.* (Anthology of Brunei Malay literature.) Kuala Lumpur: Dewan Bahasa dan Pustaka.
Andreini, E. V.
   1931 "An Old Milano Fable." *Sarawak Gazette* 61 (929): 28 [Feb. 2, 1931].
Anonymous
   1907 "A Milano Fable." *Sarawak Gazette* 37 (496): 99 [May 3, 1907].
al-Attas, Syed Muhammad Naguib
   1968 *The Origin of the Malay Sha'ir.* Kuala Lumpur: Dewan Bahasa dan Pustaka.
   1970 *The Mysticism of Hamzah Fansuri.* Kuala Lumpur: University of Malaya Press.
Awang bin Ahmad
   1989 *Pengantar Sastera Lama Brunei.* (Introduction to Brunei traditional literature.) [Bandar Seri Begawan]: Dewan Bahasa dan Pustaka Brunei.
Barker, Alex W.
   1992 "Powhatan's Pursestrings: On the Meaning of Surplus in a Seventeenth-Century Algonkian Chiefdom." In Alex W. Barker and Timothy R. Pauketat, eds., *Lords of the Southeast: Social Inequality and the Native Elites of Southeastern North America,* pp. 61–80. Archaeological Papers of the American Anthropological Association no. 3. [Washington, D.C.]: American Anthropological Association.
Boudriot, C. F.
   1854–55 [Testimony]. In *Reports of the Commissioners Appointed to Inquire into Certain Matters Connected with the Position of Sir James Brooke. Parliamentary Papers* 19 (1): 112.
Bowen, John R.
   1991 *Sumatran Politics and Poetics: Gayo History, 1900–1989.* New Haven: Yale University Press.
Brown, Carrie C.
   1972 "An Early Account of Brunei by Sung Lien." *Brunei Museum Journal* 2 (4): 219–31.
Brown, Charles Cuthbert
   1952 "Sejarah Melayu or 'Malay Annals': A Translation of Raffles MS 18 (in the Library of the R.A.S., London) with Commentary." *Journal of the Malayan Branch of the Royal Asiatic Society* 25 (2–3): 1–276.
Brown, Donald E.
   1970 *Brunei: The Structure and History of a Borneo Malay Sultanate.*

Monograph of the Brunei Museum Journal. [*Brunei Museum Journal*] 2 (2).

1980 "Hiranyagarbha—The Hindu Cosmic Egg—and Brunei's Royal Line." *Brunei Museum Journal* 4 (4): 30–37.

1984 "Brunei Through the *Sha'er* and *Silsilah*." *Solidarity* 99: 10–15.

1988 *Hierarchy, History, and Human Nature: The Social Origins of Historical Consciousness*. Tucson: University of Arizona Press.

Brunei

n.d. "Undang2 No. 4 Tahun 1961, Undang2 Taraf Kebangsaan Brunei, 1961." In *Surat2 Perlembagaan Negeri Brunei*, pp. 115–35. [Kuala Belait]: Brunei Government Printer.

1988 *Brunei Darussalam in Profile*. London: Shandwick.

Chomsky, Noam

1986 *Lectures on Government and Binding: The Pisa Lectures*. 4th ed. Dordrecht: Foris.

D[alton], J[ohn]

1968 [1831] "Mr. Dalton's Essay on the Diaks of Borneo." [Published in the *Singapore Chronicle*, March and April 1831.] In J. H. Moor, ed., *Notices of the Indian Archipelago, and Adjacent Countries; Being a Collection of Papers Relating to Borneo, Celebes, . . . &c*, pp. 41–54. Singapore, 1837. Reprinted London: Frank Cass, 1968.

Damit @ Muhammad bin Haji Aminuddin, Awang Haji

1986 "Awang Semaun Menarah Gubang." (Awang Simawn planes a dugout canoe.) In Matassim Haji Jibah, ed., *Pertuturan II*, pp. 103–6. [Bandar Seri Begawan]: Brunei Museum.

Davison, Julian, and Vinson H. Sutlive, Jr.

1991 "The Children of *Nising*: Images of Headhunting and Male Sexuality in Iban Ritual and Oral Literature." In Vinson H. Sutlive, Jr., ed., *Female and Male in Borneo: Contributions and Challenges to Gender Studies*, pp. 153–230. Borneo Research Council Monograph Series, vol. 1. Shanghai, Va.: Borneo Research Council.

[Dickenson, J. T.]

1838 "Notices of the City of Borneo and Its Inhabitants, Made During the Voyage of the American Brig Himmaleh in the Indian Archipelago, in 1837." *The Chinese Repository* 7 (3): 121–36; 7 (4): 177–93.

Earle, Timothy, ed.

1991 *Chiefdoms: Power, Economy, and Ideology*. Cambridge: Cambridge University Press.

Fatimah binti Mohd. Daud

1990 "Kerajaan Islam di Brunei: Suatu Tinjauan Sejarah." (Islamic government in Brunei: A historical view.) *Pustaka* 3: 27–34.

Foley, John Miles

1990 *Traditional Oral Epic: The "Odyssey," "Beowulf," and the Serbo-*

Croatian Return Song. Berkeley: University of California Press.

Freeman, J. Derek

1979 "Severed Heads That Germinate." In R. H. Hook, ed., *Fantasy and Symbol: Studies in Anthropological Interpretation*, pp. 233–46. New York: Academic Press.

Fried, Morton H.

1967 *The Evolution of Political Society: An Essay in Political Anthropology*. New York: Random House.

George, Kenneth M.

1991 "Headhunting, History, and Exchange in Upland Sulawesi." *Journal of Asian Studies* 50 (3): 536–64.

Hall, D. G. E.

1981 *A History of South-East Asia*. 4th ed. New York: St. Martin's.

Hall, Maxwell

1955 "The Last Slave-Raid in Sabah." *Malayan Historical Journal* 2 (2): 162–69.

Hang Tuah Merawin

1971 "Serita Tugau, Raja Melanau. Tugau, The Melanau King." 5-page Melanau manuscript; 5-page English translation. Miri, Sarawak.

Harrisson, Tom

1949 "Gold & Indian Influences in West Borneo." *Journal of the Malayan Branch of the Royal Asiatic Society* 22 (4): 33–110.

1960 "Birds and Men in Borneo." In Bertram E. Smythies, [ed.], *The Birds of Borneo*, pp. 20–72. Edinburgh: Oliver and Boyd.

Havelock, Eric A.

1963 *Preface to Plato*. Cambridge, Mass.: Harvard University Press.

Hose, Charles

1926 *Natural Man: A Record from Borneo*. London: Macmillan.

Hose, Charles, and William McDougall

1912 *The Pagan Tribes of Borneo*. 2 vols. Reprinted 1966. New York: Barnes & Noble.

Hoskins, Janet

1987 "The Headhunter as Hero: Local Traditions and Their Reinterpretation in National History." *American Ethnologist* 14 (4): 605–22.

1989 "On Losing and Getting a Head: Warfare, Exchange, and Alliance in Changing Sumba." *American Ethnologist* 16 (3): 419–40.

Hudson, A. B.

1970 "A Note on Selako: Malayic Dayak and Land Dayak Languages in Western Borneo." *Sarawak Museum Journal* 18 (36–37): 301–18.

Hunt, J.

1846 [1812] "Sketch of Borneo, or Pulo Kalamantan." Appendix 2 in Henry Keppel, [ed.], *The Expedition to Borneo of H.M.S. Dido for the Suppression of Piracy, with Extracts from the Journal of James*

Brooke, Esq. of Sarawak, vol. 2, pp. xvi–lxiv. London: Chapman and Hall.

Hyginus

1975 "Fable 197" [c. 1st century B.C./A.D., from 1400 B.C. sources]. In Charles Doria and Harris Lenowitz, eds., *Origins: Creation Texts from the Ancient Mediterranean*, p. 125. Garden City, N.Y.: Anchor/Doubleday.

Irwin, Graham

1955 *Nineteenth-Century Borneo: A Study in Diplomatic Rivalry.* Reprinted 1965. Singapore: Donald Moore.

Ismail bin Pg. Ibrahim, Pg. Hj.

1982 "Permainan Gasing (Top Playing)." *Brunei Museum Journal* 5 (2): 104–18.

Jaafar bin Muhammed Sah

1988 "Sultan Abdul Majid ibni Sultan Muhammad Shah." *Pustaka* 1: 31–33.

Josselin de Jong, P. E. de

1961 "Who's Who in the Malay Annals." *Journal of the Malayan Branch of the Royal Asiatic Society* 34 (2): 1–89.

Kater, C.

1876 "Uitrusting van een Dajak ter Wester-Afdeeling van Borneo die uit snellen gaat; Beschrijving van Wan Masjehoer, Djaksa te Sintang." *Tijdschrift voor Indische Taal-, Land- en Volkenkunde* 24 (1–2): 234–37.

Keppel, Henry

1853 *A Visit to the Indian Archipelago in H. M. Ship Maeander, with Portions of the Private Journal of Sir James Brooke.* 2 vols. London: Richard Bentley.

Kimball, Linda Amy

1979 *Borneo Medicine: The Healing Art of Indigenous Brunei Malay Medicine.* Ann Arbor: University Microfilms International for the Anthropology Department, Loyola University of Chicago.

Kratz, E. U.

1993 "Durhaka: The Concept of Treason in the Malay *Hikayat Hang Tuah.*" *South East Asia Research* 1 (1): 68–97.

Lawrence, A. E.

1909 "A Milano Fable." *Folklore* 20: 83–85.

1911 "Stories of the First Brunei Conquests on the Sarawak Coast." *Sarawak Museum Journal* 1 (1): 120–24. Reprinted 1969, *Sarawak Gazette* 95 (1342): 305–6 [Dec. 31, 1969].

Lord, Alfred B.

1960 *The Singer of Tales.* Cambridge, Mass.: Harvard University Press.

McKinley, Robert
    1976 "Human and Proud of It! A Structural Treatment of Headhunting
        Rites and the Social Definition of Enemies." In G. N. Appell, ed.,
        *Studies in Borneo Societies: Social Process and Anthropological Ex-
        planation*, pp. 92–126. Center for Southeast Asian Studies, Northern
        Illinois University, Special Report no. 12. DeKalb, Ill.: Center for
        Southeast Asian Studies.
Maxwell, Allen R.
    1984 "Prasasti Melayu Kuno: Daftar Buku dan Cerita Ringkas." (Old
        Malay inscriptions: A summary and bibliography.) *Beriga* 4 (Jul.–
        Sept.): 65–71. Bandar Seri Begawan, Brunei.
    1987 "Ethnohistory in Sarawak: A Mostly Untapped Resource." *Sara-
        wak Gazette* 113 (1499): 7–14.
    1988 "Collation of Six Versions of the Brunei Epic, the *Sya'ir Awang
        Simaun*." Unpublished manuscript.
    1989a "A Survey of the Oral Traditions of Sarawak." Special issue
        no. 4, part 1, Sarawak Cultural Heritage Symposium. *Sarawak Mu-
        seum Journal* 40 (61-I): 167–208.
    1989b "Origin Themes in Orang Ulu Origin Myths." Special issue
        no. 4, part 3, Orang Ulu Cultural Heritage Seminar. *Sarawak Mu-
        seum Journal* 40 (61-III): 231–49.
    1989c *Sya'ir Awang Simaun*, Version "A." Five 5¼" disks, 155-page
        manuscript.
    1989d *Sya'ir Awang Simaun*—Version "B." Three 5¼" disks, 92-page
        manuscript.
    1989e *Sya'ir Awang Simaun*—Version "D." Nine 5¼" disks, 367-page
        manuscript.
    1990 *Sya'ir Awang Simaun*—Version "C." Three 5¼" disks, 272-page
        manuscript.
    1991 *Sya'ir Awang Simaun*—Version "E." Four 3½" disks, 339-page
        manuscript.
    1992a *Sya'ir Awang Simaun*—Version "F." Four 3½" disks.
    1992b "Outline of the Episode Contents of the *Sya'ir Awang Simawn*."
        2d revision. 6-page manuscript.
Md. Yussop bin Bakar, Haji
    1989 *Adat Perkahwinan Orang Melayu Brunei di Mukim Saba.* (Mar-
        riage ceremony of the Brunei Malays of the parish of Saba.) [Bandar
        Seri Begawan]: Dewan Bahasa dan Pustaka Brunei.
Meilink-Roelofsz, M. A. P.
    1962 *Asian Trade and European Influence in the Indonesian Archipel-
        ago Between 1500 and About 1630.* The Hague: Martinus Nijhoff.

Metcalf, Peter
 1982 *A Borneo Journey into Death: Berawan Eschatology from Its Rit-uals*. Philadelphia: University of Pennsylvania Press.
Miller, Charles C.
 1942 *Black Borneo*. New York: Modern Age Books.
Mills, L. A.
 1960 "British Malay, 1824–67." Rev. ed. *Journal of the Malayan Branch of the Royal Asiatic Society* 33 (3): 1–424.
Milner, A. C.
 1982 *Kerajaan: Malay Political Culture on the Eve of Colonial Rule*. The Association for Asian Studies Monograph no. 40. Tucson: University of Arizona Press.
Mjöberg, Eric
 1929 *Durch die Insel der Kopfjäger, Abenteurer im Innern von Borneo*. Translated by T. Geiger. Leipzig: F. A. Brockhaus. (Original: Borneo, Huvdjägarnas Land, Stockholm, 1927.)
Moens, J. L.
 1939 "Srivijaya, Yava en Kataha." *Journal of the Malayan Branch of the Royal Asiatic Society* 17 (2): 1–108. [An abridged translation of the original in the *Tijdschrift voor Indische Taal-, Land- en Volken-kunde* 77 (3), by R. J. de Touché.]
Mohd. Jamil al-Sufri, Pehin Orang Kaya Amar Diraja Dato Seri Utama Awang Haji
 1971–73 *Chatatan Sejara Perwira2 dan Pembesar2 Brunei*. (Historical notes on Brunei heroes and officials.) 2 vols. [Bandar Seri Begawan]: Dewan Bahasa dan Pustaka Brunei.
 1977 "Islam in Brunei." *Brunei Museum Journal* 4 (1): 35–42.
 1990a *Latar Belakang Sejarah Brunei*. (Background to Brunei history.) [Bandar Seri Begawan]: Jabatan Pusat Sejarah.
 1990b *Tarsilah Brunei: Sejarah Awal dan Perkembangan Islam*. (Brunei genealogical history: Early history and the development of Islam.) [Bandar Seri Begawan]: Jabatan Pusat Sejarah.
 1990c "Islam dari China?" (Islam from China?) *Pustaka* 3: 23–26.
Morris, H. S.
 1953 *Report on a Melanau Sago Producing Community in Sarawak*. Colonial Research Studies no. 9. [London]: Her Majesty's Stationery Office.
 1978 "The Coastal Melanau." In Victor T. King, ed., *Essays on Borneo Societies*, pp. 37–58. Hull Monographs on South-East Asia, no. 7. Oxford: Oxford University Press.
Muhammed Abd. Latiff
 1980 *Satu Pengenalan Sejarah Kesusasteraan Melayu Brunei*. (An in-

troduction to the history of Brunei Malay literature.) [Bandar Seri Begawan]: Dewan Bahasa dan Pustaka Brunei.

Muhammad bin Abdul Latif
1988 "Kemasukan Agama Islam di Brunei." (The entrance of the Islamic religion into Brunei.) *Pustaka* 2: 7–16.

Muhammad Hadi bin Abdullah
1988 "Islam di Daerah Tutong." (Islam in Tutong District.) *Pustaka* 1: 19–22.

Nais, William
1989 "Overview of the Bidayuh Culture." Special issue no. 4, part 2, Malay, Melanau and Bidayuh Cultural Heritage Seminars. *Sarawak Museum Journal* 40 (61-II): 367–71.

Needham, Rodney
1976 "Skulls and Causality." *Man* 11 (1): 71–88.

Nicholl, Robert
1975 *European Sources for the History of the Sultanate of Brunei in the Sixteenth Century*. Penerbitan Khas bil. 9. Bandar Seri Begawan: Brunei Museum.
1976 "The Sixteenth Century Cartography of Borneo." *Brunei Museum Journal* 3 (4): 96–126.
1980a "The Mediaeval Cartography of Borneo." *Brunei Museum Journal* 4 (4): 180–218.
1980b "Brunei Rediscovered, A Survey of Early Times." *Brunei Museum Journal* 4 (4): 219–37.

Parry, Milman
1930 "Studies in the Epic Technique of Oral Verse-Making. I. Homer and Homeric Style." Reprinted 1971. In Adam Parry, ed., *The Making of Homeric Verse: The Collected Papers of Milman Parry*, pp. 266–324. Oxford: Clarendon Press.

Pigafetta, Antonio
1969 *The Voyage of Magellan: The Journal of Antonio Pigafetta*. A translation by Paula Spurlin Paige from the edition in the William L. Clements Library, University of Michigan, Ann Arbor. Englewood Cliffs, N.J.: Prentice-Hall.

Pigeaud, Theodore G. T., ed.
1960–63 *Java in the 14th Century, A Study in Cultural History: The Nagara-Kertagama by "Rakawi" Prapanca of Majapahit, 1365 A.D.* 5 vols. 3d ed. Koninklijk Instituut voor Taal-, Land- en Volkenkunde, Translation Series 4, 1–5. The Hague: Martinus Nijhoff.

Pringle, Robert
1970 *Rajahs and Rebels: The Ibans of Sarawak Under Brooke Rule, 1841–1941.* [London]: Macmillan.

Ranjit Singh, D. S.

   1984 *Brunei 1839–1983: The Problems of Political Survival.* Singapore: Oxford University Press.

Renoir, Alain

   1987 "Repetition, Oral-Formulaic Style, and Affective Impact in Mediaeval Poetry: A Tentative Illustration." In John Miles Foley, ed., *Comparative Research on Oral Traditions: A Memorial for Milman Parry,* pp. 533–48. Columbus, Ohio: Slavica.

Rosaldo, Michelle Zimbalist

   1977 "Skulls and Causality." *Man* 12 (1): 168–69.

Rousseau, Jerome

   1990 *Central Borneo: Ethnic Identity and Social Life in a Stratified Society.* Oxford: Clarendon Press.

Rutter, Owen

   1985 [1929] *The Pagans of North Borneo.* Singapore: Oxford University Press.

Sahlins, Marshall D.

   1968 *Tribesmen.* Englewood Cliffs, N.J.: Prentice-Hall.

St. John, Spenser

   1974 [1862] *Life in the Forests of the Far East.* 2 vols. Kuala Lumpur: Oxford University Press.

Sandin, Benedict

   1971 "The Bisayah of Limbang." *Sarawak Museum Journal* 19 (38–39): 1–19.

   1980 *The Living Legends: Borneans Telling Their Tales.* [Kuching]: Dewan Bahasa dan Pustaka Malaysia, Cawangan Sarawak.

Sellato, Bernard

   1989 *Hornbill and Dragon/Naga dan Burung Engggang: Kalimantan, Sarawak, Sabah, Brunei.* Text in English and Malay. Jakarta/Kuala Lumpur: Elf Aquitaine Indonesia—Elf Aquitaine Malaysia.

Service, Elman R.

   1971 *Primitive Social Organization: An Evolutionary Approach.* 2d ed. New York: Random House.

Shelford, Robert W. C.

   1916 *A Naturalist in Borneo.* Edward B. Poulton, ed. London: T. Fisher Unwin Ltd.

Shellabear, W. G.

   1967 [1896] *Sejarah Melayu.* [New ed.] Kuala Lumpur: Oxford University Press.

Sturtevant, William C.

   1968 "Anthropology, History, and Ethnohistory." In James A. Clifton, ed., *Introduction to Cultural Anthropology: Essays in the Scope*

and Methods of the Science of Man, pp. 451–75. Boston: Houghton
Mifflin.

Sweeney, Amin
1971 "Some Observations on the Malay Sha'ir." *Journal of the Malaysian Branch of the Royal Asiatic Society* 44 (1): 52–70.

Teeuw, Andreas
1966 "The Malay Sha'ir: Problems of Origin and Tradition." *Bijdragen
tot de Taal-, Land- en Volkenkunde* 122 (4): 429–46.

Vayda, Andrew P.
1969 "The Study of the Causes of War, With Special Reference to
Head-Hunting Raids in Borneo." *Ethnohistory* 16 (3): 211–24.

Wilkinson, R. J.
1959 [1932] *A Malay-English Dictionary (Romanized)*. 2 vols. London:
Macmillan.

Winstedt, Richard O.
1969 [1961] *A History of Classical Malay Literature*. [2d ed.] Kuala
Lumpur: Oxford University Press.

Wolters, O. W.
1967 *Early Indonesian Commerce: A Study of the Origins of Srivijaya*.
Ithaca, N.Y.: Cornell University Press.
1970 *The Fall of Srivijaya in Malay History*. Kuala Lumpur: Oxford
University Press.

Andrew McWilliam

Severed Heads That Germinate the State
History, Politics, and Headhunting in Southwest Timor

In the latter part of the year 1850, an anonymous Dutch traveler (referred to only as "D") set out from the Dutch administrative center of Kupang in the far west of Timor to undertake a journey into the "unpacified" interior of the island. He traveled into the sprawling and mountainous domain of Amanuban, which, from the early years of the nineteenth century, had maintained a warlike anti-Dutch resistance to the colonial administration. The observations of "D" provide some of the only recorded eyewitness European accounts of the political situation in this part of Timor at the time. His report offers a uniquely pertinent perspective on the fierce internal political struggle that characterized the period. He writes:

Amanuban used to be a single state and one Radja, who lived at Niki Niki, had uncontested power. Several times this state has had hostilities with the Dutch authorities. . . . The last expedition took place under the Resident Hazaart[1] and was not successful. Since that time there have been splitting tendencies within the domain itself. From time to time some *Fettors* and *Temukung* [indigenous headmen], who are not satisfied with the erratic authority of the Radja, have split away and have attempted to become independent. It has come about that Amanuban has split into two parts; one part, which is administered and taxed by the Radja of Niki Niki and the under-regents who remain faithful to him, and another part under the headmanship of the people who have split away and have become au-

[1] He is probably referring to the expedition of 1822, the last in a series of forays into the Timor hinterland. The main result of these military expeditions was to deplete severely the finances of the Dutch outpost in Kupang and to curtail any further serious attempts to "pacify" the interior until the turn of the twentieth century (see Veth 1855: 97).

tonomous and, more or less, independent. They are continously in a state of war with the Radja of Niki Niki and his minor regents and they are also fighting among themselves. (D 1850: 166)

The leader of this breakaway faction is identified by "D" as Nagawasa (i.e., Nabuasa) who, in his words:

used to be of the status of *meo*; that is, the head and administrator of everything to do with warfare and the defence of the state. [But now] . . . all those small states that have split away from the Radja in Niki Niki are more or less dependent on this *meo*. This happened because in time some of those *Temukung* and their people who were too weak to stand alone, have attached themselves to this Nagawasa. In that way his village, which was once small, has grown in size and population. It is now the largest of all settlements in this region of Amanuban. (D 1850: 167)

Prior to their departure from the barricaded stronghold of the *meo* Nabuasa, "D" and his party were presented with a freshly smoked human head taken from the region of Niki Niki. They were asked to present the head to the Dutch resident in Kupang as "the best proof of the righteousness of [their] bond with the Company [the old term for the Dutch East Indies Company]" (D 1850: 172).

The testimony of "D" establishes the historical reality of a political division within Amanuban during the nineteenth century. In this perspective, a headhunting warrior (meo) clan leader named Nabuasa achieved a position of political dominance and independence. The nature of his clan's political domain, its organizational structure, and the pivotal role of headhunting in the development and maintenance of the political unit form the subject of this paper.

Headhunting and State Formation in Timor

The scenario described by "D" for the state of Amanuban, then the largest indigenous state in West Timor recognized by the Dutch colonial government, was typical of the region as a whole during the nineteenth century. The territory proliferated in small semi-independent political states and petty chiefdoms, each composed of a cluster of clans surrounding a ceremonial ruling center to which tribute was delivered. Most areas were also subject to periodically fierce internal feuds and unrest. This situation was in large part the legacy of centuries of protracted struggle between Dutch and Portuguese colonial interests in eastern Indonesia. Among the prizes contested by these interests was control of the lucrative export trade in beeswax and white sandalwood, which grew in abundance on the island of Timor (see Boxer 1947).

Ethnographers of Timorese political history (especially Cunningham 1962; Middelkoop 1963; Schulte Nordholt 1971) have all mentioned the inherent instability of Timorese indigenous states and their propensity to fracture into smaller, mutually antagonistic units. Schulte Nordholt, a former Dutch colonial administrator (*controleur*) in north central Timor, has written that "the ruler is the unifying force but the urge for superiority on the part of the constituent units is sometimes so strong that unity breaks down" (1971: 449). The result, in historical terms, was a kind of dynamic ferment in which political communities struggled with two equally compelling forces of integration into larger federations and dispersal into multiple semi-autonomous entities.[2] Schulte Nordholt and other writers, however, offer only brief and limited explanations of the nature of this disintegration. We gain little understanding either of the processes that created division or of the form the resultant political organization of the breakaway community may have taken.

In presenting what amounts to a political analysis of headhunting in West Timor, I argue that during the turbulent period of the nineteenth century, warfare and the pursuit of headhunting represented a key dynamic in the formation and transformation of the indigenous Timorese states. Based on a partial reconstruction of its oral traditions, I show how the ritual management of ceremonial violence served as the creative basis for the Nabuasa name group to attain autonomous political power. This group achieved legitimacy for an extensive system of clear hierarchical forms and functions through adherence to a particular cultural pattern of diarchic political order. This order was represented through systems of conceptually male and female functions that overlay a complex

[2] The situation is not dissimilar to that described by Geertz for nineteenth-century Bali, where centripetal forces and the unifying effect of mass ceremony under this or that lord vied with centrifugal forces of dispersive segmentation and organizational pluralism (1980: 19).

of unstable and shifting alliances. Of particular interest in this regard was the application of a rich corpus of conventional metaphors, cast in a dualistic form, which provided political coherence to an otherwise fragmented environment of localized clan segments.

Ultimately, the historical conditions that had initially favored the imperialistic ambitions of this warrior clan shifted and undermined its status. In 1906, with the support of Dutch military forces, the Nabuasa domain was finally reincorporated under the control of the aging ruler of Amanuban in Niki Niki. Since that time, the history of the Nabuasa domain in southern Amanuban has been one of gradual political decline and sublimation once again to outside powers. From Dutch colonialism to the Japanese imperialist interregnum, contemporary Timorese social life is now strongly conditioned by the pervasive influence of the modern Indonesian state. The memory and legacy of the heroic autonomous past nevertheless provides a continuing important source of self-identification and sense of place for the communities of southern Amanuban.

The Nabuasa group and the people of Amanuban as a whole form part of the largest ethnic group in West Timor, known as the Meto (see Map 1).[3] They presently number over 750,000. For the most part, the populations of the mountain interior pursue near-subsistence agriculture focused on an annual crop of rainfed maize supplemented with rice, cassava, beans, and fruits, as well as small-scale animal husbandry. Settlement patterns are dispersed, with the majority of people living in small kin-based hamlets of up to 30 nuclear families. In the contemporary context, up to a dozen hamlet settlements form the administrative jurisdiction of a village. Today, the thirteen village areas and some 25,000 people who once formed the core area of Nabuasa control now form part of the subregency (*kecamatan*) of southern Amanuban within the modern Indonesian state system.

Despite the significant changes to the political and economic

[3] The people of this region are referred to by a variety of names. These include Timorese, Dawan, and Atoni pah meto and its contraction, Atoni. I prefer the term *Meto*, which means indigenous or native, hence *atoin meto*, or indigenous people. The term is usually applied in contrast to the phrase *atoin kase*, meaning foreigners.

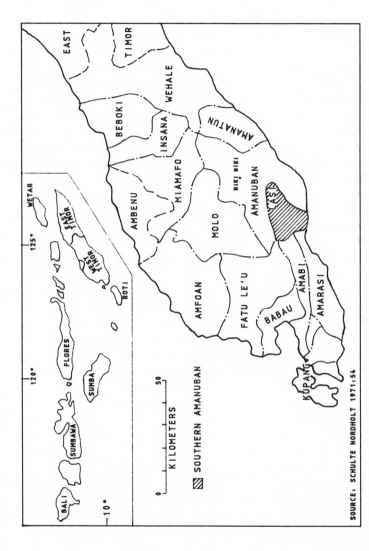

SOURCE: SCHULTE NORDHOLT 1971:54

Map 1. West Timor. From Schulte Nordholt 1971: 54.

character of the region, many of the older patterns remain in evidence. Of particular importance in this respect is the continuing relationship between kinship, marriage alliance, and land tenure. In Meto society, a primary form of affiliation refers to all people who share the same name (*kanaf*). Membership in name groups is reckoned on the basis of paternal affiliation. All name groups are widely dispersed and reflect a history based on migratory patterns of shifting agriculture and warfare. The result is that in any Meto hamlet, one finds a mixture of name-group segments, one of which is dominant. Typically, the leading group is also the original settler of the area and controls the largest area of arable land. Subsequent settlers gain access to usufruct land rights by marrying women of the original settler community and other groups who have already settled. Over time, a loose hierarchy or precedence of alliance relations is established. Groups that take women in marriage are politically subordinate to their wife-giving affines. Meto people describe this relationship as one between "females" (wife-takers) and "males" (wife-givers). In addition, because typically it is also the wife-givers who provide land rights to their affines, a related hierarchy of nested claims to land also develops. Later settlers acknowledge the land claims of those who preceded them. This order of precedence has its roots in the nineteenth century, when the meo name group, Nabuasa, and its senior allies constituted the symbolic and political source of this order of social relations. The legacy of that particular history is still very much in evidence in patterns of land holdings and settlement structure, local political leadership, and the continuing ties of kinship that link hamlets and villages to one another.

The Role of the *Meo* in Timorese Society

The principal meaning of the term *meo* among the Meto is "cat," but it carries the secondary meaning of a man who has taken a human head in warfare. In the past, the title of meo connoted warrior status and represented an avenue for young men to achieve prestige and renown. The meo was considered *pa'e* (a hero) and was variously referred to as an *atoin monef* (a masculine man) or as *nakfatu* (invulnerable; literally, stone head). Becoming a meo was also probably part of a young man's rite of passage into adulthood and marriage. In this regard, Schulte Nordholt has commented that "the headhunting raid and marriage, death and life, are inseparably linked together" (1971: 356; see also Spyer 1984: 67).

Because of the marked seasonality of Timor's climate, Meto warfare was mainly undertaken during the dry season. Thus, the end of the monsoon rains brought with it both the anticipation and the dread of headhunting. With it came the opportunity for young men to attain the status of meo. Generally speaking, this title was open to all male members of Meto society who participated in a successful headhunting raid.[4] Thenceforth they became *asu makenat* (dogs of war) and were entitled to wear the insignia of the office, such as silver armbands, horsehair leglets, and elaborate headdresses studded with silver and gold coins.

Ritual violence and the cult of headhunting formed an integral part of the social and political landscape of central West Timor prior to the twentieth century. Headhunting's significance both as a ritual event and as a political strategy can be gauged from the following tales of former military engagements. They provide exemplary images of the vitality and murderous nature of the headhunters' exploits. The first story derives from a commentary by a Nabuasa elder living in the present-day village of Olais, formerly the center of Nabuasa power. Implicit in the commentary is the recognition of Olais (Lasi) as a ritual center for the management of headhunting raids.

Formerly, if my ancestors wished to attack a fort, a cannon (*ken uf*) would be tied in place in the direction of the persons to be executed. [Then,] call-

[4] Schulte Nordholt (1971: 345) claims that certain clans were denied the right to become meo, but he does not elaborate this point. Spyer (1984: 64) argues that logically these clans would be those which held custodian rights over the land and agricultural rituals. I would support Spyer's conclusion with the proviso that it is conventional in Meto society to differentiate the name group internally, and meo-ship need only be denied to the part of the name group that actively maintained the custodial duties. Two examples of internal differentiation that occur through segmentation and dispersal of the group are the internal distinctions based on elder/younger "lineages" (a function of the birth order of brothers) and female/male distinctions determined by whether an individual traces membership to the name group from a root female or male ancestor. (See note 9 for further clarification.)

Illus. 1. "Hillmen of Timor just brought into Kupang by Missionaries," described by F. McKenzie as a "rough looking tribe." A number of men wear warrior insignia, including headdress and anklets. Based on the designs of their woven waistcloths, they are probably men of Amanuban. Photo by F. McKenzie, June 1924.

ing the younger brothers with burning and noise (from the cannon), they would take to their horses and arrive at night. Arriving here (in Lasi) and traveling to fight, assembling here and going to attack, Oemenu Takain (an enemy stronghold in the present-day district of Kupang). Arriving there a trap was laid, while my ancestors' younger brothers followed behind. Then, as the residents slept soundly, they [the raiders] set fire to all the houses and stood at the gate of the enemies' house. [Here] they [the enemies] were slaughtered. All the men were killed, the women captured and held. Then when they [the raiders] arose [to leave] the women were left behind [but] they carried off the young female children. Four human heads were [also] taken and carried to the river where the brains were re-

Illus. 2. The finery of the meo's costume. Two contemporary Meto men from Insana wearing clan ceremonial dress. Photo by author, 1990.

moved properly and the heads were raised to dry so that clinging skin did not rot . . . and the heads were roasted for up to one week with fine dry wood. Then whoever wished to become a *meo* [initiated headhunter] was given a head and went outside the settlement to hide with the head . . . each night making a fire. When ten men were ready to *nabuk* [undergo the celebratory rites], they entered the settlement at one time. Having attained meo(ship) in this way and been made (ritually) cool they could re-enter [the community]. Each head from wheresoever was hung facing the direction of its land. (L. Nabuasa, Olais, 1986)

The second story, or rather group of narrative extracts, is taken from one of the headhunting texts collected by the Dutch missionary Middelkoop during the 1930s. In text D, the narrator (Abraham Toto) describes his participation in a raid against the

Nabuasa people, in collaboration with a rival group from Amanuban, many years before. One exchange is related as follows:

When the cries became so thunderous, we understood that the Nauwasa
[Nabuasa] people from Amanuban were all there, the guns crashed continually, they were firing at us. So we were standing ready and Nai
Faot called out the war cry. . . . Then Nai li Nauwasa shouted, saying . . .
"Auw. . . . Lak, hero; Auw! Lak, hero, wait for me." Having finished shouting, the flame of the rifle flashed from there towards us. . . . The Nauwasa's guns crashed continually behind us. We people of Amanuban and
Mollo, we fled and while we were going we bit the new ears of maize and
kept ourselves still as death. Behind us guns crashed like thunder. Nai Lak
Selan suddenly sat down on an ant-hill—then his gun crashed, a Nauwasa
man was flung dead to the ground. Well then we kept on climbing the
slope, but when they reached the man who fell down dead, they stopped,
they did not follow us anymore. . . . After that we crossed the yellow river,
we decided to be on the alert, it was black as tree leaves with Nauwasa
there. (Middelkoop 1963: text D, 177–79)

At a later point in the narrative, Toto describes how it came
about that one of the headhunters from Nabuasa was killed and
beheaded.

The long-legged headhunter drew his sword, held it by the blade in his
hand, felt all over the fallen headhunter (*meo*) from his toes to his head
(for it was dark), and cut off his head. After having cut off his head, he
stamped on the forehead, then he pronounced the warcry. . . . Next morning we examined the attire of the dead headhunter; oh no, oh no, this man
was like a big buffalo; this man looked splendid and so did his attire; his
wraps were beautiful, his wrists were covered in silver bracelets, bone
armlets completely covered his upper arm, his head-hunter's kerchief, his
silver leglets with black hair—everything—was splendid. He wore a beautiful new rifle belt, there was red hair on his [hair]comb and a silver plate
on top of it. . . . We brought this fine headhunter (a man of Nabuasa) to Ka-
pan tunan [near the present-day town of Kapan]; we incorporated him into
the *nono* [fertility cult] there. (Middelkoop 1963: text D, 217–19)

In addition to the individual attraction of headhunting and warfare as a means of achieving personal renown, in the context of the
political community it is apparent that certain clan groups were
accorded the title of meo explicitly to expand the boundaries and
defend the political domain from invaders. These groups were
known as *meo naek* (great meo) and provided leadership in mat-

ters of warfare and defense. In the ritual speech of the Meto, this role is described as the responsibility to *natik pah he manuan am natik nifu he manuan* (to kick the land so that it becomes wide, to kick the lake so that it becomes wide). In Timorese terms, the development of society is a historical expansion from the "confined lands" (*pah ma'lenat*) to the "wide lands" (*pah manuan*). The metaphor of confinement implies a range of associations, such as overcrowding and land shortage, leading to acrimony and feuding. Traditionally, the typical response to this situation was simply for part of the community to shift residence and seek open, unsettled, or "wide" lands. By the nineteenth century, this process was mainly achieved through warfare and expropriation of land and people by the coercive leadership of the meo naek. These important meo name groups, usually numbering four or a multiple of four (as in the rajadom of Insana, which was said to have had sixteen appointed warrior clans; Cunningham 1962), were located at the nominal periphery of the political domain. These places were referred to as "gates" (*eno*) of the domain and constituted the limits of the political influence of the ruling center. An example of this arrangement is recorded by Middelkoop. In a reference to one meo naek of Mollo (a former prominent rajadom) at the "gate" of Amanuban, the chiefs were said to have commented: "Lif Toto is strong to cut down the weed, strong to press down the grass [reference to his ability as a warrior and headhunter]; thus let him go to the entrance . . . let him be as the horns of Mollo, the teeth of Mollo" (Middelkoop 1963: text D, 155).

The formal position of the meo naek in the political community tended to become hereditary, to the extent that the group maintained its position of preeminence in matters of warfare.[5] This is in contrast to the "minor" meo from subsidiary clan groups, who participated in headhunting but whose status remained only honorary. The distinction was articulated in the contrast between the great meo (meo naek) and subordinate "small" meo (*meo ana* or *meo kliko*). The "minor" meo provided a support function for the warrior leadership, smoothing the way to the enemy village,

[5] Here I differ from Schulte Nordholt (1971: 344), who claims that the title of meo is not an hereditary one. For the male members of the Nabuasa kanaf group, the title is certainly inherited, and Nabuasa men are often referred to by this honorific title.

scouting the terrain, and laying the ambush (Middelkoop 1963: 111). In the myths of Amanuban, it is widely accepted that the Nabuasa clan formed one of the four great meo of the territory. The clan groups, Sole, Nome, Nabuasa, and Teflopo, are said to be the traditional warrior chiefs, the four bulls, the four males (*keus ha ma moen ha*) of Amanuban. Each was delegated to settle the periphery of the territory in order to expand its boundaries and to maintain a flow of harvest tribute and the spoils of warfare to the ruling center, the raja (*uis amnanut*: the "high lord") of Niki Niki. For this reason, each was also accorded the title of *a'su pah* (he who carries the land on his head).

The historical relationship between the ruling center and the peripheral warrior chiefs, however, remains somewhat unclear. On the one hand, the warrior clans were clearly structurally subordinate to the ruling political and ritual center. Their position was delegated by the center. Thus Cunningham has written that "unity of the princedom could be secured through force, particularly toward remote village areas who might be wooed by a neighbouring lord or seek independence for themselves. A dominant local lineage, with its own warriors, might assert its independence and the warriors of the lord [meo naek] were responsible for their subjection" (1962: 120).

Conversely, however, the very peripherality of the warrior chiefs, in both geographical and political terms, afforded opportunities to act independently. Middelkoop has said as much in relation to the meo chiefs and provides a number of examples where rulers have expressed their dependency on the warrior clans (1963: 10). Unfortunately, he does not provide details of the precise political relationship between the groups. Nevertheless, it is clear that an inherent ambiguity existed within the organizational structure of Meto political domains, creating political tension between the center and the periphery.

It is precisely this process that may have been operating when "D" made his journey into Amanuban in 1850. The great meo Nabuasa not only had asserted his independence from the ruling center of Niki Niki, but had also amassed sufficient authority and power to challenge the rule of the center itself. In order to understand the nature of this process and the basis of the Nabuasa claim more clearly, it is necessary to turn to the testimony of the contemporary descendants of the Nabuasa group and their allies. Their perspective on the past not only illuminates their own specific political history but offers more general insights into the role of warrior clans within the structure of former Timorese political systems as well.

Trunk Speech and Images of Political Power

Among the Meto, knowledge of the past exists only insofar as it can be spoken or enacted through ritual by living members of society. Oral narratives on the past serve to locate people and validate their claims in a given territory and a given order of political organization. These inherited words of the ancestral experience are sometimes described as *uab uf* (trunk speech). History in these terms is conceptualized as a botanical metaphor in which time is projected from a putative origin trunk (*uf*) to a contemporary tip (*tunaf*) or flowering (*sufan*). To speak the past of one's name group is to recount an organic process of growth and dispersal from the mythical origin.[6]

This community knowledge of the past is recorded through formal verse, or ritual speech (*natoni*), which differs from ordinary speech (*uab meto*) in a number of important respects. Though it utilizes much of the vocabulary of ordinary speech, the style of speaking is elliptical and poetic. It is structured in the form of canonical parallelism, found throughout eastern Indonesia, whereby there is a tendency to speak in a series of dyadic or paired sets of phrases that are generally synonymous in meaning and systematically, hence canonically, applied (Fox 1988: 23–24).

In the contemporary context, this detailed knowledge of the past tends to be restricted to a few older individuals, usually men. Younger people often possess a schematic understanding of the ritual words of the ancestors, but this may be limited to the bare outline of particular political relationships or key phrases. In the following discussion, I draw on elements of the ritual knowledge of

[6] The representation of life processes in a botanical idiom is a pervasive metaphor among the cultures both of Timor and of the wider region of eastern Indonesia. See, for example, Fox 1971, 1988; Traube 1986; Lewis 1988.

two particularly able ritual speakers of the Nabuasa kanaf. Their profound ability to narrate the past and express detailed exegetical commentaries provides the basis for understanding the political organization of the former autonomous Nabuasa territory. This is not to say that their image of the past is uncontested, for beyond the region of southern Amanuban there is considerable divergence of opinion. However, within the boundaries of the former Nabuasa domain, the great majority of people acknowledge some prior Nabuasa authority and therefore accept the words that accompany this claim.

The oral histories preserved by the elders of the Nabuasa group acknowledge the interdependent link with the former raja of Amanuban and the ritual center of Niki Niki. As a warrior group, the Nabuasa's skill was *natik pah, nasiken pah* (to kick-expand the land, to seize the land). In one of the oral histories that describes their relocation to the boundaries of the domain, the following words are recalled:

The ancestor said, "My place is	*Nai nak, Au he tokom*
to guard the open spaces.	*manusuah panat*
I do not speak in disputes	*Au ka uab lasi kaufam*
and I do not discuss disputes	*ma amolok lasi kaufam*
[except] if I go to war	*kalu het nao het makenat*
and go to fight,	*at nao het maken*
[except] if I go to behead	*kalu het nao ma oteta*
and go to execute."	*nao het maet oke.*

The chiefs of Amanuban respond by directing the meo Nabuasa to the periphery:

Never mind, let us	*Maut het*
direct and delegate	*malek am malul*
so that he guards us [in]	*henati in pao kit*
Bonak, Hauhonit,	*Bonak Hauhonit*
Sasi, and Oe Ekam	*Sasim Oe Ekam*
[and] tames for us	*he namaukit*
the wild bird, the wild chicken,	*kol fui, maun fui*
and the wild deer, the wild pig.	*am lu fui, faif fui.*

The oral history then records how the Nabuasa ancestor expanded the domain into an area known as Bonak, Hauhonit, Sasi, and Oe

Ekam, an area of some 600 square kilometers in the southwest of Timor, which the contemporary Nabuasa group and its allies still occupy. The reference to wild animals points to the resident populations at that time who remained outside the political control of the ruling center and consequently did not deliver up annual harvest tribute. The "taming" of these populations achieved this objective.

As a formally appointed warrior group, the Nabuasa clan also delivered up harvest tribute to the ruling center. Nabuasa tribute took the form of plundered booty and the spoils of war. This is expressed in ritual speech as

Hunting the fresh meat,	*Nuananam sis mate*
tapping the young honey,	*hel nanam oin makuke*
carrying and entering the palace	*nekin tam neu sonaf*
to offer and present to	*on a hau ma fati*
the lord of Banam (Amanuban).	*Banam tuan.*

These prestations refer to the harvested products of the forest, but also are a veiled reference to the acquisition of enemy livestock and severed human heads accumulated in warfare. An important qualification, however, which contemporary Nabuasa elders are quick to make, is that although historically the Nabuasa group acknowledged a ceremonial tie with the center and offered military protection and tribute as part of this obligation, they were not dependent on the ruler. This relationship was expressed to me in the following terms:

Nabuasa became a cat	*Nabuasa anfain meo*
and a dog [of war].	*ma anfain asu*
He guarded Nope [the ruler], but	*In apanat Nope mas*
Nope did not govern	*Nope kanaplenatfa*
Nabuasa.	*Nabuasa.*

This idea illustrates the essential ambiguity of warrior clans within the political structure. They guarded the center on their own terms. Though they acknowledged a prior delegatory authority from the center, this authority was only as strong as the support it was accorded. The origins of the Nabuasa disaffection from the center are, however, no longer clear. One version recalls a time when Nabuasa presented the center with smoked human heads that had become rotten and maggot-infested. This insulting prestation is known in formal terms as

| The rotten meat that stinks, | *Sis apunut afot* |
| the honey of the cannibal cutter.[7] | *oni akut akeut.* |

From this point, the Nabuasa clan no longer offered tribute to the ruler in Niki Niki, and instead became a rival center of power, drawing its own tribute from allied groups under its protection. Thus it is claimed in the Nabuasa corporate view that, at this time, *Banam in Usif nua* (Amanuban had two lords): the weakened ruler (clan Nope) in Niki Niki, powerless to stop the decline of his authority, and an emergent autonomous domain under the warrior clan, Nabuasa.

When individuals speak of uab uf (trunk speech) in terms of the political structure of the Nabuasa system, they refer to the earliest complete formation of that structure. Although it is understood that the political order developed piecemeal and gradually, it is nevertheless conventionally expressed as emerging complete at one time. This reflects a persistent characteristic of Meto conceptions of politics, whereby order is constantly superimposed upon the flux of shifting alliances and contingent events by adherence to an inherited corpus of cultural codes for describing the state. Thus it is apparent that the development of the autonomous Nabuasa position in fact occurred in a number of stages. One established the group's position in the new territory surrounding the mountain region of Lasi; a subsequent phase involved an expansion westward to consolidate its power base. The latter involved a modification in the internal order of political relations.

Order and Authority in the Nabuasa State

The site that the Nabuasa group and its supporters selected for settlement is named Pupu tunan. Here the group established a fort (*kot*) on a narrow raised shelf of land that formed a ridge extending

[7] There is no evidence that cannibalism ever figured prominently in Timorese society. The practice is generally regarded with abhorrence, since it is usually associated with the alleged cannibal desires of witches (*alaut*), who are said to consume the internal organs of their victims. However, a degree of ritual cannibalism associated with headhunting appears to have been quite common. Favored parts of the severed head prepared for ritual consumption were

from the top of the mountain (Lasi). Access was via a narrow path-
way from the mountain, and the land fell away precipitously on
three sides. Thus, in the manner of many older settlement sites
in Timor, considerations of defense were paramount. In times of
war, the population would seek protection in the barricaded central fort.

In the conceptual organization of the political unit, the Nabuasa
ruler occupied the center or navel (*usan*) of the system. Enclosing
the center in a protective ring were a series of named clan groups
that held various functions within the political system. There
were certainly other groups resident within the domain, and, as
the historical record reveals, their number grew considerably
during the mid-nineteenth century. But, in terms of the "trunk
speech," the latter settlers are collectively placed under more
prominent named figures.

In basic outline, there were three sets of political relationships
that formed the central core of the Nabuasa political domain. Together they constituted the ritual and political order. Immediate
political support for Nabuasa derived from the four principal allied clans known as the "father people" (*atoin amaf*), named as
Benu, Neonane, Sopaba, and Toislaka. These clans held the dual
responsibility of supplying harvest tribute to the Nabuasa center
and acting as soldiers and headhunters in times of war. As pro-
viders of agricultural produce, these clan groups set aside special
garden areas (*etu*) and livestock for the production of ceremonial
food for their leader. In this regard, informants cite the words:

They weed the garden	*Sin tof lene*
and give tribute to their lord	*ma tol usif*
carrying the cover and rice basket,	*nekin tobe ma taka*
cooked pig and steamed rice.	*faif peti ma flol pastele.*

In times of war, the four amaf were the principal military per-
sonnel for Nabuasa active in headhunting outside the region. In
this role they were minor meo (meo ana) and were obligated to of-

---

the brain and the fleshy parts at the base of the skull. These were sometimes
boiled with tamarind pulp or citrus. By this practice, the headhunters sought
to ingest something of the vital force (*smanaf*) of their victims. The precise
meaning of the phrase in the quoted text is unclear to me but may refer to this
practice. See also Middelkoop 1963: 140 and Schulte Nordholt 1971: 360.

fer up the severed human heads captured in warfare to the Nabuasa center. There is a general view that human trophy heads
were given as prestations at the time of the presentation of agricultural produce. It is possible, therefore, to view the harvest of
agriculture and the metaphorical harvest of warfare as complementary elements that represented the combined products of the
domesticated sphere within the polity and of the wild space in the
conceptual outside.[8] Benu, Neonane, Sopaba, and Toislaka may be
viewed as mediators of the boundary between outside and inside, between the tame and the wild. They were politically active
in both the wet season, the conceptually inactive, cool, "female"
time of planting and growth, and the dry season, with its emphasis on male mobility, the heat of warfare, and ritual feasting. The
symbolic integration of these dualistic themes was directed at the
ritual promotion and safeguarding of life and the living community, including the ancestors.

In addition to these four core groups, there were a number of
other name-group segments accorded politico-ritual titles within
the domain. The groups Sila and Nuban were referred to as amaf
and held positions similar to the four main allies to the extent
that they were "weeders of the garden" and provided food prestations to the center. They are distinguished, however, as amaf
"within the Nabuasa house." They served in the stronghold com-
pound itself and supervised its organization. They were said to
"sit in the settlement and to guard the house" (*tokom bi kuan ma
apao ume*) and did not participate actively in headhunting raids.
According to one version, it was they who received the guests of
the meo naek Nabuasa as well as the smoked trophy heads accumulated in war. It is in this sense that they are referred to as
"those who convey the prestations and carry the betel bag" (*asaha
maus ma asnin kabin*).

In the immediate region of Lasi, two clan groups were appointed
guardians of the "gates" (*eno*) to the settlement area. These positions are identified with the groups Leo and Toislaka, the latter

---

[8] Schulte Nordholt has identified explicit associations here in relation to the
harvesting hook (*kait*). This was used both in the rituals to gather up the
smoked trophy heads after a successful raid and in the rituals for the first fruits
of agriculture, know as "the head of the maize, the head of the rice" (*pena
nakan, ane nakan*). Schulte Nordholt 1971: 352–53; see also McWilliam 1982
and Spyer 1984: 244.

being one of the four principal allies to Nabuasa. The conceptual opposition between the two defenders of the Lasi stronghold expresses many aspects of the cultural order of the polity. The Leo group guarded the eastern entrance to the mountain settlement of Lasi from a settlement know as Panite. It was referred to as the guardian of the "head gate" (apao eno nakan). In this capacity, the Leo group was entrusted with meeting visitors and prospective settlers who were presenting themselves to the meo naek Nabuasa. The visitors would be accompanied down the narrow path to the central complex.

In contrast, the Toislaka group occupied a settlement site, Bonsain, at the base of the mountain on the western slopes. This was known as the "foot gate" (eno haen). As the guardian of this gate, the Toislaka clan prevented intruders from gaining access to Lasi from the west. Any persons attempting to enter the area from this direction were summarily executed. A Nabuasa elder explained this arrangement to me in the following terms: "Whosoever entered via the Panite [head] gate would live. But those who came via the Bonsain [foot] gate would be executed. If entering via the eastern gate, Nabuasa would receive and place them, but the western gate was prohibited because it was the wide gate. If not forbidden, people could enter without the knowledge of Nabuasa and become [his] enemies.

In this contrast between the two gateways to Lasi, a holistic conception of the domain is implied. The eastern gate, associated with the rising sun, is the gate of life. The western gate, associated with the setting sun, is the gate of death. The opposition is also marked by the contrasting metaphor of the wide (manuan) gate and the (implicitly) narrow or confined (ma'lenat) gate. An attempt to enter Lasi from the open, underpopulated spaces reversed the historical movement from the confined to the wide spaces and implied a threat that was summarily dealt with. Finally, the conceptual orientation also encompassed a body symbolism of the political system in which Nabuasa occupied the navel (usan) and the eastern head and western foot marked the boundaries. This association was consistent with Meto orientation to the cardinal points of the compass, in which east (neonsaet, sunrise) and west (neontes, sunset) comprise the dominant axis and north (li, left) and south (neu, right) are derivative, and implies an orientation based on a human form facing the rising sun.

In addition to the named amaf, the Nabuasa leadership also drew around them four clans with a special honorific title of *usif* (lord). These four groups, Telnoni, Isu, Ataupah, and Tenistuan, are referred to as "the four lords, the four males" (*Uis ha ma Moen ha*). They arrived in the Lasi area by separate routes, but each represented a disaffected ally of the old ruler of Amanuban in Niki Niki. Their subsequent relationship with the Nabuasa center was one of mutual support and alliance. In formal speech it is stated that they were

United together and	*Nabianok am*
linked together	*natalbok*
and in mutual support	*ma suikman*
and mutual respect	*ma tolan*
with their bull, their male,	*nok sin kesu sin mone*
who is Nabuasa.	*es a Nabuasa.*

Nabuasa offered them the protection of settlement in Lasi, and to each was appointed four amaf groups from the area to provide harvest tribute from communal gardens and support in the case of warfare. In the words of ritual speech, the role of the sixteen amaf in relation to the four usif was to "weed the garden and tap the lontar palm" (*tof lene ma anhelin tua*). In other words, their role was identical to that of the four core groups, which supported the Nabuasa ruling center, providing ceremonial harvest tribute to their respective leaders and acting as warrior defenders.

The final significant figure in the organization of the autonomous political unit was the name group Nubatonis. The role of Nubatonis within the polity reflected an ancient concern in Timorese culture with the importance of diarchy as a defining characteristic of the state. The development of the politicial domain under Nabuasa leadership was constituted as both a political and a religious system. The continuing prosperity of the wider political community was underpinned by an ongoing communication with the hidden world of ancestors and spirits. As a warlord, the Nabuasa clan maintained ritual and political control over the conduct of warfare and headhunting. The "great meo" was said to be the "lord of the earth" (*Pah tuaf*) and was accorded the title of "custodian of the people" (*abain toh*) to the extent that the clan leader held executive authority over the people of the domain and the right to settle newcomers within the territory. This position was conceptually and preeminently masculine. Complementing this role was that of the clan group Nubatonis, which was conceptually female in designation. The Nubatonis clan leader was known as the *a na'amnes* (he who holds the sacred rice); he held the primary responsibility for the ritual control of the monsoon rains and ritual authority over the land and forests of the domain. In complementary opposition to Nabuasa, Nubatonis was said to be the custodian of the land (*abain pah*). The primary task of the Nubatonis group in Lasi was to manage the timing of the monsoon rains through prayer and blood sacrifice. These rituals were conducted at spiritually important locations around the domain, usually forested mountain tops and important water sources.

In addition to this role as guardian of the earth and its products, Nubatonis held the major responsibility for the agricultural management of the land. As the delegated authority from Nabuasa, Nubatonis supervised the cultivation of garden lands and arbitrated disputes in the first instance. When farmers sought to cultivate new tracts of forest, they would request the right from Nubatonis. The farmers paid a tax known as the silver coin and coral bead (*noin sol mese ma inu fua es*), which entitled them to cultivate the land for up to five years, after which the area would revert to the custodianship of the a na'amnes. The majority of the tax was presented to the Nabuasa chief.

The Nubatonis group, therefore, held a powerful and influential position within the domain. However, as senior members of the Nabuasa group stress and as contemporary descendants of the local Nubatonis group attest, the authority was subordinate or complementary to the overall delegatory political authority of the warleader Nabuasa. This conclusion is supported to the extent that a second clan group, named Neonbota, was later elevated to the position of a na'amnes in the Lasi area and shared ritual responsibilities with Nubatonis. Taken together, the relationship between the a na'amnes and the meo naek embodied a symbolic unity between the "male" authority of Nabuasa and their jurisdiction over warfare and the political community, and a conceptual "female" authority over the ritual management of the land and its resources under Nubatonis and Neonbota. The success of the political system rested upon the efficacy of this diarchy.

The Expansion of the Polity

At a certain point in the development of the autonomous Nabuasa domain, a significant expansion occurred westward from the stronghold area of Lasi. The impetus for this second expansionary phase is recalled in one of the narrative histories I recorded, with the following passage:

Then our ancestor	*Okat na Nai on a*
spoke, saying,	*te uaban, uab nak*
"This our land has been	*i hit pahat ontak*
liberated and is empty.	*tafet kan luman*
Later in days to come	*of he neno namunit*
men will pillage us again	*atonim beuntenkit*
and control us again.	*ma nobintenkit*
It is better that	*nalekot*
[we] direct again	*maleka ten*
and delegate again	*ait malulu nten*
so that we seize our land	*he tatautan hit pah*
or enter our land definitely."	*ai tatnatam hit pah.*

What followed was a dispersal of designated clan groups into the dry savannah forest of southwest Amanuban from the mountainous central stronghold of Lasi. The reality of this historical event is supported by the testimony of contemporary resident populations of the area, the majority of whom locate their former natal settlements in the region of Lasi. Moreover, in these villages, the longest settlement claim does not extend past five generations, suggesting a date for the expansion during the latter years of the nineteenth century. All resident groups within this territory acknowledge the political and historical primacy of the Nabuasa clan and trace their original rights to settlement in the region to the delegatory authority of former Nabuasa leaders.

In outline, the organization of this expansionary process of Nabuasa influence was based on a multiplication of the core model, namely, four subsidiary clans or amaf (father) groups surrounding a ruling fifth that occupied the center. The leading role in this dispersal was taken by the Nabuasa group itself. Though

East ————————————————————— West

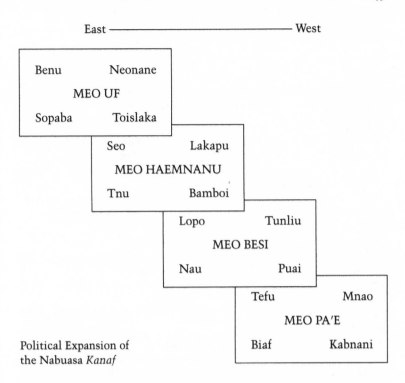

Benu   Neonane

MEO UF

Sopaba   Toislaka

Seo   Lakapu

MEO HAEMNANU

Tnu   Bamboi

Lopo   Tunliu

MEO BESI

Nau   Puai

Tefu   Mnao

MEO PA'E

Biaf   Kabnani

Political Expansion of
the Nabuasa *Kanaf*

the Nabuasa leadership, the classificatory "elder" line (*tataf*), remained in Lasi, "younger brother" lines of affiliation (*olif*) were
directed to the periphery to secure the territory. This resulted
in the creation of four subterritories under the direct control of
the Nabuasa group. The senior "elder brother" line, known as the
meo uf (trunk or origin *meo*), continued to play a central role with
the traditional four supporting groups, Benu, Neonane, Sopaba,
and Toislaka. An outline of the structure of the three "younger
brother" Nabuasa regions is presented in the accompanying figure. In each case, the warrior clan group Nabuasa takes the central
position and is accorded a specific meo or headhunter title. Thus
the *meo haemnanu* ("long-legged" meo) was chief in the territory
of Oe Peliki, the *meo besi* ("invulnerable" meo) ruled in Oe Ekam,
and the *meo pa'e* ("hero" meo) was the leading Nabuasa group in
the district of Polo. They became the "lords of the land" (*pah tuaf*)
in their respective areas of jurisdiction and controlled the settle-

ment of immigrants and the collection of harvest or tribute. In matters of war, however, Lasi and the senior Nabuasa leadership, the meo uf, continued to dominate. The indigenous representation presented in the figure articulates only the principal named groups of the areas. These main groupings gradually accommodated immigrant settlers under their authority.

This extensive area of territory was claimed through warfare. These campaigns are recalled in the narrative tales of each domain using the typical metaphors associated with the headhunter tradition. In the territory of Oe Ekam, for example, in relation to the exploits of the meo besi, the following verse segment was noted:

Safe and Buki,	*Safe ma Buki*
Bonak and Hauhoni	*Bonkam Hauhonit*
the long-legged horse,	*bi kase haemnanu*
the long-shafted spear,	*ma auni haemnanu*
extended the land	*es natik pah*
and extended the water	*ma natik nifu*
in order that [it become]	*hen*
wide and great,	*manua ma naek*
in order to chase out	*hen liu*
the wild bird	*kol fui*
and the feral chicken	*ma maun fui*
to evict them from this place.	*hem poi nako bale le i.*

Each of the four Nabuasa political centers were supported by four subsidiary allied clans known as amaf (father) groups. The four original political allies, Benu, Neonane, Sopaba, and Toislaka, remained in Lasi supporting the senior Nabuasa leader, the meo uf. In the expanded domains, each Nabuasa leader appointed a series of new political allies, or amaf. In each case, the first named amaf group of each domain took on the ritual responsibilities for agriculture. Seo, in the domain of meo haemnanu, Lopo, in the domain of the meo besi, and Tefu, in the domain of the meo pa'e, were accorded the title *a na'amnes* (he who holds the sacred rice) and collected tribute and taxes from subordinate groups who settled in the respective areas. In this regard, these particular amaf groups held a conceptually female role. However, this gender designation was not absolute, because the four fathers in each of the new Nabuasa domains were also divided into two conceptual groupings of male and female. The first two named groups in each area were classificatorily male to the extent that they were responsible for warfare and headhunting raids outside the territory. They were the *atoin makenat/atoin amaunut* (men of war/sorcerers). Hence the paired groups—Seo-Lakapu, Lopo-Puai, and Tefu-Mnao in the respective expansion areas—held this position.

The latter two groups in each domain were conceptually "female" and were said to provide a defensive role for the respective Nabuasa strongholds in the new territories and to cultivate food gardens for their warrior leaders. Thus, they were said to

become women in the house	*fain bife ambi ume nanan*
as servers of food,	*on a tuthais*
becoming as	*fain on a*
the doorstep and mantle	*teli ma sutae.*
[of the Nabuasa house].	

The fact that senior allies under Nabuasa leadership could be both a na'amnes (and therefore conceptually female in this role), and symbolically male headhunter warriors highlights the contingent nature of dual classification within the society, a concept simultaneously relative and context-sensitive.

Each of the Nabuasa subterritories was said to have had two principal gateways oriented east and west, similar to the original settlement of Lasi. The eastern one was the "cool gate" (*eon manikin*), associated with the allies to the east. Its counterpart, the "hot gate" (*eon maputu*), was associated with the conceptual outside, enemy clans, and the threat to peaceful life from the west.

The expansion of the Nabuasa clan and the addition of three subterritories formed the conceptual masculine half of the greater political domain. Accompanying this development was a parallel expansion of the senior allied groups, resident in Lasi, under the political direction of the senior Nabuasa leadership. They formed the conceptual "female" half of the domain.

In the formation of the Lasi political assemblage, it was noted that Nabuasa drew around it four usif (lord) groups, namely Isu, Telnoni, Ataupah, and Tenistuan. By the time of the expansionary phase, the clan groups Isu and Telnoni, with their respective amaf allies, had established themselves immediately northeast of the Lasi settlement area. Ataupah and Tenistuan were directed westward into the open savannah territory. The Ataupah group, with their supporters Tanu, Noislaka, Neonleku, and Bosoin, settled near the Baki River. Here they established a forward stronghold adjacent to the extensive uninhabited grasslands to the north, which formed a buffer zone between Lasi and the enemy lands of Mollo. The Tenistuan clan group shifted far to the west, settling a region to the south of the Nabuasa meo pa'e known by the name Oe Kiu (tamarind water).

The presentation of this expansion in schematic terms masks a strong internal dynamic in the relations between the constituent parts. There is little sense of an ancient dynastic order in the reproduction of political relations. Rather, what emerges in the indigenous perspective is the adherence to a particular cultural pattern of political order that overlays a complex of unstable and shifting alliances. In the case of Tenistuan, for example, the position of its four original allies had weakened at the time of the expansionary period. In their place were elevated seven named allied clan groupings: Kause feto,[9] Kause mone, Neonbanu, Tse, Leobisa, Benu, and Tasesab. These clan groups were divided into the conceptual categories on *mone* (male) and *feto* (female). The "male" group included Benu and Tasesab, which functioned as headhunter warriors for Tenistuan. The remaining clan groups acted as guardians of the Tenistuan "house" and cultivated gardens for their leader. Collectively, the role of these amaf groups was to *apao musu ma tof lene* (guard the enemy and weed the garden).

The emergence of four distinct territories under the authority of the usif groups created a loosely federated political domain comprising eight core subsystems: four areas under the direct control of the Nabuasa clan, and four areas under the authority of the usif, which nevertheless continued to recognize the political preeminence of the Nabuasa meo uf of Lasi (Map 2). This relationship was described to me as one in which Nabuasa maintained the authority to speak and wage war (*natoin ok am maken ok*) for the collectivity. The political configuration created in this period of

---

[9] The name *Kause feto* (lit.: female Kause) is an example of internal differentiation in the name group. This occurs when an unmarried woman of the group bears a child and no father is recognized. In such cases, if the child is a boy, the female appellation, *feto*, is added to his name. Subsequently his children will also take the name Kause feto, as will his son's children.

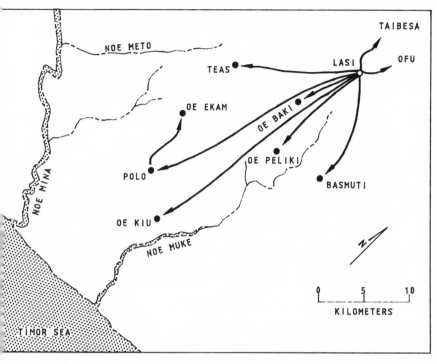

Map 2. Nineteenth-century expansion of Nabuasa allies into southern Amanuban.

expansion was also described in terms of the alliance between the "sweet" and the "bitter." The usif clans were known as the *usi mina* (the sweet lords) in contrast to the Nabuasa clan leaders, the *usi menu* (the bitter lords). This gave rise to the phrase *mina menu* as a shorthand description of the wider domain.

The Political Economy of Headhunting

In the foregoing section I have sketched the outline of the Nabuasa domain as it is represented by knowledgeable contemporary descendants of the area. What remains implicit in this expanding political unit is the formal basis of its political integration. What explicit elements of allegiance tied the subsidiary domains to the Nabuasa center? The principal answer, I believe, was headhunting, and specifically the capacity of the Nabuasa clan to control the organization and means of ritual combat. This was achieved primarily through the protective efficacy of the Nabuasa war ritual (*le'u musu*). The le'u musu was crucial to Nabuasa power and the maintenance of a central position within the political order. In simplistic terms, the le'u musu complex might be described as enmity magic, concerned with the conduct of warfare and, primarily, with the taking of human heads. It formed one aspect of a generalized belief in the properties of le'u, which carried the sense of the sacred or taboo and was intimately connected to the hidden world of ancestors, spirits, and the supreme being (*uis neno/uis pah*) of the Meto religion. One shorthand term for the indigenous religion of the Meto people, for example, is *hau le'u, faut le'u* (the sacred tree, the sacred stone). Though ultimately all le'u is one,[10] for practical purposes it is possible to distinguish two broad categories of le'u: fertility le'u (*le'u nono*) and enmity or hostility le'u (*le'u musu*). The former was said to be sleeping when the enmity le'u was invoked.

The name of the Nabuasa le'u musu was *menu mafu na nabuasa* (bitter disorienting Nabuasa). It was from this enmity magic that the clan took the le'u name Nabuasa, and thenceforth operated under its protective spell. In the period of intractable warfare and political expansion of Nabuasa hegemony during the late nineteenth century, this le'u musu was considered of vital importance to the success of any military exercise. All subsidiary groups within the federated polity fought wars and skirmishes under the protective cover of Nabuasa hostility power. This is not to say that all feuding between enemy groups was undertaken with the expressed authority of the Nabuasa. Ongoing border disputes and buffalo rustling could continue unresolved for years. However, in formally constituted periods of hostility where headhunting came to the forefront, to act without the cover of the Nabuasa le'u musu would have been folly.

The focus for headhunting raids was the Nabuasa hostility cult

[10] Middelkoop has described five general types of le'u, or ritual, which included a generalized fertility magic connected with agriculture and the name group (*le'u nono*), pregnancy and childbirth ritual (*le'u fenu*), ritual knowledge for taming and increasing buffalo herds (*le'u abanat*), ritual knowledge for coloring cotton threads used in textile manufacture (*le'u kinat*), and finally enmity ritual (*le'u musu*), used in headhunting and warfare (1963: 23).

house (*uem le'u musu*). It was from here that headhunting raids outside the domain were formulated, initiated, and concluded. The cult house stood in the stronghold of the Nabuasa leader in Lasi. Within, it held the sacred objects of the le'u musu, including swords, flintlock rifles, gunpowder, specific herbs and roots, and special clothes and ornaments worn by the meo. These items were considered powerful in themselves, imbued as they were with the sacred le'u.

Although the Nabuasa chief was known as the *le'u tuan* (the lord of the le'u), the cult house was guarded by two trusted individuals from the allied groups, Sopaba and Saebani. In their capacity as guardians of the hostility magic, they were referred to as "female" meo (meo feto) with respect to Nabuasa, the "male" meo (meo mone). This category distinction was said to be directly related to the function of the "female" meo as guardians of the cult house, in much the same way that we noted above for the lesser meo in the expanded polity. However, it is also acknowledged that these two clan groups were affinally related to the leading Nabuasa line as wife-takers and were therefore structurally "female" in relation to their "male" wife-givers in the conventional categories of Meto marriage relations.

In discussing the Nabuasa le'u cult house I have had to rely on the memory of older residents: the structure fell into disuse prior to Japanese occupation of Timor during the Second World War, and only the crumbling stone base remains in evidence today. The old men recall a conical thatched structure supported by two large wooden posts (*ni le'u*). Upon these posts were hung the various elements of the le'u musu, divided into male and female aspects. The part of the enmity magic known as the "male" le'u was hung on the eastern post, guarded by Sopaba. The "female" part was hung on the western post, guarded by Saebani. In ritual speech these two aspects of the hostility le'u are referred to as follows:

> *Le'u mone: hoen Nabuasa até, lomit atoin hum leko;*
> *le'u bife: hoen Saebani até, lomit bife hum leko.*

These phrases translate as "Male le'u: the slaves of Nabuasa, we like a fine-faced man; female le'u: the slaves of Saebani, we like a fine-faced woman." They refer to decapitated human heads of both sexes that formed the ritual offering to the le'u. Smoked and dried, the hunted heads were stuck on poles surrounding the cult house or fixed in the branches of the large banyan tree, the *nunuh nakan* (head tree), which still stands on the site, emptied of its trophy heads. The structure of the former cult house was completed with sixteen short posts that supported the edges of the conical roof, consistent with designs of cult houses still found today in north central Timor. At the top of the structure was the Nabuasa white flag (*pen pen muti*), flown when the le'u musu was invoked and warfare was in progress.

In times of war, the participant headhunters would assemble at the cult house to invoke the le'u musu and prepare for raids on enemy settlements. An important feature of these ritual preparations was the formulation of the appropriate war cry curse (*fanu mak ne*), which, it was believed, would ensure victory if the correct formula was found. The war cry represented a manifestation of what Middelkoop has described as a deep-rooted belief in transcendental justice (1960: 61), whereby one's enemies would be struck with terror at a legitimate war cry demanding that justice be done.

The participants assembled at the cult house also received what is termed the *pius metan ma nen koa* (*pius metan* is the black cloth used to pack the guns and a bamboo cylinder, *nen koa*, which when filled with gunpowder was sufficient for one shot of a gun). Each participant was then placed under the protective spell of the le'u musu, which was said to offer the headhunters invulnerability to the enemies' bullets and the ability to disorient their victims. This involved smearing the bodies of the headhunters with a mixture of betel nut juice and a variety of le'u substances, accompanied by an incantation.

The invocation of the le'u musu created a context of ritual heat. Both the participants and the community entered this state of heat (*maputu*), which was only removed through a process of ritual cooling (*nasapu nahaniki*) by which the headhunters and their severed human heads were reincorporated into the community. The heat of the taboo curse sphere invoked through the le'u musu was antithetical to life and placed the participants in touch with the spirit powers. Ordinary activities in the community were suspended throughout this period.

These elaborate ritual aspects of headhunting and the "sacred" nature of the headhunters' journey have led Middelkoop to argue that headhunting in Timor was connected with the idea of tribute that had to be paid to the unseen transcendental beings with whom the ancestors were linked (1960: 70). There is certainly sufficient evidence to support this position, but I would argue that it is equally important to recognize the historical and political context in which headhunting raids were undertaken. In the present study it is clear that the ceremonial aspects of headhunting, and the undoubted success of the cult under Nabuasa leadership, were vital elements in the prestige accorded the political center. These factors added to the general recognition that the Nabuasa kanaf group had a "great name" (kana naek) and reputation in the region. This, I would argue, was instrumental to the development of the Nabuasa group influence. Nabuasa political centrality was a direct consequence of the ritual management of war, including the formulation of the war cry, the control of weapons and gunpowder, and the belief that the enmity cult magic could deliver invulnerability in the face of enemy response.

There were two important consequences of the headhunting successes that contributed to the development of the political order under Nabuasa authority. First, headhunting offered many opportunities to accrue wealth. This took the form of enemy slaves, livestock, and personal valuables, plundered from enemy communities or from the richly adorned headhunters themselves. Toto's story of the executed Nabuasa warrior related earlier illustrates something of the elaborate finery of the meo costume. Much of this booty accrued to the participant headhunters, highlighting an important individual motivation for seeking the status of meo. Schulte Nordholt has argued that in Timor, "The looting of the corpse was almost as important as the taking of the head, as the meo was richly adorned with strings of coral beads and silver discs—the articles paid as bridewealth to the bride-giving group in return for a woman, a smanaf, by means of which a source of new life could be incorporated in the bride-receiving group" (1971: 347). Headhunting, therefore, offered opportunities to secure propitious marriages with powerful allies through the acquisition of bridewealth valuables and, in the process, to amass considerable material wealth, albeit not without some risks.

The relative amount of plundered booty expropriated by the political leaders of the Nabuasa settlements and their allies is uncertain. Though the severed enemy heads were the primary prestation of the participant headhunters to the Nabuasa center, it is likely that a considerable number of female slaves, captured buffaloes, and other booty accompanied these offerings. Success in the management of warfare and headhunting, however, had considerable indirect economic benefits as well. As the ritual and political center, the Nabuasa clan in Lasi and its subsidiary "younger brother" settlements to the west claimed the authority to derive tribute from the subordinate allies and other groups brought within the sphere of Nabuasa influence through warfare. This was one of the important consequences of the split with the rival ruling center of Amanuban under the raja Nope in Niki Niki.

The Nabuasa center profited not only from the harvest gifts of agricultural produce delivered to the respective power centers by the amaf groups at the end of the wet season, but also from the export trade in beeswax (to supply the flourishing Javanese batik industry) and sandalwood. Tribute to the center was referred to as "head money" (*noni nakan*) and represented an explicit acknowledgment of the Nabuasa leadership as the "head" of the political community. Each year, for example, tribute known as the "head of the honey and the white beeswax head" (*oni nakan ma nini nakan*) was collected from wild beehives and directed to the center. The Dutch traveler "D" also noted that "through this trade [in sandalwood] the population has become rather wealthy in a way one does not see in other parts of Timor. Men and women are richly decorated with silver rings and discs. . . . Sandalwood is the most important form of income for the headmen. These goods must be collected by the general population of which nine-tenths is given to the heads" (1850: 172). The income from the trade of these resources could be used to acquire, among other things, the principal means of warfare, namely, muzzleloader rifles and gunpowder. In this way, warfare and headhunting not only served the political interests of the ruling group but also provided the means to sustain its political position.

The headhunting complex and its associated coercive results also contributed to a second important benefit from which Nabuasa leadership derived political kudos. As the acknowledged Pah tuaf (lord of the earth) of the southern district of Amanuban, the Nabuasa meo uf of Lasi maintained ultimate executive authority over the land and utilization rights to its resources. This control was not identical to ownership, but referred to the authority or right to determine who could settle and cultivate particular tracts of arable forest land. The expansion of the territory under Nabuasa control was a major result of the warfare and headhunting pursued during the late nineteenth century. However, control over land was only meaningful in terms of the people who could utilize it and recognize the Nabuasa meo as their benefactor. This seems to have been a factor in the significant population development of the Lasi area, where, according to "D," Lasi became the largest settlement in the whole of Amanuban with an estimated population of 3,000 people. This was clearly a significant center, particularly in the light of Venema's estimate that the population for the whole of Amanuban in 1916 was 29,909 (1916: 208). Van Lith, a Dutch administrator (controleur) of south central Timor in the early part of the twentieth century, has also commented on the development of Nabuasa influence as one in which "the authority of the Radja diminished further as new clans had been driven away from other places and come to this region [Lasi] and established themselves with the blessing of the monarch [i.e., Nabuasa]" (1921: 77). He compares the process of settlement to the Trojan horse strategy of the Greek king Agamemnon, whereby new settlers under the protection of the Nabuasa ruler settled land ostensibly belonging to the raja of Niki Niki and then undertook war against him. In receiving rights to settle designated tracts of land from the Nabuasa leadership, immigrant groups took on the responsibility of guardianship for that area. In doing so, the immigrant groups took on the status of kua tuaf (hamlet masters) under the general authority of the respective headmen of the area. Subsequent settlers into the area achieved rights of residence from the established kua tuaf, usually through marrying into the communities. Newcomers acknowledged the precedence of settlement of their wife-givers, and thereby received cultivation rights to plant their staple maize and upland rice crops. To this day, land claimants in the region acknowledge this process of nested claims to land, the claims of one group resting upon those that preceded them. In the late nineteenth century, the Nabuasa meo uf of Lasi was at the apex of this structure of precedence in which subordinate groups directed a flow of tribute to the political center in exchange for the continuing right to "eat" from the land. The subordinate allies were collectively referred to as Nabuasa's *muti ma natu* (silver and gold) for the good reason that they represented the organizational basis for Nabuasa power. To the allies Nabuasa was the *aneot ahafot::apaot apanat* (the canopy and cover::the defender and guardian), exemplary images of central authority and lordship.

In the contemporary Nabuasa perspective, the high point of Nabuasa influence accompanied the expansion of the allies into the southwestern regions of Amanuban. Modern history, particularly since the imposition of Dutch administrative control over Amanuban during the first decade of the twentieth century, represents a continuing process of disintegration and erosion of Nabuasa influence. A turning point occurred soon after 1906 when the Dutch government, in support of the raja of Niki Niki, entered the region of Lasi to seek formal subjugation and enforce the *pax nederlandica*. Safe Nabuasa, then the meo uf in Lasi, submitted without resistance. From that time the Nabuasa name group and its allies in the various subdivisions of the region acknowledged both the legitimate authority of the Dutch administration and the reinstatement and reinforcement of the Nope clan as raja of Amanuban. In such an environment, the continuation of headhunting and generalized warfare also became untenable, and as a consequence, the central Nabuasa domain of Lasi lost much of its authority.

The significance of the heroic past expressed by knowledgeable Nabuasa elders and noted ritual speakers of the area nowadays is muted. The mass conversions to Christianity in the 1960s and the intrusive authority of the modern Indonesian state have created a new ruling ideology that colors the practice of everyday life. Since the Second World War, increased immigration to the region has also brought a significant rise in population and a greater mix of people from different territories. The regions formerly under the political control of the Nabuasa clan and its allies have been divided into thirteen separate villages, each with its own local village-government structure. At the same time, continuity with the past and the political relationships created in the former period are still much in evidence. They persist in patterns of land tenure and land claims, which rest upon rights devolved through Nabuasa permission. They are reflected in the individuals elected as village headman, who are consistently drawn from descendants of the former ruling Nabuasa groups and their political allies. Moreover, the reproduction of marriage alliance and the networks of kin connected by the narrative thread that links one to another reflect a pattern of political and ritual order established before the twentieth century under the warrior group, Nabuasa. In these and other ways, the Nabuasa case study and the vision of the past offered by contemporary informants provide an intriguing perspective on the nature of the indigenous state in West Timor and the generative opportunities offered by the political celebration of ceremonial violence.

The political history of the indigenous Meto states of West Timor, particularly prior to the twentieth century, is one of extraordinary complexity. These states appear as highly fluid, changeable structures reflecting a dynamic tension between centripetal and centrifugal political forces. Processes of political integration of Meto populations into united federations compete with equally persistent forces of disintegration and dispersal into small, quasi-independent and mutually antagonistic territories. The general picture obtained from both the mythic and the historic records attests to the endemic competition and rivalry arising from the flux of changing circumstances.

This situation was clearly exacerbated by colonial intervention in the political process. For it was quickly recognized, in that time-honored strategy of divide and rule, that there were certain advantages in signing treaties with as many specific rulers and claimants to power as came forward. The subsequent proliferation of "legitimate" rulers and chiefs resulted in the gradual fragmentation of the opposing indigenous political forces, rendering them powerless (Fox 1977: 70). It was not until the late nineteenth and early twentieth centuries, following a sustained program of pacification and a rationalization of the political map by the Dutch colonial government, that the indigenous territories of West Timor were consolidated into stable self-governing political systems.

These elements of Timor history have led some commentators

to disavow the traditional existence of any developed indigenous political system above that of the segmented clan. Forman, for instance, has suggested that "the indigenous states of Timor were a product of Portuguese and Dutch historiography" (1977: 100). But this, I would argue, is overstating the case, and devalues the evidence of the Timorese oral tradition, which, despite the competing claims of different groups, clearly and invariably supports the existence of quite complex political entities with clear hierarchical forms and functions. These political forms are frequently expressed in recurring cultural themes and indigenous metaphors of political order. They strongly suggest that the concept of the state, or some allied form of federated political order, has a tradition in Timor that predates colonial meddling (see also Friedberg 1977).

The ideal model of the traditional political integration in West Timor appears to have been based on a concept of ritual communication for describing the state. In this conception, the territory was composed of four political subdomains (actually double pairs) surrounding a sacral fifth ruling center to which harvest tribute was directed. This arrangement reflects an ancient pattern found in the Hinduized states of Southeast Asia (Heine-Geldern 1956). In relation to the political domains of Timor, both Cunningham (1962) and Schulte Nordholt (1971) find compelling evidence for the validity of this model, notwithstanding certain regional variations.

In all cases, the ritual or sacral center was key. Schulte Nordholt has argued that "it is the ruler who symbolizes the unity of the realm. More than that, it is because of him that the realm is an integrated unit. That is why his place is in the navel of the realm" (1971: 396). An essential aspect of this unifying center is an inherent dualism of female ritual authority and male temporal power. The former is associated with the sacred le'u, the rituals of the earth, and the spiritual well-being of the domain. The latter aspect has to do with the exercise of control over the political community. In the eastern domains of West Timor, this resulted in a ruling diarchy comprising a conceptually immobile female (*feto*) ritual lord, sometimes referred to as the "one who sleeps" (*atupas*), and an active masculine (*mone*) executive counterpart who realized the potency of the ritual lord in the outer domain. Further west, the masculine aspect predominated (Schulte Nordholt 1971: 439). There was no "female" ruler as such, but to the extent that the center maintained control over the rituals and sacred le'u valuables of the domain, it embodied the female principle.

The female-male complementary dualism of the ruling center was duplicated in the relationship between the center and its constituent peripheral subterritories. The outer "male" domains fed the center through the delivery of harvest tribute and provided the defensive perimeter for the conceptually inner "female" domain. Each subdomain of the wider unity was also conceptually ordered in terms of female and male conceptual categories. In this way, the constitutive model of the indigenous polity embodied a dynamic symbolic system in which key contrasts of center/periphery and female/male provided the basis for both the reproduction and the transformation of the state. Each level of the Timorese political order mirrored the elemental unity of a husband (*mone*) and wife (*fe*), of marriage alliance between clan groups, of the male and female ancestors (*ena/ama, nai/bei*), and of the supreme being of the Meto religion with its dual aspect of father sky (*uis neno*) and mother earth (*uis pah*). The relative size of any autonomous political community was dependent upon the capacity of a prominent clan to harness political power under its central ritual authority. Thus, in principle, there was no limit to the number of political powers that could be accommodated within a domain, provided they acknowledged the authority of the center, which alone could legitimate their status within the territory (Fox 1982: 5). In practice, the inherent tension within this process frequently resulted in a collapse of the fragile unity, when the authority of the center was challenged or undermined.

The case study of the Nabuasa clan and its political allies reflects many of the elemental processes of Timorese state formation discussed above. Originally one of the four peripheral "male" warrior clans for the ruler Nope in Amanuban, the Nabuasa achieved political and ritual centrality in the process of challenging that authority. The polity was organized on the cultural distinctions of inner and outer domains based on four points surrounding a central fifth, and was articulated by a flow of harvest tribute to the new ruler. At the ritual center of Lasi, we also find a diarchy of ritual authority and temporal power with conceptual female and male distinctions. Here, however, there is no neat contrast between a "female" ritual authority and a "male" temporal power. Though the Nabuasa ruler is clearly the political powerholder, the warrior leader is also the ritual authority of the enmity le'u, the "male" le'u (le'u atoni). Female ritual authority—in this case, the "female" le'u (le'u bife)—is delegated to the name group Nubatonis, the ritual guardian of the earth. The relationship is duplicated in the role of the ritual sacrificers (a na'amnes) within the subsidiary "younger brother" Nabuasa domains. This distinction represents a variation on the traditional model of Timorese political systems proposed by Schulte Nordholt and Cunningham. It may be explained, I believe, by the special significance of warfare, and particularly the cult of headhunting, in the development and expansion of the territory. Political power achieved by the Nabuasa group evolved from, and indeed was found upon, the ritual management of ceremonial violence and the control of the sacral headhunting le'u (le'u musu). Female ritual authority, though important to the ritual management of agriculture and therefore part of the legitimizing authority of the ruling center, was always subordinate to its male complement. For the Nabuasa name group, headhunting served both as the basis for achieving political autonomy and as the integrative theme in the organizational structure of the subsequent political order.

Acknowledgments

Research for this paper was undertaken in West Timor between 1984 and 1987. During this period I was employed on an Indonesian-Australian development project in southwest Amanuban. The paper is based on a section of my dissertation completed at the Australian National University in 1989.

The title of the paper was suggested to me by Janet Hoskins and is adapted from the fine paper on headhunting by Derek Freeman, "Severed Heads That Germinate," in R. J. Hook, ed., *Fantasy and Symbol: Studies in Anthropological Interpretation* (London: Academic Press, 1979). I am also indebted to Michael Vischer for assistance with translating some segments of Dutch reports written in a particularly archaic style.

References

Boxer, C. R.
1947 "The Topasses of Timor." *Koninklijk Vereeniging Indisch Instituut*. Mededelingen no. 73.

Cunningham, C.
1962 "The People of the Dry Land: A Study of the Social Organisation of an Indonesian People." Ph.D. thesis, Oxford University.

D
1850 "Reis naar het rijk van Amanoebang op Timor in October 1850." (Journey to the realm of Amanuban in Timor in October 1850.) *Tijdschrift voor Nederlandsch-Indie* (Journal for the Dutch Indies) 13 (2): 153–79.

Forman, S.
1977 "East Timor: Exchange and Political Hierarchy at the Time of the European Discoveries." In K. L. Hutterer, ed., *Economic Exchange and Social Interaction in Southeast Asia: Perspectives from Prehistory, History and Ethnography*. Michigan Papers on South and Southeast Asia, no. 13. Ann Arbor: Center for South and Southeast Asia Studies, University of Michigan.

Fox, James J.
1971 "Sister's Child as Plant: Metaphors in an Idiom of Consanguinity." In R. Needham, ed., *Rethinking Kinship and Marriage*. London: Tavistock Publications.
1977 *Harvest of the Palm: Ecological Change in Eastern Indonesia*. Cambridge, Mass.: Harvard University Press.
1982 "The Great Lord Rests at the Centre: The Paradox of Powerlessness in European-Timorese Relations." Unpublished paper, Asian Studies Association of Australia, May 10–14, 1982, Monash University.
1988 *To Speak in Pairs: Essays on the Ritual Languages of Eastern Indonesia*. Cambridge: Cambridge University Press.

Friedberg, C.
1977 "The Development of Traditional Agricultural Practices in Western Timor: From the Ritual Control of Consumer Goods Production to the Political Control of Prestige Goods." In M. J. Rowlands and J. Friedman, eds., *The Evolution of Social Systems*. Proceedings of a meeting for the research seminar in Archaeology and related subjects held at the Institute of Archaeology, University of London. London: Duckworth.

Geertz, C.
1980 *Negara: The Theatre State in Nineteenth Century Bali*. Princeton: Princeton University Press.

Heine-Geldern, R. von
    1956 *Conception of State and Kingship in Southeast Asia.* Data paper, Southeast Asia Program, no 18. Ithaca, N.Y.: Cornell University Press. [Revised version of an article published in *Far Eastern Quarterly* 2 (1942).]
Lewis, E. D.
    1988 *People of the Source: The Social and Ceremonial Order of Tana Wai Brama on Flores.* Dordrecht: Foris Publications.
Lith, P. C. A. van
    1921 "Memorie van het eiland Timor." (Memorandum of Timor.) In *Memorie van overgave* (Memorandum of service), Inter Documentation Centre. Zug. Switz 1982, (5) 778, 32. Microfiche.
McWilliam, A. R.
    1982 "Harvest of the Nakaf: A Study of Headhunting Among the Atoni of Timor." Litt. B. thesis, Australian National University.
    1989 "Narrating the Gate and the Path: Place and Precedence in South West Timor." Ph.d. thesis, Australian National University.
Middelkoop, P.
    1960 *Curse, Retribution and Enmity, as Data in Natural Religion, Especially in Timor, Confronted with the Scripture.* Amsterdam: J. van Campen.
    1963 *Headhunting in Timor and Its Historical Implications.* Oceania linguistic monographs, no. 8. Sydney: University of Sydney.
Schulte Nordholt, H. G.
    1971 *The Political System of the Atoni of Timor.* The Hague: Martinus Nijhoff.
    1980 "The Symbolic System of the Atoni of Timor." In James J. Fox, ed., *The Flow of Life: Essays on Eastern Indonesia.* Cambridge, Mass.: Harvard University Press.
Spyer, P.
    1984 "Hunting Heads for Alliance: The Recreation of a Moral Order in Atoni Exchange." Masters thesis, University of Chicago.
Traube, E.
    1986 *Cosmology and Social Life: Ritual Exchange Among the Mambai of East Timor.* Chicago: University of Chicago Press.
Venema
    1916 "Nota over Zuid-Midden Timor." (Report on South Central Timor.) In *Memorie van overgave* (Memorandum of service), Interdocumentation Centre. Zug. Switz 1982, (5) 778. Microfiche.
Veth, P. J.
    1855 "Het Eiland Timor." (The island of Timor.) *De Gids* 8 (1): 546–611, 695–737; (2): 55–100.

Jules De Raedt

Buaya Headhunting and Its Ritual
Notes from a Headhunting Feast in Northern Luzon

Headhunting was an important historical practice for the roughly 1,000 Buaya people of Kalinga in the highlands of northern Luzon, the Philippines. It extended back beyond human memory, and was defined as a human sacrifice to the highest of the spirits. Since about 1930, headhunting has been on the wane, but it has not completely died out. In the mid-1960s, I attended a headhunting feast (*sagang*) in one of the 185 households in this largely endogamous region.

I was told by several witnesses that everything in the feast I attended was done as in the old days, but conditions had changed so much that I am skeptical of this claim. There was a good deal of excitement among the participants, but some of it was unreal. There was no head at the ceremony, only the knife that had been used in the killing. (Many of the guests did not know that there actually had been a killing; they could not be told in order to protect the killer.) The presence of a head puts the village into a state of frenzy and exhiliration, with lots of ribald and even debauched behavior. The feast I saw had elements of this mood, but also contained admissions of the ways that times had changed. Some people said this was only an echo of what the Buaya consider a "real headhunting feast"—but its ritual symbolism reveals many subtle understandings about the power of the unseen that the Buaya would say still operate today (De Raedt 1969: 679–778).

I describe here the village shrine, the prescribed stages of the headhunt, and the ceremony that I actually witnessed. I provide notes on some activities that did not occur, but that I was told were usually part of the celebration. This headhunting feast must be studied in the context of changes in Buaya life that have been felt over the past half century, especially shifts in concepts of leadership. The greatest leader in traditional Buaya society was a headhunter, who usually was also a wealthy man and a legal expert. Since the government has abolished headhunting, new avenues for leadership have emerged to take its place—expecially schooling and government service. World War II veterans who had killed at least two people were given the status of "headhunters" in the ceremony that I saw, and were allowed to perform the ritual boasts. At present, the Buaya have largely submitted to the government ban on headhunting, but they allowed me to attend this feast in the 1960s to understand some of its earlier importance to their ritual life.

The Village Shrine

The village shrine (*sangasang*) where heads were stored after a headhunting feast was the most revered and feared shrine in the village. Less than twenty years before the ceremony I describe, skulls could still be seen in the shrine, where they were watched over by the village guardians, also called *sangasang* as a group. The guardians were portrayed as both beasts (*kakayap*) and demons (*alan*), greedy and aggressive denizens of the above, below, upstream, and downstream, and also protective friends (*bulun*) and companions (*bulbulun*).

The shrine was located at some distance from the village, on the way to the river, so that the guardians could keep both human and mystical enemies out. The shrine itself was a cluster of plants, including the strongest and tallest bamboo in the area, whose big thorns made an impenetrable thicket. Decorative plants and trees with red and yellow flowers were added to the shrine. Whenever a new head was placed in the shrine, brush was cleared away and the decorative plants were made visible.

If a shrine was not erected at a new site settled by these shifting cultivators, it was said that a *bingil* would appear—a person covered with old wounds and pus, and smelling like rotten flesh, with his tongue hanging out, like a severed head. Illness or death would plague the settlement until a shrine was erected. The bingil could only be propitiated by a headhunt or a large animal sacrifice and a chase (*dagdag*) in which all the village residents took part.[1]

The village guardians craved heads and had to be given food offerings during large animal sacrifices. When headhunting could no longer be freely practiced, people said that meat brought in the shrine during a big sacrifice had to be enough to feed the guardians. But in general, the villagers acknowledge that they can no longer care for the guardians properly.

Old shrines are now allowed to deteriorate, and weeds and other plants that were once removed to protect the red and yellow flowers are now left to grow freely. Some of the old shrine sites are almost unrecognizable. Current village residents do not receive as many signs from them, and many hope that the guardians have left for good. But they are concerned about the effects of this loss of protection on their own well-being, which was once assured through the sacrifices of their religion. "A pig is only a pig," they say, implying that a human head comes closer to taking care of the grave human problem the headhunting ceremony was intended to cure. Since the shrines have been neglected, it is said that many new illnesses have come in, labeled with new names and diagnoses from the hospital. If headhunting were still permitted, the Buaya say, these illnesses could be cured more easily.

The shrines still play some role in village life because of the taboos that surround them[2] and because illness and insanity are

---

[1] For this rite, an effigy of the bingil is tied to a pole where the shrine will be erected, with a banana trunk as its body, rags hung on it for clothes, and an old raincoat. A broken pot on top represents the head. Bamboo tubes are struck with other objects to make noise and to drive the bingil out of the village. The participants chase it out toward the effigy, then strike the banana trunk with spears of the same kind used in headhunts and run away to the village. A medium who joins them in the chase becomes possessed by the bingil and pursues them back to their houses. Her tongue hangs out like the bingil, and her touch is said to kill any person she catches. When the participants have arrived back at the house once haunted by the bingil, the bingil-medium says he will no longer molest them and leaves, to stay at the village shrine with the other guardians.

[2] No pollutants can be brought near a shrine, nor any funeral meat. It would be disrespectful to spit or urinate nearby, so no children are allowed to play there. Cutting some of the plants can result in illness or insanity. The shrine is said to be inhabited by the souls of the persons whose skulls were stored there, represented by pieces of red hardwood carved to show a face and eyes. The skull itself may rest on a pile of stones, beside five long upright river stones.

often attributed to violations of these taboos. *Sangasang* affliction causes shivering, trembling, and a hanging tongue, as well as unpredictable laughing, shouting, dancing in the middle of the night, chasing at the slightest provocation, and biting both oneself and others. The spirits of the village shrine who cause these illnesses are named: the leader is Tayadan (Shiver), assisted by watchmen named Pakkuyan (Shout), Payudan (Sentinel), and Takang (Gaping Mouth). These aggressive male spirits possess a female spirit medium and ask for specific objects to appease them: Tayadan is given a hunting spear and a red string to tie his dogs, and his dogs are given red rice, meat, and broth. The medium possessed by this spirit shivers as if with fever, then gobbles up the dog food from a coconut shell. Animals are sacrificed to try to cure the patient, but sometimes this affliction is fatal.

The guardians can make themselves visible to village residents through casual encounters or spirit mediums. They usually take the form of wild dogs with long tails (pets have their tails trimmed), roosters, cats, snakes, bees, centipedes, water buffalo, and horses. All of these are seen as threatening potential killers. If a dog appears full of wounds, it is a sign that the village is threatened with a calamity. People must then perform big sacrifices to feed the guardians until the signs stop. Near the end of the last century, the Buaya remember a series of such signs that preceded a punitive expedition from Tuao that attacked the Buaya village of Buntuk. The village was burned and many people died, so the signs retain a strong psychological reality for current inhabitants.

Other smaller shrines in the house or at the village gates can also receive pig sacrifices, but only the village shrine asks for human victims. The same spirits are addressed in headhunting rites and animal sacrifices, but headhunting was traditionally necessary for the most serious cases of human misfortune, and had to be carried out at regular intervals to cure or prevent disaster.

The Headhunt

Headhunting is described by the Buaya as undertaken for religious, social, and psychological reasons. The religious reasons stem from the idea that a severed head produces a general state of welfare in the village, protects it against epidemics and famine, and assures that food will be plentiful. The Buaya claim that during the headhunting days, disease was less common, there were fewer premature deaths, and health and nutrition were better. Headhunts were also sometimes called to cure the apparent insanity of sangasang affliction. Socially, taking at least two heads was a step to leadership in an achievement-oriented society. Leaders were also expected to be wealthy and have legal expertise. Headhunting also satisfied psychological needs, including revenge for killings or adultery, the conclusion of mourning, or simply the urge to kill.

When the Buaya discuss headhunting, they mention such personal motivations for it as the desire for loot or glory, childlessness, grief over the death of a close relative (a child or first cousin), wounded pride (due to an unfaithful wife), the new interest of a paramour, or the inability to provide for the household. The man found in the killing an opportunity to take out his grief or humiliation on the person he would kill. Even when the motivations were strictly personal, the presence of a head required the full religious ritual. It was not usual for the man to leave in a huff on a do-or-die suicide mission, however. Most headhunts were organized and undertaken on the advice of a female religious leader I call the prophetess. She would call for a headhunt because of illness, declining fortunes, or the need for revenge.

The organized headhunt (kayaw) began with a chicken sacrifice to divine how each member of the party would fare. The prophetess would become possessed by dwarves (bulbulun di mangayaw, "friends of headhunters") who guide the men on a headhunt and produce a small, sometimes shining good-luck stone. She would rub the stone on the leader's head, and allow it to disappear and "enter" his body to protect him. She would also place ten betel quids, with a stone on each of them, on a plate with strings of beads laid over them and a red piece of cloth on top (the alung di mangayaw, "veil of the headhunters"). These would be stored in the house shrine of each participant during his absence. Any disarrangement of these ritual quids would be a sign that someone had been killed or wounded.

The headhunters themselves would wear a similar red or yellow head veil, and would look for signs that their dwarf "friends" were coming to meet them in the shape of snakes, centipedes, large

lizards, or wild roosters. Headhunters were allowed to wear tattoos of red and black, which gave them a fearful appearance. They
traveled in large parties (from 10 or 20 to as many as 100 to 200
members) playing bamboo gongs struck with an aggressive and en-
ticing rhythm. Secret paths through the jungle were followed to
avoid detection, and the musical instruments were used to make a
shrine for their dwarf "friends" at the final resting place. The
bamboo gongs were set up, circled by ritual quids and pebbles,
with strips of red and yellow cloth tied into a red knot, along with
decorated rolls of chewing tobacco and betel nut. This "no tres-
passing" sign was said to act as a blockade against the guardians of
the enemy's village shrine, who would be distracted by chewing
the ritual quid and so would not attack the invading party.

The prophetess accompanied the fighters, and would begin the
attack with a high-pitched yell, throwing her sacred spear toward the enemy village. Then the attackers would throw bamboo
spears weighed down with rocks and would prepare to invade the
enemy village with axes (see Sugguiyao and Sugguiyao 1964: 183–
87 for a vivid description of such engagements). Victims of the
ambush could be men, women, or children; it made no difference
for either the social honor of the killer or the religious purpose of
the act of killing. In raids where many people were killed, each
headhunter would take home only one head.

It was best if a living person could be brought back, usually
a child. The child would then sit on an inverted mortar in the
middle of the dancing arena in the captor's house yard during
feasting and dancing. Sometimes the child would be danced with
like a trophy, held up by the headhunter and abused before the
others. The next morning, the child would be killed at the village
shrine. The Buaya say that the meaning of the headhunt is more
clearly stated if a living victim is brought back, since the sacrifice
and bloodshed should be at the village shrine. However, this happened very rarely, and in the 1960s they could recall only one case
where it had been done.[3]

---

[3] Once the kinsmen of a child who had been kidnapped for a headhunting
feast came to the kidnapper's village to plead for the return of the child while
the feast was in progress. A very high ransom was paid, but the child died a
month later. It was explained to me that once a person has been captured and
dedicated to be sacrificed, he or she will be doomed to die. The death could
have been caused by the abuse, exposure to elements, lack of food, and shock
during the days following the capture.

The head was the next best thing to a live human victim, but it was also possible to bring back hair and fingers. Government pressure and the greater distance needed to travel to find an enemy resulted in an increase in other parts of the body used as substitutes. The fingers were kept in bottles and could be easily stowed away. The hair was mounted on a "head" crudely carved out of a piece of wood. In the one case that I witnessed, the knife used to kill the victim was the only symbol available—but it was nevertheless considered appropriate in the absence of anything better.

When the raid was finished, the prophetess would call on the soul of the victim to follow the body part that was carried off. Then the attackers would run home as fast as they could. Someone might stay behind to plant sharpened sticks in the ground where the pursuers were expected to pass. When they approached their own village, the headhunters would shout to show they had made a catch. The women would respond with a high-pitched yell and greet them at the gates. Two long reeds would be planted on either side of the path and knotted at the top to block the village guardians of the enemy village, and to keep the soul of the head from entering their own village.

The head would be kept outside until the feast could be held. The headhunters themselves would walk up a house ladder held upright at the village gate to show their ascendance. A small rite would be performed to protect the headhunting party from the contagion of death: they would be crowned with a headband of red and yellow bark cloth with "plumes" of red flowers and leaves tucked between the head and the headband.

The Headhunting Feast

The headhunting feast that I observed was conducted with some secrecy because the practice had been banned. There was no actual head, but the ritual baskets called *sakulang* where the head is usually stored were draped with red cloth, decorated with red hibiscus flowers, and planted in the center of the house yard. The tallest basket was the one where the head would have been placed, and it was flanked by others, connected with rattan, that held food offerings intended for the spirits.

It was almost night before everything was ready. The prophetess and other mediums left the house and gathered around the baskets, wearing head plumes like those headhunters wear. The gongs were played and, with a high-pitched yell, the mediums began to dance around the baskets, with a long tongue-like cake held in their mouths and dangling out. One of the village guardians, Iladeldelan (The Licker), asked for these cakes, and they were flung away at the end of the dance to satisfy him. However, later in the rite he would come back to lick the victim's blood.

The mediums first caressed the baskets appreciatively, then clapped, and then turned toward the basket that would have held the head and stretched out their arms and hands in a gesture of derision. They asked for wine. This should be presented by an older headhunter. Here, it was a World War II veteran who had volunteered to serve as the chief spokesman. The spirits being propitiated are male, so they must be answered by a man—although the rite is carried out by the female prophetess and female spirit mediums. The mediums sprinkled the wine around for the village guardians.

Then the spirits, through the mediums, asked for the man who did the killing. He was not present, but still in hiding. He planned to make an appearance later in the night. If he showed up too soon, the secret would be revealed. The spirits were made to understand that some caution was necessary under present conditions, but that the killer would come join them later.

The poles of the baskets were oiled to make them more appealing to the spirits, and to keep them from causing illness. Then the mediums chewed betel nut and spat the red saliva at the foot of the main basket, the place where the dripping blood of the severed head might become visible. Buaya say the red saliva-spitting expresses how the celebration of the headhunt will make all the participants "glow" (*ganga*).

The mediums then requested their ritual payment (*kakala*), which usually takes the form of a fancy handkerchief or a large piece of red cloth. In the absence of the headhunter, others presented each medium with a one peso bill (about 25 cents), which they rolled up and tucked into their headbands like a head plume. They danced for a while with their emblem, then removed it and set it aside.

New spirits were called in and asked to dance with the people gathered at the feast. The headhunter should have been the first to dance, but he was still not there. So the mediums invited other men to join them in their dance, bowing derisively towards the main basket as they did so. As they danced, they became possessed by spirits, who interrupted the proceeding with short improvised songs. The spirits said they were delighted with the event, pleased with the ritual payment, and happy that the feast was having its effects. Set to the tune of a popular song, one medium sang:

The buenavista leaves tremble on their twigs	*Summamay di katanglay*
	Dallogay ta dallogay, taku udot
We shall become even more radiant.	*sumsumgay*
How I wish for the *kakala* [the head]	*Nakay kad di kakala*
so we can play ball with it.	*sa ta ita ibola, dallogay ta*
	dallogay.

If there had been a head, the spirits would have tossed it in the air like a child playing with a ball, or would have tossed it back and forth with the headhunter, to express the delight that the unseen feel at the event.

The World War II veteran spokesman suggested another rhyme to the spirits:

Behold [the head] that was installed,	*Inon didi napadan*
embellished with	*ud a nabanekelan*
adornments	*an si nadaggadaggang*
this evening	*eban situn gidgidam*
it says.	*ka-ana.*

People told me of other more spectacular things that could have happened with a head. The prophetess could have danced with the head on her head, then could have sucked its blood. One eyewitness described an event where worms falling from a decomposing head covered the face of the prophetess, who was caught in a frenzied excitement and did not know what was happening. Later, she regained consciousness after the spirit left her and vomited when she was told what she had been doing.

The extraordinary attractiveness of the headhunter is celebrated in dancing that would otherwise be considered obscene. Kalinga dancing is normally performed without touching, but at the headhunting feast I saw the medium press her body and face against the men who danced with her, moved by the spirits who possessed her. Other women joined in the singing or the choruses, and some men danced alone. This violated the usual rule that a master of ceremonies would appoint couples to dance one at a time, and was an overt admission of sexual attraction. Head-hunters at a sagang also receive small love gifts—a betel quid, sometimes with a bead hidden in it. A married woman who presented such a gift could be fined for adultery in another context, but not at a headhunting feast. The sagang marks a period of erotic license, when love affairs are permitted that would become criminal if continued after the feast.

Sugarcane wine was drunk in great quantities by both men and women—the men completing a series of six ways of drinking it (in a buffalo horn, mixed with cooked rice, etc.). After a short while, the men began to vomit, but they would then return to drink again. The house yard became muddy with wine that had been vomited. The revels lasted throughout the night in a spontaneous, uproarious style. Excessive drinking, dancing, and sexual contact was part of the feast, where people were encouraged to relax their inhibitions and enjoy themselves without restrictions.[4]

The debauchery of the sagang refers to epic songs about heroes who are celebrated for killing enemies and courting women, doing "all that which makes us happy." The headhunter is said to find more sexual pleasure than any other Buaya. The mixture of intoxication, erotic stimulation, and loud, exciting music marks a separation from the ordinary world and from the calm, serene realm of the primordial Creator. The headhunting feast glorifies killing and seduction to celebrate conquering the brevity of life with victory over an enemy.

When the mediums' dance with the men finished, the prophetess started staring wildly at the main basket, possessed by a new spirit. She opened her mouth and croaked with guttural sounds, signaling that someone had come for the head. My assistant had

[4]This is not a return to the commemoration of primordial times, as such feasts have sometimes been interpreted. Talanganay, the Creator, had an abhorrence of sex and was very calm and peaceful, free from concern about food, health, and death. His music was serene and contrasts greatly with the atmosphere of debauchery found at a headhunting feast. What the sagang celebrates is not the primordial time itself, but rather man's solution to its absence. Whereas in the Talanganay myth, sex symbolizes the absence of self-control and ethical purity, in the sagang, sex symbolizes the good things the headhunt brings to the celebrants.

been forewarned by the prophetess that this would happen, so he went to the main basket and took out the knife used in the killing. He placed the tip of the blade in her mouth. She licked it a couple of times and asked, "Is this it?"

"Yes," he answered, placing the tip deeper in her mouth and pressing it on her tongue. She closed her mouth for a few minutes, then the spirit left. The people all fell silent, frightened by what they had seen. The spirit who came to lick the knife was Iladelde-lan (The Licker) from the village shrine. He was said to have tasted the blood on the knife, become satisfied, and left.

Ten minutes later, the prophetess became possessed by a dwarf who called for the erection of a symbolic barrier (gibaw) against epidemics at the village gate. A headhunt followed by the erection of a barrier was a standard defense against an approaching epidemic; the procedure sealed the village so outsiders could not come in, as a kind of quarantine. It was agreed that the barrier would be set up. Then there was a break while people waited for the arrival of the man who had taken the head.

The prophetess asked the killer to come present the ritual payment (kakala). She served him from a bowl of wine, "so that he would not be given out"—that is, discovered and sent to prison. He had come to ask the spirits for protection with this gift to the unseen. Then the mediums began to dance with him. He tried to move independently around the baskets, but the mediums, in an overt show of emotion and erotic attraction, rushed up to him and pressed their bodies against his. Their boldness showed the appreciation the spirits had for his accomplishment and their interest in his safety.

The ritual payment of betel quid that the headhunter made to the spirits was reciprocated by gifts of betel from the spirits to the people. These gifts were distributed by the mediums, who said, "There is nothing more we could desire, since we have our kakala." A water buffalo and a pig were killed and cooked, and liver, five pieces of meat, and a section of the ribs were placed in a bowl to be fed to the house spirits (see De Raedt 1989 for details on these animal sacrifices). It was almost midnight when the mediums turned to these offerings, and they had to stop because they were drunk and exhausted after so many hours of dancing and no food.

Three war veterans were asked to lead the headhunter's boast (*pokaw*), since each of them had killed at least twice. The killer whose act was celebrated at this feast could not participate, since this was his first victim. The boasts were entertaining narratives of their own exploits in the war, which amused the audience but were not directed toward the spirits.

Then the prophetess became possessed again by Iballiyagan (The Paymaster; literally, Who Produces or Brings Forth), the spirit of a new era, derived from the paymaster who "produces" the money used to pay government employees. Buaya mediums consider schoolteachers and others who receive government salaries as modern replacements for headhunters: they are people with extraordinary achievements who receive boons from a transcendant authority. The spirit asked for money to be given away the next day, silver coins presented by the killer to the spirits, then given to each participant. Another debt was also mentioned: a Buaya man had killed someone in another region in revenge for an earlier killing, and he now draws a government pension because he was disabled in World War II. The prophetess said the dwarfs have granted him special favors, so he should do a sagang to thank them. "We were his guides in getting his money. He should not be so selfish now," she said. The food was served, and I and many others finally settled down to sleep at about four A.M.

The next morning the main basket containing the knife was to be transferred to the village shrine, taking the place that the head would normally have. A plate was prepared with the pig's nose, a piece of cake, cooked rice, liver, and two betel quids, and the baskets were dismantled and lifted from their holes. The mediums, decorated with their head plumes, yelled, the men shouted, and gongs were beaten as they marched to the shrine and planted the baskets into the ground to erect the symbolic barrier (gibaw). Wine was passed around and poured at the foot of a grapefruit tree. Then the knife was placed with rice cake and two betel quids in one basket, the offering plate in another. The prophetess called out: "Ikadeldelan [The Licker], go and lick the enemy! Let him be brought here to the village shrine! Do not fail to give us a substance [a head], but we will do it secretly [behind the government's back]."

Loud yelling followed, then the prophetess added: "Tiwong [Insanity], go out and be crazy! Bring us one of those outlaws! He can be the substance for our village shrine!" There were outlaws roaming in the mountains, and she hoped one of them would come near to the village and provoke the villagers so he could be killed with impunity. The government would not punish the killing of outlaws, and the spirit of insanity might be able to lure them closer.[5]

The mediums danced again in a circle in front of the baskets, with offering plates on their heads, as the prophetess explained: "This is done to call our souls, to let the village shrine know that we are there, and so we can bring the baskets to the shrine." Later she added, "The greedy spirits say with hunger, 'If the people would only kill, we would not eat them.' The dwarves hear this and come to accompany us on a headhunt. At the sagang, they give the head to the spirits. The greedy spirits come to take the head, and the dwarves to see the merrymaking, for they are delighted at a sagang."

The spirits of the village shrine came to possess the prophetess. Payudan (The Sentinel) asked for tobacco as his payment (kakala), and all the mediums were served wine. Then those who had killed before and were considered headhunters gave wine to all the people present. Coins and beads collected in a small bowl with oil were given out by the prophetess, first to the killer and the gong players, then to all the men and women. Then two of the war veterans/headhunters prepared a final boast "to curse the head basket." They explained that the boast would keep the basket in the shrine to protect the village, show the spirits they were in control, make the people radiant (ganga) so they could resist illness, fulfill ritual requirements, scare off enemy guardians, dispel their jealousy, prevent blight, and apologize for the fact that the baskets were carried by nonheadhunters.

The main idea in all these answers is the opposition of radiance (ganga) and blight (balus). Participation in a headhunting feast makes everyone glow in the reflected glory of the headhunt. The headhunters can be proud of what they have done and are permitted to shout out boasts to the spirits. They curse the basket

[5] These particular outlaws were killed later by men of another region. The Buaya themselves did not want to look for them because they feared government interference.

once the spirits have received the head, or its surrogate, the knife. One village leader described the shrine to me saying, with much emphasis, "The plants there are planted by us." The red and yellow plants represent the radiance that the headhunt produces for the headhunter and all the villagers who celebrate his accomplishment. His act generates a glow that protects the village against illness and enemy attack. This "glow" could be interpreted as the renown of a famous fighter, which intimidates his enemies and keeps them at bay.

Every major feast is fraught with danger. The prophetess explained that when they dismantle the baskets to carry them to the shrine some of the flowers and leaves may fall off and strike the men who carry them. The men can fall ill if they are not protected by the boast, which reinforces the radiance and glow the celebration should produce. To kill is itself dangerous, and those who rejoice in it must do so very carefully. The war veteran/headhunter faced the baskets as he boasted, but this boast was intended for the spirits, to "tame the wild dogs" who guard the shrine and domesticate them with ritual offerings. Two men must offer the boast, both trying to control the dangerous element that resides in the shrine.

The mediums then returned to the house yard in silence and removed their head plumes. They danced once more to shake off the blight (balus) that might follow them home from the shrine. Then they moved to the village gate for a meal and the final seance. The next day, the closing ceremony was held.[6] At this rite, the disruptions caused by the government ban on headhunting were acknowledged. The prophetess began by serving wine to everyone, "so that they might become resistant, for the heat is coming."

She designated my assistant, an intelligent young man who aspired to become a leader, and said: "May one among you rise up." The dwarf spirit possessing her responded, saying, "I will do no

---

[6] The closing rites are usually held three days later, but no one can leave the village during that period because it has been sealed shut. I would not have been able to stay for them, so the prophetess took pity on me and held them two days earlier. If there had been a head at this rite, it would have been placed with the liver in a small cage on a platform built in the bamboo clump in the village shrine. The bamboo itself would be weeded and cleaned up before the ceremony at the shrine, and the red and yellow flowers would be revealed. Since there was no head and everyone wanted to minimize the evidence of the ceremony, no cage was made in the rite I witnessed.

more secret murders." Suddenly, she snatched an agate stone out of the air and held it over the head of an ambitious, intelligent young man who seemed destined to replace the aging village leader. The stone was placed in a bowl of oil, and the oil was poured on the heads of all present to bless them. The stone came from a man who had been imprisoned twenty years ago for killing. He had kept the stone for his protection, then had returned it to her on his release.

The dwarf spirit spoke through the prophetess to warn the young men not to show off that they had seen the basket "whose top looks like a hibiscus flower," and not to think of putting a substance (that is, a head) into it, "for the mediums have become useless now, and the killings are all over." It was a clear admission of the change of times, now sanctioned by the dwarf spirits themselves, who used to incite the men to take heads and guide them on their way. The earlier statement that the dwarf would "do no more secret murders" may have referred to objections he heard from people who said they could not be responsible for the consequences of more killing. The prophetess may also have been responding to accusations that she had incited men in other regions (Amasiyan and Taggay) to go out and kill. One man went out after hearing her speak and was imprisoned for killing. She was not fined, but she had been warned that even in a seance she should not let the dwarfs say such things through her anymore.

Recent Changes

The exuberant celebration of the sagang has now been largely replaced by peace-pact festivities, engagements, installation ceremonies for government officials, and feasts to entertain visitors from another region. People with salaries, especially teachers or mine managers, celebrate their appointments in some of the same ways that a headhunter used to mark his glorious triumph on the battlefield. The Buaya say, "Money now replaces what our ancestors did, for where can you get hands now that are stained with blood?" They also say, "The government officials and the educated are our headhunters now," and "The picking up of heads has been replaced by the picking up of rice."

The Buaya are probably still searching for new pegs to plug into the headhunting hole in the traditional triad of leadership—the war leader, the wealthy man, the legal expert. World War II veterans who have both killed and acquired money through a government pension are often classed as "headhunters" for ceremonial purposes, as I saw at the feast I attended. Men with some college, a government position as a barrio captain or mayor, or a teaching job have a similar prestige. Many of these new categories are elected—the barrio captain and his six councillors, the two barrio police, and the treasurer and secretary. Others are created through schooling but are validated in traditional ways, since teachers are usually assigned to their native regions.

The government has abolished headhunting, but its new order of power has also led to the emergence of new spirits. I have mentioned Iballiyagan (The Paymaster); there is also Urayon (The Director), who stands for dependence on government guidance. During the seances, the mediums speak of how the dependence on spirit protection must now work alongside dependence on government guidance (*urayon*). "The people accept the government as their master," they say, but they do not mean that the Buaya have accepted that the government can do whatever it pleases. In the past, the dwarf spirits accompanied the headhunters and gave them a nickname, "servant" (*ba-un*), which showed that the headhunters needed the dwarf spirits' guidance. Now that nickname is also applied to the government officials in the village: they are still the "servants" of the spirit powers that once guided the headhunters on their way.

Note

I was still a Roman Catholic priest when I did fieldwork in among the Buaya for over two years in the mid-1960s. My rapport with the people grew steadily because, among other things, I learned to speak their language. The headhunting feast that I witnessed near the end of my stay was funded by me, since the headhunter was too poor to shoulder the expenses by himself and, according to the culture, he had to do it in order not to be victimized by his exploit. I did not ask whom he killed and have no record of the man's name. As far as I know, he was never arrested. He did not bring the head home out of fear that he would be caught. Of course, I did not report the event to the authorities. But since the murder had already been committed, I did not feel any qualms about sponsoring the feast, so I could witness it for the record.

References

De Raedt, Jules

  1969 "Myth and Ritual: A Relational Study of Buwaya Mythology, Ritual and Cosmology." Ph.D. dissertation, University of Chicago.

  1989 *Kalinga Sacrifice*. Cordillera Studies Center, University of the Philippines, College Baguio, Baguio City, Philippines.

Sugguiyao, Miguel, and Rosario Sigguiyao

  1964 "Kalinga Primitive Culture." *Saint Louis Quarterly* 2 (2): 181–200.

Anna Lowenhaupt Tsing

Telling Violence in the Meratus Mountains

Stories of headhunting, raiding, and war so often guide us to imagine the perspective of fighters—whether the leaders who strategize for victory over enemy lives or the young men who test their manhood in violence. Even stories of the women left behind and their personal losses reinforce a contrast in which public commitment to battle is the other term. But what of whole communities harassed, even constituted, by threats of violence?

During my research in the Meratus Mountains of South Kalimantan, Indonesia, I was continually impressed by the importance of fear in defining Dayak communities.[1] Vulnerability is almost an ethnic self-stereotype for Meratus Dayaks: vulnerability to headhunters, soldiers, and police, to officials, to more powerful ethnic groups, to spirits. Vulnerability distinguishes the familiar local from the power and danger of the foreign. I am not talking about the quaking, superstitious dread so commonly described by missionaries as a characteristic of primitive people. Meratus fears are sensible concerns about the regional organization of violence as it has taken shape within national and international regimes of militarization and economic expansion.

A memory of my own arrival at these issues provides an entry for discussion in which it is difficult to exclude oneself to exoticize Meratus fears. As I was hiking for the first time into the mountains, an old man ran out of a hut near the trail, waving his arms for me to stop. He was excited, out of breath, and toothless—and thus a little hard to follow—but I got his message: "You are an

---

[1] Kalimantan is the Indonesian section of the island of Borneo. The term Dayak refers generally to non-Muslim indigenous people of Borneo.

American. Bring us guns. Bring us planes. Build an airport here. Otherwise surely we'll be wiped out."

This was the kind of request I had thought existed only in the CIA imagination. I was embarrassed. My first thought was to look behind me to see whom else he could be addressing; as a minority woman graduate student, I was used to thinking of myself as a peon, not an agent of American imperial might. Yet I am an American. The old man's request brings up my own complex position of fear and privilege, and the interweaving of my personal ties with Meratus friends and the global power relations of which we are each part. Even now, he reminds me that writing an article on fear can never be just a dry academic exercise; Meratus Dayaks, like other "indigenous peoples," indeed could be wiped out. A neutral stance seems not just impossible but unforgivable.

Yet what are the political and ethical possibilities for writing about violence? No simple positioning against abuse and terror is available. Global violence makes local violence often seem the only hope against annihilation: Military buildups in the Third World create the possibility of national autonomy from neocolonial force as they also stifle the aspirations of ethnic minorities. CIA schemes and generals' dreams stalk each other, shaping commonality in opposition. At the local level, too, violence is two-faced. Minority leaders who fight back restrain the tide of national terror, but at the same time, their ferocity deepens asymmetries of gender and rank within their own communities. And even where historical events make our political choices seem easy, writing politically about violence is still difficult—and never ethically unambiguous. To write of the forceful defense of Dayak communities, however sympathetically, may inspire Western readers to think of savagery; to write of the suffering of innocent victims—as this reminds Westerners of local rights—may annoy Dayak readers who see themselves denigrated as passive losers. To describe the politics of violence is to dip into material that is frightening, confusing, and hotly contested. At best, it must be a risky experiment that speaks to some more than others. This essay is a modest attempt to think about the politics of violence and minority status at local and regional levels. It is not the airport the old man requested, but, for better or worse, only one story perhaps worth telling.

To describe Meratus concerns about violence, it also seems important to turn away for a moment from the common U.S. desire to protect exotic and vulnerable "indigenous peoples." This agenda makes it too easy to imagine "traditional lifeways " without knowing the local situation. (A striking example of international concern for tribal protection gone awry is the recent controversy over the representation of the southern Philippine Tasaday as isolated and therefore vulnerable "Stone Age people." See Moloney 1988; Berreman 1991.) Protectionist frameworks that contrast ancient harmonies with the destructive intrusions of the late twentieth century are inadequate for understanding the Meratus situation; they would deny the history and internal complexity of Meratus communities and posit Meratus knowledge of regional-to-global integrations as extremely recent. Instead, the Meratus I knew insisted that contemporary ethnic harassment and military intimidation is significantly continuous with a long regional history of headhunting and warfare in which they have often been victims. To make any respectful sense of Meratus politics, one must begin, I think, from an appreciation of this local perspective.

One example of this perspective, to which I will return: Meratus believe the government periodically sends out headhunters to take Meratus heads, just like those mounted, they believe, by precolonial kingdoms in the region. Headhunting scares are enormously frightening. They convince most Meratus to take government compliance very seriously. Yet they create a particular kind of oppositional stance as well: not only are Meratus calling state policy violent, but they also refuse the state's categories in which Dayaks, not state raiders, are the headhunters. Indeed, Meratus relations with the state are negotiated within a crosstalk of mutually incomprehensible accusations of violence. Just as state officials accuse Meratus of the violence of savages—those outside state rule and modern history—Meratus say that the history of state rule itself has been the source of violence. Meratus stories point to the violence of those state projects, whether national development and administration or precolonial ritual, that in other versions appear only as bringing order to troubled frontiers.

This essay explores Meratus talk about violence as I listened to it in the early 1980s. The stories I begin with are not technically headhunting stories at all, but stories of soldiers and revolutionaries. Such stores alerted me to the ways in which Meratus cast themselves as subject to unpredictable violence—as, indeed, they showed unpredictable violence to be inherent to the character of regional and national authority. Given Meratus appreciation of the continuities of regional history, might it not be provocative—and even sensible—to consider these tellings "headhunting" stories?

With this in mind, I turn to nineteenth-century Kalimantan headhunting, which connects my essay to the others in this volume and illuminates the context in which Meratus stories of power and fear developed. Without records or even tales of particular raids in southeast Kalimantan, I rely only on general descriptions of headhunting; my point is to tell something of regionally available political models of violence, which helped shape Meratus appropriations and responses. My own experience in a relatively recent headhunting scare then brings my discussion back to the contemporary era, as the regional history of headhunting informs Meratus understandings of current state tactics of administration.

My final section turns to the ways Meratus constitute themselves as potential survivors as well as victims of such tactics. I examine how violence is used rhetorically in contemporary community politics, and particularly how a storytelling style allows witnesses of violence—whether headhunting, war, fights, or police harassment—to establish their bravery in retrospect. Ambitious men use threats and stories of violence to show their leadership abilities—and to remind their listeners of their common vulnerability. Brave men's talk of violence thus reconstitutes communities of the fearful; together they tackle the serious business of survival.

Anthropological Starting Places

In mid-twentieth century anthropology, which appears from a 1990s standpoint to constitute the "classic" standard of the discipline, violence was discussed mainly in relation to issues of regulation. On the one hand, social structure was described as regulating—ordering, controlling—a Hobbesian violence (e.g., Evans-

Pritchard 1940). On the other hand, regulated violence could reinforce the social order, or even regulate other things, such as ecological balance (e.g., Rappaport 1968). It is in contrast to these
frameworks that new work on the constitution rather than the
regulation of violence seems particularly exciting. Michael Taussig (1987), for example, explores the "culture of terror" created by
the colonial encounter in Colombia: colonial fears of native savagery produced savage strategies that terrorized the local popu-
lace. In this analysis, discourse and physical bodies are mutually
implicated (see also Feldman 1991). Talk of killings, like killings
themselves, inspires fear, threats, and further killings; it is impossible to discuss violence divorced from its context in tellings
of violence. This approach seems particularly relevant wherever
fears of savagery legitimate official violence in the name of order
aimed toward subjugated populations—whether on the streets of
Los Angeles or in the Meratus Mountains.

Taussig's approach to violence also shifts anthropologists' attention from the imagined autonomy of local cultural arenas to the
mutual constitution of local and global cultural processes. The
Colombian discourse of violence he describes crosses back and
forth between peoples of European, Indian, and African descent.
Although much less ambitious in scope, my project also reconstitutes anthropological notions of the "local." Rather than begin
with Dayak institutions of violence and move out from this base
to show their impact on regional dynamics, I argue that Dayaks
are made significant local groups—for example, as victims or perpetrators of headhunting—in relation to wider regional discourses
on violence and social identity. This analytic reversal is particularly important in my argument that the state, as imagined in the
Meratus Mountains, is key to constructing Meratus notions of
political agency. Meratus do not speak of themselves as an autonomous group that must adjust to state expansion; instead, they
talk of Meratus communities as made possible in the first place by
their marginal relationship to state rule (see Tsing 1993).

My understanding of state-oriented models of political agency
in southeast Kalimantan leads me away from much of the literature on tribal identities and archaic and minority cultures. Thus,
for example, exchange models—in which group identity is constructed through reciprocal exchanges with similarly constructed
others—have not been particularly helpful to me in understanding

Meratus politics and culture. Much twentieth-century literature on headhunting in Indonesia takes exchange models as a beginning for understanding the cultural logic of headhunting raids and rituals. (See George 1991 for a recent discussion of this literature.) Perhaps because Meratus see themselves as victims rather than as headhunters, I never heard Meratus discuss violence in relation to exchange. A victim's perspective looks out toward wider configurations of power rather than to the reciprocal equivalence of social units.

Instead, I join the recent literature on Southeast Asian headhunting in revamping the relation of culture and history. Recent ethnographers, including Kenneth George (1991), Janet Hoskins (1987), and Renato Rosaldo (1980), have described headhunting traditions within local and regional histories that make the past relevant to the present. These authors struggle against earlier anthropological conventions that identified headhunting with timeless and archaic tradition, separated from history; these conventions left in place the problematic possibilities of conflating headhunting and savagery. In contrast, George, Hoskins, and Rosaldo suggest the humanity of headhunters by showing their history. Their work facilitates analysis of contemporary talk of headhunting as it enters the ongoing and continuous construction of history, rather than marking the break between a timeless precolonial past and a historicized present. In this spirit, I argue that Meratus rumors of government-sponsored headhunting forays must be situated in local understandings of the history of violence in southeast Kalimantan. These understandings highlight continuities between past and present state-building practices: in particular, the systematic deployment of violence at the borders of state rule.[2]

[2] A series of articles in *Oceania* (Drake 1989; Erb 1991; Forth 1991) has shown the prevalence of rumors of government headhunting and construction sacrifice in contemporary Indonesia. These articles offer fascinating details of the local traditions and regional political dynamics in which such rumors flourish. My essay adds to this emerging literature. In contrast to the cases cited, however, I try to pay more attention to the effectiveness of stories and rumors in creating and contributing to a contemporary climate of violence, rather than see them as secondary reflections on other, nonviolent matters. The power of headhunting rumors draws from Meratus understandings of a continuous history of violent state rule. The rumors are not a *metaphor* for contemporary conflicts that reconstitute the divide between ancient times and the present; rather, they participate in building the ongoing violence of state-local relations.

Systematic Random Violence

I use the term Meratus (or Meratus Dayak) to refer to Dayak shifting cultivators of the Meratus Mountains of South Kaliman- tan. Meratus typify themselves as living in the forests just outside the everyday reach of more powerful, more organized, and more violent peoples. To both the west and the east, Meratus are flanked by the regional majority population, known as Banjar. Banjar are cosmopolitan Muslims who trace their heritage to pre- colonial court centers of the Barito River delta or their affiliates on the south or east coast. Before Dutch colonial rule, Banjar kings claimed control of all southeast Kalimantan, including the Mera- tus Mountains; at least sporadically, Meratus paid tribute to court centers in various directions. Meratus have also been in long-term if somewhat uneven contact with various other Dayak groups, who are contrasted with Meratus through the regional label Du- sun. In northern sectors of the mountains, for example, Meratus border Balanghan Dusun. Comparing themselves to both Dusun and Banjar, Meratus find themselves politically vulnerable and disorganized. They imagine themselves in the position of periph- eral political subjects surrounded by multiple authorities.

Many of the older Meratus men and women I knew had lived through a number of major armed clashes in southeast Kaliman- tan, including those associated with World War II, the Indonesian revolution, and a regional rebellion that began in the late 1950s. In each case, most Meratus were socially peripheral to the fighting and had only indirect contact with the "general's-eye" views of the conflicts endorsed by patriots and partisans on each side. Yet the presence of armed men in the Meratus Mountains—whether passing through, hiding out, or pursuing opponents—was a fright- ening manifestation of power, and in coming to terms with this power particular partisan causes were less important than the fighting force itself. For example, several Meratus from the central mountains recalled for me the awesome spectre of a column of World War II Japanese soldiers marching across the rough terrain with their hiking sticks, heading from east coast military bases to the more populated west side administrative centers. The moun- tain people hid from them in the forested hills, avoiding contact when possible.

In each of these periods of armed conflict, most Meratus in the central mountains tried to stay out of the way by making their houses and swiddens in lonely places far from the main transmountain trails. Those who were visited by soldiers spoke of hosting each side in turn with professions of total loyalty, hoping to avoid retribution. To appease the fighting anger of the soldiers, they gave rice and chickens freely to whatever armed men got close enough to demand them. Those who witnessed violence recalled only its unpredictable targets and its terrible effectiveness—not its contribution to a cause.

Perhaps these stories of the past were particularly striking to me because elsewhere in my experience I had so often heard war and revolution recalled as moral tales. I grew up in the United States hearing about World War II as the war against fascism in which it was impossible not to take a side. Similarly, most urban Indonesians discuss the 1945–49 revolution as a heroic struggle for independence from colonial rule. I was used to war stories that told of courage, fear, or even disillusionment for a cause; it mattered which side you were on. In these Meratus recollections, however, the point was to stay out of the way of the senseless ferocity of both sides.

Indeed, these recollections made me aware of the Meratus sense of historical continuity in regional relations of power and violence. Meratus stories of headhunting raids offer a very similar scenario. As I will discuss in a later section, Meratus were subject to both Banjar and Dusun headhunting and slavetaking raids in the nineteenth century. The stories Meratus told me of this period also stressed appeasing powerful groups on every side and hiding in the forests to evade their inevitable violence. The particular campaigns in which headhunting raids were mobilized had little resonance in Meratus tales. The headhunters cared little about the particularities of their victims; they were searching for human sacrifices. Their targets seemed random even as they created the pervasive possibility of violence for those within the areas they roamed. Meratus tales do not show the unfolding political plans of the raiders; instead, raids appear to be a structural feature of regional power relations. Similarly, Meratus narratives of twentieth-century warfare draw on expectations of the systematic random violence endemic to regional power asymmetries. In these stories violence is not a moral issue, nor an issue of tit for tat. Violence is not to be justified or condemned; it is the prerogative of power.

Let me turn to some particular stories of the Indonesian revolution. When the Dutch colonial administration returned to reconstitute the "Netherland Indies" after World War II,[3] they found themselves up against a well-developed nationalist movement that declared Indonesian independence in 1945. Four years of difficult fighting and negotiating ensued before Indonesia won its full independence from colonial rule. In southern Kalimantan, a good number of Banjar were deeply involved with the nationalist struggle. (Yet through much of the southern Kalimantan countryside, the period is still remembered, following colonial usage, as *jaman astrimis* [or *jaman satrimis*], "the era of extremists.") One of the areas in which Banjar nationalists sometimes hid from their colonial adversaries was the Meratus Mountains, and it was through Banjar nationalist evasions and colonial government chases that Meratus got to know the revolution. In the Meratus stories I heard, each side was portrayed as armed, dangerous, and likely to kill someone merely because they got close enough to form a target.

One respected older man who had been an energetic bachelor during this period told me the story of how one particular Meratus man was killed by Banjar nationalists. Two nationalists were roaming through the hills to stay out of the way of the colonial authorities when they arrived one afternoon at a Meratus community festival and joined the party. Their arrival put the Meratus elders who held government titles (such as village head, assistant village head, neighborhood head, etc.) in a difficult position. They had received instructions from the government to apprehend all the nationalists they encountered, and they worried that they would be punished if they refused. They had also heard that these two Banjar were carrying a hand grenade, and they were afraid. The eventual victim in this story was one of these title holders, an assistant village head I'll call Ma Jawa. (Meratus adult men's names take the form Ma *X*, where *X* may be, but is not necessarily,

[3] In 1945, the Allies returned governing power to the Netherland Indies Civil Administration (NICA). NICA governed in Kalimantan between August 1945 and December 1949.

the name of a child.) Here is a section of the story I was told, re-constructed from notes.

Ma Jawa wasn't brave enough to say anything. I was sitting at the food stall [erected in the ritual hall for the purposes of the festival] holding my bush knife, [i.e., preparing for a fight]. Finally, another guest asked the na-tionalist to show him the hand grenade. The nationalist said [referring to the power of the grenade], "It will get ten times darker than this before it rains." Everyone thought fighting was about to begin, and they all ran out of the ritual hall.

[The other nationalist] asked where everyone was going. Grandfather L said, "This is a mess." [The nationalist] said, "Well, we're leaving." The two of them went out and came up to Ma Jawa. "Who are you?" they asked, and he told them. Then they left.

Two weeks later, they appeared again. Ma Jawa was visiting his wife's relatives in A——. I was in the house when [the nationalist] came in and tried to grab Ma Jawa. Ma Jawa jumped out. Half the people were running away. [The nationalist] caught Ma Jawa by cornering him in a swamp. They tied him up and called him a dog of the Dutch. Grandfather L tried to oppose them, but they threatened him and he ran away, telling every-one else to run too.

They brought Ma Jawa to a deep pool in the A—— River and held him under water. When he was almost dead, they hung him on a tree and slit his throat. Everyone from A—— had run away.

The grisly details of Ma Jawa's murder were stressed in every story I heard about the event. This was not just a murder but a spectacle of horror reminding Meratus of their collective vulnera-bility. Of course, this was fighting for a cause, and the narrator here shows some knowledge of this cause: as a local government title holder, Ma Jawa was a "dog of the Dutch." But there were (and still are) enough of these titles going around in the Meratus Mountains that a large proportion of mature, ambitious men have had one at some point. The stigma of Ma Jawa's title hardly sug-gests that others could feel secure. From the Meratus perspective, Ma Jawa did not distinguish himself to the nationalists; he merely let himself be identified and stayed too close.

This narrator went on to tell a story of how one of these same two nationalists was unexpectedly shot by one of his comrades as he crossed a river on another hike though the mountains. (He knew their names, which I have avoided for both privacy and ease of reading in the story above.) This story increased a sense of random and pervasive violence. Furthermore, he told of the even more overwhelming and unpredictable threat of the other side: the colonial government. After the incidents above, various Meratus elders were arrested by the colonial authorities for not apprehending the nationalists. And then the military made a direct appearance in the narrator's life, forcing him into a strategy of appeasement in which he feigned the naiveté and goodheartedness of an imagined primitive:

The B—— hall was surrounded by Dutch [employed] military. The commander came in and told me not to run away. I told him I had never heard of [the Banjar nationalist leader] Hasan Basri. The commander picked up one of the children and threatened the boy. I told him that some men had come, but I thought that they were government men because they were wearing green uniforms and wearing guns. The commander told me to report it if they came again.

The army had closed off all the doors and windows because they were afraid of the nationalists. They had captured two Meratus men from a different area. They let them outside on a rope to relieve themselves, and they got away. The soldiers stood around and shot in every direction. They told me to go find the men who escaped. I tried to get them to stop shooting so I wouldn't be hit. When my uncle came that night with a torch, I told them not to shoot him.

These stories bring up lots of issues about the narrator's self-positioning, for certainly he told these stories to make a point about his own abilities. But I defer this discussion until later in this essay to finish introducing the Meratus experience of violence. I have already stressed the ways that Meratus cast themselves as socially and culturally peripheral to the perpetrators of violence; they neither support nor oppose soldiers, but rather appease them or flee from them. This does not simply create an identity as victims and outsiders, however. Violence and its narration bring Meratus *into* the regional organization of knowledge and authority, convincing them of the pervasiveness of power. In stories of violence, Meratus create themselves as peripheral political subjects as well as victims.

The specificity of Meratus positionings can be better appreciated by comparing these stories to the perhaps better-known "peasant" critique of war by those who, though they are not beneficiaries of war, serve as its recruits. I think, for example, of a story a Dusun man living near the Meratus Mountains told me about the time he was drafted to serve in the Indonesian army in the takeover of East Timor.[4] When he arrived in East Timor, he found that the non-Muslim shifting cultivators he was supposed to fight were, in his words, "Dayaks like us." He and his buddies reached an agreement with the "enemy" not to fire seriously at one another, and as a result, he claims, his was the only group sent at that time to make it home with no casualties (on either side). His is a criticism of war from the inside, from a position that differentiates minority ("Dayak") foot soldiers from Javanese generals. His everyday experience of ethnic and class stratification has become, in this war story, a solidarity across enemy lines against the orders and interests of generals. In contrast, Meratus stories depict every soldier as a fully empowered representative of the system of knowledge and power for which he fights. Meratus speak from the borders of cultural citizenship rather than from the bottom of its hierarchy. Their land is sporadically traversed by soldiers; at these times, they host soldiers and agree to all their demands. Yet they are not daily engaged in the social world that the soldiers represent. They know its internal stratification mainly through its expansive exercises. It is in creating this peripheral engagement with regional systems of power that a "headhunting" model of power and violence seems particularly relevant.

Headhunting and Power

In many ways, Meratus lifeways are comparable to those of the best-known Dayak group in the anthropological literature: the Iban of Sarawak (e.g., Freeman 1970; Sutlive 1978; Padoch 1982). Like the Iban communities described by J. D. Freeman, Meratus communities are relatively open and egalitarian. Ideals of autonomy and personal independence are strong, and social networks are flexible. However, one contrast stands out sharply: whereas the Iban recall an aggressive heritage of headhunting, Meratus identify only as the victims of regional headhunting practices.

[4] East Timor was a Portuguese colony until 1975, when it briefly became independent. Indonesian forces then invaded East Timor and, despite an armed resistance that has continued to have considerable strength, annexed the area as a province of Indonesia.

Freeman's descriptions of nineteenth-century Iban headhunting are also both familiar-sounding and misleading for thinking about southeast Kalimantan in the same period. Freeman stresses the egalitarian organization of Iban headhunting raids and the prestige goals of individual men: "Any mature man who had the occasion to mount an attack . . . could become a *pun ngayau* (lit. originator of war). . . . I would emphasize that when an Iban became a member of a fighting group it was *by his own choice*, and that in joining an attack (always in the hope of taking a head) he was doing what he most wanted to do" (1981: 36, emphasis in original). In contrast, headhunting in southeast Kalimantan in the nineteenth century was rather more connected to stratification. European accounts from this period report Dayak headhunting as organized by and for chiefs to provide heads for occasions such as the funeral of a chief or the erection of a new house. Local accounts suggest that headhunting was also a practice of the various Indic/Muslim kingdoms on the south and east coasts, particularly to provide heads to commemorate royal construction projects.

It is probably impossible to find accounts of the particular groups that harassed Meratus in the nineteenth century. Thus it may help to begin instead with widespread patterns of organized aggression in the region. Jerome Rousseau's composite version of nineteenth-century headhunting and warfare in the stratified Dayak societies of "central Borneo" (1990) seems a useful orientation:

Headhunting took place primarily after the sowing, when there is a lull in farm work, or after the harvest. . . . There were strategic limitations to the number of participants in an expedition: not all able bodied men could go away, otherwise the house would be left undefended. . . . Slaves could participate. . . . Even small operations had to be approved by the chief. (265–66)

Sometimes a base camp was set up in the jungle. . . . On a major expedition, a path might be built to facilitate retreat. Wood shavings were prepared to set fire to the house; they attacked its fleeing occupants as it burned. Even in such cases, the purpose was not to exterminate the enemy but to take a few heads and prisoners, and loot. (266)

After victory, the attackers cut off the heads of dead or dying enemies, and hid the bodies of their own dead in the jungle to prevent their heads from being taken; they then retreated as rapidly as possible. (266–67)

Rousseau conceptually differentiates "headhunting" (for heads), "warfare" (for political control), and "raids" (for plunder and slaves), yet his descriptions suggest that many forays blurred these lines. Large expeditions, in particular, were planned by chiefs and other leading men to take heads, captives, and loot at the same time as they established a group's political power. Indeed, Rousseau and other writers (for example, for southern and eastern Kalimantan, Scharer 1963; Bock 1985 [1881]) stress that headhunting was closely associated with the capture of slaves. Stratified Dayak groups used slaves not only for labor but also for sacrifices. It appears that heads and sacrifices of war captives were used for the same kinds of event.

Some occasions called for sacrifices of slaves, such as the erection of a new house . . . or a curing ritual for an ailing chief; a slave was also sacrificed after the death of a chief to serve him in the other world. Only recent captives or bought slaves were used for this purpose. (Rousseau 1990: 176–77)

Headhunting was particularly appropriate at the erection of a new longhouse. . . . Alternatively, a human sacrifice would serve the same purpose: a live victim was thrown in a pit and crushed by the main post of the house. (275)

Scholars of Bornean social life have long organized their work along a great divide between primitive "Dayaks" of the interior and cosmopolitan "Malays" of the coasts. This follows a locally important ethnic contrast. Yet in considering the history of southern and eastern Kalimantan, connections as well as disconnections across this line stand out. The Indic/Muslim kingdoms of the south and east coasts seem to have engaged in slave capture, warfare, and headhunting raids not unlike those of stratified Dayak groups farther upriver, at least according to contemporary Banjar raconteurs of precolonial traditions. (Banjar are the "Malays," that is, *urang malayu*, of southeast Kalimantan.) Indeed, Banjar royalty and Dayak chiefs shared a common—although uneven—engagement in the political and economic networks of the regional-to-global slavery, spice, and forest-products trade; the local power consolidations and struggles in which headhunting and captive sacrifice played a part cannot be separated from the history of these common networks (see, for example, Peluso 1983).

Contemporary Banjar speak of a noble tradition in which human heads or sacrificed captives were required to consecrate new buildings. Patterns of warfare and headhunting thus seem to have linked the politics of precolonial Banjar nobles and southern and eastern Kalimantan Dayak chiefs.

The Dutch colonial apparatus worked hard to consolidate violence in its own hands by the beginning of the twentieth century. Neither headhunting nor local warfare could be considered a "custom" in Kalimantan after Dutch suppression made even talk of their occurrence illicit.[5] Understandings of the relation of power and violence, however, have continued to draw from the precolonial period. Reminders of headhunting and captive sacrifice are not uncommon. Banjar told me that the regional government uses water buffalo heads to substitute for human heads in commemorating state construction. The Balanghan Dusun, a Dayak group living in the northern Meratus Mountains, continue to practice prestige-graded feasts that once culminated in a feast requiring a human sacrifice; now a drop of blood from the finger of the host provides a substitute. And perhaps there continue to be occasions on which headhunting and human sacrifice are deemed appropriate. Journalists and Christian missionaries in West Kalimantan reported that the army authorized Iban to take Chinese heads in the late 1960s during a state drive to push Chinese Indonesians out of rural areas (for example, Peterson 1968; Coppel 1983). From a somewhat earlier period, consider Rousseau's report from East Kalimantan: "In 1945, the Long Nawang Kenyah captured two Japanese soldiers. One was killed [as a sacrifice; that is, by a series of nonlethal stabs by the whole group in turn]. The other was kept for the chief, who was away at the time, so that he could have a victim of his own" (Rousseau 1990: 269 n. 2).

So far, I have introduced these patterns of regional headhunting

---

[5] However, Erb (1991) suggests that contemporary Indonesian stories of human sacrifice for construction projects may derive, at least in part, from *European* customs. European missionaries working in Flores told her that "quick lime" made for mortar for construction in Europe was strengthened by adding live animals or flesh and blood. The missionaries thought that earlier missionaries in Flores may have teased the people about the possibility of adding humans instead of animals, thus leading to contemporary fears of construction sacrifice. This raises the possibility that stories of construction sacrifice in Kalimantan may have been further elaborated, rather than deflected, by Dutch colonial rule.

and captive sacrifice from the perspective of an outside observer who is willing to exoticize and stabilize "custom" for the sake of a quick sketch. My sketch draws, at least indirectly, from local accounts of "custom," but surely there are also very different kinds of local perspective. Participants in raids and sacrifices presumably would have much more to say about particular political mobilizations, life experiences, or social negotiations than about fulfilling custom (see Rosaldo 1980). But in turning back to Meratus experiences, in this essay I have much more to say about the perspectives of potential victims.

Government Headhunters

The tales Meratus told me about precolonial headhunting raids tended to be sketchy, generalized depictions of the problem. They offered few clues about specific times, identities, or campaigns. Yet they did give me some important impressions. For example, the stories depicted large well-organized groups of men under well-defined leadership; these were the fighting forces of powerful communities. The raiders arrived from a variety of directions and sources; people gave long lists of place and ethnic names—most of which I could not identify—to tell of the raiders. Some of the names they listed may have been titles for the raiders themselves: for example, people spoke of the *urang laskar*, the "laskar people," who came to attack; *laskar* is an Indonesian word (but not in ordinary Meratus use) for "soldier." The urang laskar seem to have been one kind of government headhunter. Stories of headhunting raids added historical depth to contemporary depictions of the dangers of regional power.

Those who told me stories of headhunting raids in the past did not stress fighting back. Local practice was to run away—or to be difficult to find in the first place. The armed response of which people did speak involved shooting raiders with blowpipe darts. The blowpipe is a weapon best used when hiding unseen in the forest. It is the preferred weapon of patient hunting, not collective warfare. According to Rousseau, central Bornean raiders rarely used blowpipes, but instead wielded swords, spears, and, when available, firearms (1990: 265). Although government officials and Banjar villagers think of Meratus skill with blowpipes as an aspect of their savage potential, Meratus self-depictions mention it only in relation to self-defense.

In the 1980s, blowpipes were not in everyday use among the Meratus I knew best. I saw blowpipes in the rafters of people's houses kept mainly as heirlooms and objects used in rituals; few men hunted with them. Trade networks through which the Meratus I lived with had most recently obtained dart poison had been disrupted some years before; hunting with dogs and spears had become much more popular. My conversations about the headhunting raids that caused people to retaliate with blowpipe darts referred to a period long before the people I spoke with were born. In this context, I assumed headhunting to be a concern of the distant past. Perhaps you can imagine how disoriented I was, then, to find myself in the middle of a headhunting scare.

In the spring of 1981, rumors spread on the western slopes of the Meratus Mountains that government headhunters were on the loose. People connected the raids with malfunctioning oil drills in the oil fields operated by Pertamina, the Indonesian state oil company, about 70 kilometers to the north. The government, people said, had ordered the Javanese oil workers to get heads to ritually restabilize the machinery. The raiders came to the Meratus Mountains because they knew it as the most vulnerable sector within the entire region. According to my Meratus friends in the western foothills, the police and army had been alerted to let the raiders do as they pleased. One man reported that the army had authorized 500 headhunters and 500 thieves to get the ritual resources necessary for regional oil production.[6]

Everyone was terrified. Hiking from one community to another, or even from one house to another, became a treacherous, frightening journey. Seeming traces of armed intruders appeared everywhere; disturbing stories proliferated. My housemates reported meeting strangers hiking at night without apparent destination. Our neighbors glimpsed unknown men huddled beneath the trees.

---

[6] Why Pertamina? The Meratus I know have had almost no contact with Pertamina and no particular wrongs to pin on them. Rather than a moral condemnation, Meratus rumors were an acknowledgment of the official power— and therefore violence—of which Pertamina partook. Meratus rumors participated not in a logic of inverted reciprocity, in which accusations of violence are turned and returned to their source, but rather in a peripheral acknowledgment of a more powerful Other.

One man claimed he passed a stranger on the trail wearing a "chain-mail shirt"; was he referring to an unusual uniform? I, too, didn't know what to make of odd occurrences while hiking on the forest trails. Several times my companions and I smelled cigarette smoke as if someone had just been there. We listened too intently to rustling noises in the bushes. Once we came upon a fresh half-eaten lunch, left on a rock by the side of the trail and looking just abandoned.

People were even afraid to work in their fields. My friends dragged me to isolated swidden sites asking me to play my tape recordings of community festivals loudly to simulate the sounds of a crowd. Finally, the news reached us that the body of a be-headed child had been found where she had been fetching water from a stream near a community more than a day's hike to the south of us.[7] My friends were relieved that the victim was not someone they knew personally. Over the next days, our lives slowly returned to a more relaxed tenor and a calmer pace.

The scare brought out stories of previous scares. A few years before, people said, raiders had been sent out to find heads for the construction of a major hydroelectric dam project to the south. Every time one of the region's important bridges needed repair, people said, fresh heads were sought. Indeed, all major public construction, they said, inspired headhunting raids: and the recent government drive for "development" (*pembangunan*, Indonesian) only meant more "building" (*bangunan*, Indonesian). From the Meratus perspective, the terms are hard to differentiate: "development" *is* state-sponsored "building." People described their roles as those of the victims of development in a rather literal sense: they provide the heads that fertilize construction.

When I next visited the Banjar towns to the west of the Meratus Mountains, I tried to collect stories that might give me a different sense of what was happening during the headhunting scare. The

[7] Janet Hoskins usefully inquires about the significance of the gender of the child, and about why the headhunters were satisfied with one victim. It makes sense to me that the victim described was a girl, since, as I argue elsewhere (Tsing 1990), Meratus discuss women as the Meratus Everyman figures who are least able to transcend local vulnerabilities. I myself was surprised at the time by the idea that one victim was considered sufficient, particularly given the number of separate headhunter sightings. I think people assumed the head to be necessary for a particular ceremonial occasion; things calmed down because of the general sense that the occasion has passed.

Banjar I spoke with agreed about the principles and importance of construction sacrifice, whether human or otherwise, but they knew nothing of recent rituals or repairs at the Pertamina oil fields. However, they had another story of violence and the state from this same time period: a cutthroat motorcycle gang, they said, had been invading people's houses to rape and murder; the police couldn't touch them because they were invulnerable to bullets. Perhaps this was a differently positioned version of the headhunting-raid rumors; perhaps not. In any case, taken together, the scares give some sense of the contrasting kinds of violence people fear.

Meratus fears of the violence of development have flourished in a context in which police and military officers continue to be their most prominent contacts with state policy and administration. Police and military officers are the only state officials to tour the Meratus Mountains; civil servants rarely come beyond the surrounding Banjar district seats. Furthermore, Meratus expect police and military officers to be armed, intimidating, and often arbitrary in their actions. Just as with soldiers, Meratus offer their very best hospitality to touring police officers, hoping to appease their anger; yet they also are not surprised by arbitrary fines and frightening demands. (For example, one young Meratus man who wore army-style pants to visit a police officer touring in the mountains was ordered to strip on the spot.) In this context, government headhunters are seen as only another example of state administrative policies. For Meratus, intimidation and appeasement are ordinary elements of the acquiescence to state authority that constitutes Meratus citizenship.

Fierce Eyewitnessing

So far I have introduced Meratus dilemmas as if a homogeneous "Meratus" perspective existed. Yet it does not. I have also deferred a presentation of the specific perspectives of the ambitious men who make themselves community leaders, which is particularly important for a discussion of violence and self-representation. Anthropological convention is to begin with such perspectives—often never to go beyond them. But Meratus leaders define themselves *against* self-typifications of local culture and community, and thus it seemed useful to present these typifications first. In the Meratus setting, leaders are those who represent themselves as transcending local vulnerabilities. Though these leaders would not, I believe, deny the relevance of the dilemmas I have set out so far, they also refuse to be caught by them. They mediate with the state because they are courageous enough to meet the agents of violence on their own terms; they are not held back by fear.

Leaders are those who can turn the violence of regional power to support their own leadership. Leaders aren't afraid of the police; they threaten to call the police on others. In fact, the police are unlikely to come when invited by Meratus leaders, but the very arbitrariness of police actions makes them a convincing threat. And only the fearless would dare to deal with them. Leaders constitute their authority through reminding their neighbors of their common vulnerability to aggression.

Many of the stories of violence I heard were told by ambitious men who used them to remind an audience of both ordinary fear and the unusual leadership-making possibilities of bravery. By situating themselves as eyewitnesses to past violence, narrators argued for their abilities as capable political actors within current local and regional affairs. They had been survivors before; they had stories to tell that gave them the power to impress and perhaps even to intimidate others. These stories created the ability to protect communities even as they helped compose communities within the boundaries of fear. Meratus communities are shifting, tentative alliances; many men (and occasional women) take on leadership roles for at least some time in some context. Stories of violence help to shape both leadership and community as they establish brave leaders and the followers they impress.

This framework makes it possible to reread the stories of war and revolution I included earlier with their contemporary political uses in mind. The narrator who told of Ma Jawa's murder was also telling stories about himself: he was right there to see everything; holding his bushknife, he was ready to fight if necessary; he survived to tell the tale. The story offers him the glow of retrospective bravery; he is not destroyed but reinvigorated by the violence of revolutionaries and colonial soldiers.

This kind of self-positioning is perhaps even easier to hear in another story this man told about his involvement in the 1958–

65 Banjar rebellion. The rebels—including many disgruntled nationalist revolutionaries who now endorsed an Islamic political plan for regional autonomy—made their largest base in the dense woods on the east side of the Meratus Mountains; rebels and central government troops traveled and sniped at each other back and forth across the mountains (see, e.g., Manihuruk et al. 1962: 160–81). Some Meratus were killed; some scattered into the forest, farming only in tiny, isolated plots. The narrator here, however, lived in a less heavily crossed area; he tells of how he kept the rebel soldiers (and later, pursuing government troops) at bay by offering them rice and chickens. In this story, too, he turns around his pain and fear to gain from the soldiers' violence: they make him a local title-holder in their movement. And his leadership allows him to protect others from rebel destruction and discipline. Thus, his story simultaneously invokes the pervasiveness of fear and the necessity for leadership.

The rebels killed people if they stole, gambled, committed adultery, or didn't tithe. If you stole, they cut off the tips of your fingers. If you got pregnant, they split your stomach. They wanted an Islamic state. They came and hit me on the head once because they heard I had seen a theft and hadn't reported it. They arrested me for three nights and then sent me home and made me the local Head of Order.

Once Ibnu Hajnar [Ibnu Hajar, the leader of the rebellion] and 30 men stayed at the A—— hall. They told us to bring 30 kerosene cans of cleaned rice. I went to meet them. The second wife of Ibnu Hajnar was there, and I was told to carry her across the river while Ibnu Hajnar hung on to my arm. He had his automatic pistol in my back as we crossed.

That evening Ibnu Hajnar wanted to know why we had been gambling. I brought him a chicken and some eggs. I told him that gambling here was a custom that began with our ancestors; it was different than gambling in the market towns. Ibnu Hajnar said it was all right for us to gamble, but we shouldn't let outsiders join.

All these movements—the Japanese, the nationalists, the rebels, the Headscarf Militia [the central government's response to the rebels]—none of these ever bothered this village.

In the last line, the narrator boasts of is ability to ward off the forces that might destroy his local sphere. Without his hospitality and mediation, he implies, the community might have been annihilated. In this conclusion, all the terrible uses of force he had recounted become points of personal prestige: he had experienced their ferocity, entertained it, and turned its aggression away from him.

I heard this story one evening as a group of men sat around talking politics, weaving between the past and the present. One of the underlying tensions that animated that evening's stories was an unresolved dispute in which both sides had threatened to call the police on each other. (None of the disputants were present, however.) The narrator of this story had offered to mediate, and his stories of surviving past violence took on the significance of a claim to the leadership skills he would need for this mediation. He was not a man who was easily scared, his stories told us. He knew how to forge a community in the midst of violence.

Talk of violence is central to local politics because political leadership and community are negotiated through such talk. To summon up spectres of violence establishes a bid for leadership; to acknowledge one's vulnerability accepts community membership under that leadership. In this dynamic, varied threats converge: one can mention the police and Banjar authorities, or claim genealogical connections with more powerful and dangerous Dayak groups, or recall tales of headhunters and soldiers. Local politics is cooked up within multiple threats.

I was particularly struck by the importance of men's talk of violence as I listened to dispute mediations. Dispute mediation always takes place in an atmosphere of potential violence because people fear the possible and unpredictable intervention of the police or army. (As one young man involved in a dispute put it, only half sarcastically, the police will "beat up everyone, even if you're truthful [and therefore innocent]."[8]) Indeed, dispute mediators as well as disputants whip up this fear by threatening to call the

---

[8] All quotations in the following section are taken from a 1981 dispute settlement at which I was present. The dispute is discussed in some detail elsewhere (Tsing 1984: ch. 13). The situation involved a young man who had raped his wife's younger sister. When the younger sister complained to her father, the son-in-law argued that he wanted to marry his young sister-in-law and had just been avoiding the formalities. The father-in-law felt insulted and started a public quarrel, which the neighborhood head tried to mend. The settlement I discuss here patched up the quarrel between father-in-law and son-in-law; the young woman never argued an independent dispute case, nor was one argued for her.

police on each other. In this context, men negotiate their personal autonomy and community status by alternately alluding to, threatening, and backing away from violence. Consider, for example, one man's refusal of violence as a statement of community compliance. He calls up the history of headhunting and human sacrifice to make his point:

Imagine me fighting, uncle. Where would I have the strength? . . . I even sharpen my work knife at your forge, uncle; don't think I would ever fight with you. Not me, uncle. If I didn't depend on your forge, uncle, my knife wouldn't even be sharp. Don't think of fighting. Fighting—that would be like hanging a head in my doorway. Or erecting an iron sacrifice post. That's not like me.

This man is not a headhunter: he says he is a decent—fearful—member of the community. He is not the one who organizes human sacrifices; he is ordinary, that is, vulnerable. But his statement also takes him out of the arena of leadership; if he is vulnerable, he is also not an effective political actor in the context of violence.

Other, braver positionings are possible. Indeed, these very sentiments of demurral inspired defiance, as one proud young man transformed the headhunters' violence into that of a hunter: "If I followed the musings of my own heart, I'd hang a deer's head in my doorway. Why not?" The animal sacrifice is not so far, he implied, from the human.

These fragments are taken from a transcript of a mediation between a quarreling son-in-law and father-in-law. The first statement was made by a relative of the son-in-law who here made his peace with the father-in-law (the statement's "uncle"), thus abandoning the son-in-law. The response was the son-in-law's attempt to make it alone—to show enough toughness to sustain his side of the argument. He went on to tell the story of a time he was ambushed in a somewhat distant village. He survived, the braver to tell the story. Without such brave stories, he had no case to make; he might as well have settled at once.

Tales of violence escalated as the father-in-law recalled how he had beaten his son on one occasion, to get him to behave; the son-in-law (whose own two children were still babies) responded by saying that he had strangled a dog. Meanwhile, the mediator threatened to let regional officials know about the dispute if the two men didn't apologize. Just "letting go" of the case, he argued, could bring on the whole force of regional violence:

Now uncle [the quarrelsome son-in-law], if you don't submit, it will be even heavier; I'll just surrender the case. I'll let go of it.

But neither man was ready to express any fear as each held out for his own political initiative. Here is the father-in-law:

Don't try to scoop me up like a shrimp. . . . I'll face any government offices. I've met the police; I've met the army.

And the son-in-law:

Those offices, what can they break? Not even shrimp paste, maybe just *tandoi* fruits.

   If you take me to [the police post at the market town], I'll come along all right. If you take me to [the regency seat], I'll come too. We'll need lots of money to bribe [the officials].

If he is serious about holding his own within the argument, a disputant must show his ability to act politically. And here, to act politically means to be able to stand up to regional authority with its threats of violence. To act politically also means to make oneself a potential community leader; a man is a potential leader to the extent that he can maneuver between state discipline and community fear.

   Even vulnerability to state authorities can be turned into potential leadership in this talk. Running away itself can become a form of bravery that creates possibilities for new community formation. The angry son-in-law made this move in recalling a past election-season threat of the police:

If you wanted to bring me to government offices, well, I thought, just go ahead. I thought, threats of those offices don't scare me. Last time there were elections I was threatened by [the past neighborhood head]:

   "Ma Kijul," he said, "if you don't hike down to vote, the police will come get you."

   So, I said, they can come, tens of them if they want, and as long as none of my kin here join them, I'll wait for them by myself.

   I waited, and no one came. But if they had come, uncle, I would have gone on ahead to Red Ridge. They would never have found me in the jungle there. I figured I'd probably have companions to run with.

In this recollection, the jungle (here, *jampah*, "tangled brush") becomes the son-in-law's place of safety and refuge, just as it is the most fearful place for the police who, he claims, would force Dayaks to vote. For just a moment of thought, the policemen's own fears become the possibility of Meratus strength and survival. This is a moment in which Meratus communities are constituted oppositionally to the state: they are the disorder that state order imagines and the violence that state violence engenders.

But there are other strategic options. A leader can be a reformer rather than a refugee. The mediator in this case was claiming the power of the police, rather than opposing it; it authorized him to mediate and thus to lead a community. Even the angry young son-in-law changed his tune as the evening progressed; he argued that he too could represent his community—bravely and properly—to regional officials.

Undercurrents: Hidden Agendas and Acceptable Targets

By the end of the evening, the two men had agreed to make up and continue their relationship as father-in-law and son-in-law. They had reestablished their mutual rights to respect and their essential parity within the community. However, many other issues about the dispute had never even been named at the community meeting. Without the network of gossip that proceeded and followed the mediation, who would have known of the embedded case concerning sexual assault? The son-in-law had forced himself on his wife's younger sister, a teenager. The girl had complained to her father, who had shouted at his son-in-law. The mediation concerned the ensuing bad relations between father-in-law and son-in-law; neither the teenager nor her sister, the son-in-law's wife, were much mentioned. Both sat relatively quietly at the sidelines as the men asserted their political rights.

As in many of the gatherings I witnessed, the difference here between how men talked of violence and how women did was striking. Assertive men boasted of their abilities to survive and thrive on violence; women kept relatively quiet. Some women expressed boredom and annoyance at the proceedings ("This is a vine creeping on a vine," said one woman), but in this case no woman took

Illus. 1. A Meratus community leader poses with a wooden mock rifle, 1994. The rifle is used in ceremonies that display, appease, and tap the ferocity of spirits—much like that of soldiers.

on the political challenge of publicly embracing, or opposing, violence. In other contexts, I have argued that Meratus men's gendered political privilege is constructed in part through fierce and dramatic posturings in which women rarely take part (Tsing 1990); I also have attempted to look more closely at silences about male violence against women (Tsing n.d.). Here, my point is to mention that the context of violence that inspires assertive men to boast of their survival skills has a different significance for women, children, and unassertive men. These latter groups may criticize talk of violence from the margins ("This is long, long, long," said one quiet old man), but they generally acquiesce to political leadership by tough-talking men. Their dissatisfaction is most commonly expressed in evasions of these men's leadership schemes rather than in direct challenges to their right to set political agendas.

Indeed, men's talk of violence has different consequences for different community members. In this event, this was most obvious in talk of beating children. Though sexual violence went unnamed, a man's ability to strike his children became a leitmotif of pride. The angry father-in-law introduced this theme early in the mediation; those who don't discipline their children, he argued, will find their children putting the clothes on their parents, that is, treating their elders like children. "I'm different," he stated. ". . . When I'm mad at a child, [I'll take] a stick of wood to his head."

Child-beating is a tricky subject, and it is easy for European and North American readers to associate it with inhumanity. I hasten to add that I never saw a Meratus father strike his child; indeed, I have no evidence at all that child-beating ever occurred. My point is to argue not that Meratus men beat their children, but that they sometimes publicly and convincing threaten to beat them. On several occasions I saw fathers threaten their children as other family members successfully urged the child to run out of reach. With or without an actual threat, a boast of a threat can be effective—as in the example above—to speak to a man's power and bravery. Boasts of violent potential bring Meratus talk of family violence into the same range as talk about regional violence and headhunting.

On one level, men's threats and stories address regional violence to facilitate the political survival and autonomy of Meratus communities. Stories of violence establish men's knowledge, independence, and leadership skills. On another level, these same threats and stories intimidate the very people these leaders aim, and claim, to protect.

Violence and Representation

Threats of violence operate at many levels. It is hard to understand the Meratus situation without thinking simultaneously
about global projects of imperialism, the national military expansions that work with and against them, the regional administrative tactics that both frustrate and realize national plans, the local
posturing of male minority group leaders "protecting" their communities, and the ambivalent support and evasions of other community members who may alternately feel protected, threatened,
or annoyed by the whole situation. Telling violence in the Meratus Mountains is both constrained and empowered within the
imaginative spaces of these interactions. This is certainly true for
my stories as well as those of Meratus leaders.

Writing about violence is perhaps always political. Nineteenth-
century European travelers wrote extensively about Dayak "headhunting customs" in part because they were fascinated with an
idea of savagery that headhunting, understood as custom, helped
build.[9] For today's readers, it is hard to extricate those writings
from a colonial project in which European violence—called "pacification" and "administration"—was cast as quelling savagery and
bringing peace. Indeed, Meratus tellings of violence are relevant to
an international audience in part because they remind those of
us who have already been "pacified" of the ongoing uses of such
colonizing narratives. Administration and pacification, and their
newer partner "development," continue in the name of quelling
savagery. Meratus stories that tell of the violence of national de-

[9] A relatively mild example is Carl Bock's: "The barbarous practice of Head-
Hunting, as carried on by all the Dyak tribes . . . is part and parcel of their religious rites. Births and 'namings,' marriages and burials, not to mention less
important events, cannot be properly celebrated unless the heads of a few enemies, more or less, have been secured to grace the festivities or solemnities.
Head-hunting is consequently the most difficult feature in the relationship of
the subject races to their white masters, and the most delicate problem which
civilization has to solve in the future administration of the as yet independent
tribes of the interior of Borneo. The Dutch have already done much by the
double agency of their arms and their trade to remove this plague-spot from
the character of the tribes more immediately under their control; and the Sultan of Koetai does all he can to discountenance it. Still, as has been seen, even
he is not altogether free from the superstitious weaknesses that beset Malays
and Dyaks alike" (1985 [1881]: 215).

velopment and regional administration defamiliarize forms of authority that too many of us take as business-as-usual.[10]

Yet it is not easy to write about these stories. Internationally powerful Western standards for thinking about "human rights" lend sympathy to the victims of violence. According to these standards, the more innocent the victim—that is, the less willing the victim is to be involved in aggressive talk—the more deserving he or she is. These standards make me want to emphasize Meratus perceptions of the terrors of regional/national authority and to downplay aggressive local backtalk. Meratus should have some rights to safety and self-determination, and I want my writing to work in their behalf.

Yet most of the Meratus community leaders I knew in the early 1980s would be insulted to see themselves represented merely as victims. It is important to them that they are not caught by fear; their bravery is the source of their ability to represent communities. The dilemma of representation doubles back: to offer these leaders respect by describing their brave postures runs the risk of condemning them in Western eyes. Rather than innocent victims, they might look like out-of-control savages. Indeed, these concerns have made it politically difficult for good-hearted ethnographers to discuss violence—from spouse abuse to headhunting—in the Third World. Thus, for example, precisely because nineteenth-century European accounts of Kalimantan emphasized violence as an exotic custom, most mid-twentieth-century ethnographers were able to position themselves as advocates of the value of traditional cultures only by downplaying violence and headhunting or ignoring them entirely.

Recent advocates for the rights of minorities in Kalimantan and elsewhere have taken these peaceable accounts of tradition and

[10] It may seem ironic that—if one of my goals is to destabilize colonizing assumptions—I drew so heavily on nineteenth-century European descriptions of headhunting in the middle section of this essay. I used these descriptions to introduce the cultural context of Meratus stories of violence; only by specifying their cultural location can these stories seem "real" enough to make us so-called civilized readers uneasy about our assumptions about war. (Otherwise, we tend to normalize our own war stories and dismiss those of people like the Meratus as ignorant and superstitious.) I would argue that descriptions—like theories—can be deployed for varied political ends. My use of these descriptions does not displace or erase the politics of earlier deployments but sits uneasily beside them.

juxtaposed them with the violence of national and international military and economic expansions. Communities seem worth protecting because they are innocents under attack. Yet it is important to note that in this scheme it is the ethnographers and their readers who become the heroes of community protection. It is the enthnographers and readers who are able to deal in the world of violence—refusing to be caught by fear—to represent the innocent and ward off the aggressors. Anthropologists become "fierce eyewitnesses" who survive to tell the tale. Meratus community leaders might not be pleased to leave this role to international writers.

In writing about Meratus communities, I have thus chosen to acknowledge both their vulnerability and local leaders' political strategies of moving beyond it. I would not want to imply that the leadership stances I have described are the only way of talking back to intimidation; those rare Meratus women who aspire to leadership tend to use rather different strategies, in keeping with their somewhat different relationship to regional authority structures. Yet I do want to inspire a moment of respect for Meratus men who create and lead communities in both fear and survival. Unwilling to accept representations as victims or as savages, they scheme between Meratus communities and the demands of the state to constitute themselves as ever-mobile political agents. Their strategies refuse containment as well as defeat.

Acknowledgments

This essay was written in 1990 and revised in 1992 for this volume. I have published a different analysis of some of this material in *In the Realm of the Diamond Queen: Marginality in an Out-of-the-Way Place* (Princeton University Press, 1993).

The essay is based on research in South Kalimantan conducted between 1979 and 1981 under the sponsorship of the Lembaga Ilmu Pengetahuan Indonesia, with fellowship support from the National Institute of Mental Health and the Social Science Research Council. The paper has benefited from careful readings by Janet Hoskins, as well as Shelly Errington, Diane Gifford-Gonzales, Anjie Rosga, and Carolyn Martin Shaw.

References

Berreman, Gerald D.
  1991 "The Incredible Tasaday: Deconstructing the Myth of a 'Stone-Age' People." *Cultural Survival Quarterly* 15 (1): 3–45.
Bock, Carl
  1985 [1881] *The Headhunters of Borneo*. Oxford: Oxford University Press.
Coppel, Charles
  1983 *Indonesian Chinese in Crisis*. Kuala Lumpur: Oxford University Press.
Drake, Richard A.
  1989 "Construction Sacrifice and Kidnapping Rumour Panics in Borneo." *Oceania* 59: 269–79.
Erb, Maribeth
  1991 "Construction Sacrifice, Rumours and Kidnapping Scares in Manggari: Further Comparative Notes from Flores." *Oceania* 62 (2): 114–27.
Evans-Pritchard, E. E.
  1940 *The Nuer*. Oxford: Oxford University Press.
Feldman, Allen
  1991 *Formations of Violence*. Chicago: University of Chicago Press.
Forth, G.
  1991 "Construction Sacrifice and Head-Hunting Rumours in Central Flores (Eastern Indonesia): A Comparative Note." *Oceania* 61: 257–66.
Freeman, Derek
  1970 *Report on the Iban*. London: Athlone Press.
  1981 "Some Reflections on the Nature of Iban Society." Occasional paper of the Department of Anthropology, Research School of Pacific Studies, Australian National University, Canberra.
George, Kenneth M.
  1991 "Headhunting, History, and Exchange in Upland Sulawesi." *Journal of Asian Studies* 50 (3): 536–64.
Hoskins, Janet
  1987 "The Headhunter as Hero: Local Traditions and Their Reinterpretations in National History." *American Ethnologist* 14 (94): 605–22.
Manihuruk, A. E., and Editorial Team
  1962 *Kodam X/LM Membangun*. Jakarta: Kodam X/LM.
Molony, Carol
  1988 "The Truth About the Tasaday." *The Sciences* (Sept.–Oct.): 12–20.
Padoch, Christine
  1982 *Migration and Its Alternatives Among the Iban of Sarawak*. The Hague: Martinus Nijhoff.

Peluso, Nancy
    1983 "Markets and Merchants: The Forest Products Trade of East Kalimantan in Historical Perspective." M.A. thesis, Cornell University.
Peterson, Robert
    1968 *Storm over Borneo*. London: Overseas Missionary Fellowship.
Rappaport, Roy A.
    1968 *Pigs for the Ancestors: Ritual in the Ecology of a New Guinea People*. New Haven: Yale University Press.
Rosaldo, Renato
    1980 *Ilongot Headhunting, 1883–1974*. Stanford: Stanford University Press.
Rousseau, Jerome
    1990 *Central Borneo: Ethnic Identity and Social Life in a Stratified Society*. Oxford: Clarendon Press.
Scharer, Hans
    1963 *Ngaju Religion*. Translated by Rodney Needham. The Hague: Martinus Nijhoff.
Sutlive, Vincent
    1978 *The Iban of Sarawak*. Arlington Heights, Ill.: AHM Publishing.
Taussig, Michael
    1987 *Shamanism, Colonialism, and the Wild Man: A Study in Terror and Healing*. Chicago: University of Chicago Press.
Tsing, Anna
    1984 "Politics and Culture in the Meratus Mountains." Ph.D. diss., Stanford University.
    1990 "Gender and Performance in Meratus Dispute Settlement." In Jane Atkinson and Shelly Errington, eds., *Power and Difference*, pp. 95–125. Stanford: Stanford University Press.
    1993 *In the Realm of the Diamond Queen: Marginality in an Out-of-the-Way Place*. Princeton: Princeton University Press.
    n.d. "Violence and Silences." Unpublished manuscript.

Janet Hoskins

The Heritage of Headhunting

History, Ideology, and Violence
on Sumba, 1890-1990

Headhunting is now history on the eastern Indo-
nesian island of Sumba. It is "history" in the colloquial sense that
it is no longer practiced and has been effectively stopped by governmental authorities for the past 70 years. It is also "history" in
the historiographic sense that it is a part of the past that has been
separated from the present, preserved in narrative form and reflected upon, held up as a mirror to the contemporary social order,
and studied as part of a project to create a shared image of what
has been lost. Headhunting is part of history as an ideological construct, a vision of the past now alienated from the present, although it is only sketchily represented in "history" in another
sense—the written documentation and commentary that is part
of the supposedly scientific study of the past.

But headhunting remains a part of the cultural heritage of
Sumba. In Kodi, the westernmost domain in which I did my
fieldwork in the 1980s, the descendants of headhunters proudly
showed me skulls captured from neighboring peoples and displayed in their villages, telling long stories of the exploits of their
ancestors. The local junior high school is named after a headhunter who raided Dutch forces at the beginning of the century.
And the rhetoric of headhunting often surfaces in alliances between groups, suggesting a strong continuing link between taking
wives and taking heads.

In 1985, I attended a marriage negotiation where a Kodi family from the ancestral village of Ratenggaro received a potential
suitor and his family from the once-enemy domain of Weyewa.
Guests were greeted at a large table placed in front of the house,

Illus. 1. This man's cloth from East Sumba depicts the skull tree, where human heads were hung after a victorious raid. Courtesy of the National Gallery of Australia

where the host unfurled a magnificent cloth from East Sumba depicting a cactuslike tree surrounded by warriors with raised arms. The "fruit" on the tree had eyes and mouths, and were in fact human heads mounted on a post in a bloody display of vengeance. This was the skull tree, a small wooden altar that once stood in the center of the village and displayed heads captured from the Weyewa highlands.

The first words spoken by the groom's representative commented on the skull-tree motif, which he recognized with a chuckle: "I see you were ready for us. You know we have come to bump our foreheads together and smash our kneecaps in battle. But wait a bit my friends, we haven't yet loosened our hair for combat, we aren't holding the plumed sword of vengeance." Through metaphoric reference to the trappings of traditional warfare, he both acknowledged and accepted the challenge of an agonistic confrontation. He also explicitly and directly brought the rhetoric of headhunting into the modern context of marriage negotiations.

How is a wedding like a headhunt? And why should the heritage of a violent past be evoked precisely at the moment when both sides in this encounter should be making a public show of goodwill? The answers to these questions come, I argue, from an understanding of the cultural heritage of headhunting on Sumba, and the different political meanings that it has had in eastern and western parts of the island. They also lead us to formulate a distinction between "headhunting as history"—a discontinued piece of the past that has been preserved in narrative form—and "headhunting as heritage"—a continuing tradition that contains positive elements and values that are celebrated, even when the bloody practice itself has been suppressed.

Heritage versus History

Sumbanese speakers talk about their heritage with terms in the local language that designate practices that originated in the past but continue to be important today ("the ways of long ago," *pata tana wali la mandei*). They speak of history, in contrast, with a term from the Indonesian national language (*sejarah*) that marks an idea of discontinuity, a sequence of distinct, nonrepeating events, in which individuals emerge as actors and their exploits are unique occurrences. History does not repeat itself, but if the past is seen as "heritage," it can be repeated in a somewhat different form, because it contains not specific events but somewhat richer and vaguer potentialities.

When Sumbanese speakers talk about the history of headhunting, they evoke specific ancestors or victims and their fates on the warpath. When they place headhunting within a wider heritage, it is used to represent sequences and attitudes that can be adapted to other contexts. In precolonial times, the "debts of blood" carried on by a line of descendants were part of a timeless hostility, older than any historical memory of the origins of the hostilities. Since pacification in 1915, much of the language and ritual of headhunting has been turned to new purposes, and has assumed an importance in the ideology of nationalist struggle, ceremonies to welcome visiting government dignitaries, and alliance negotiations.

The island of Sumba is divided into two main language groups, which, I argue, have different attitudes toward the past and practice of headhunting. The Kambera-speaking people of the east live in a rigidly stratified, almost feudal system, presided over by a shrinking but still influential class of hereditary nobles. These nobles have important personal interests at stake when they say that headhunting is now "history," and that the skull tree is only a bit of visual folklore that helps boost the sales of East Sumbanese textiles on the foreign market. The people of the western half of Sumba, who speak about ten separate languages, have a more competitive, achievement-oriented society, where inequalities are subject to frequent changes of fortune. They see their military past in a different light. Headhunting for them is a heritage associated with ideas of defending local autonomy, championing indigenous land rights, and defending traditional territories.

The different values given to the memory of headhunting reflect differences in both past and present ideological goals. In evoking the glorious battles of the last century, one group thinks of struggles between nobles for control of land, while another thinks of brave warriors fighting for the respect and loyalty of political followers. Where headhunting and alliance were organized according to a hierarchical system, conflicts between eastern noble families constructed class differences and permanent inequalities. Where fighting was an attribute of individual achievement and warfare was something of an equalizer, feelings of popular solidarity developed against external enemies. In the east, the skull tree became an emblem of the power of the ruler. In the west, it has come to stand for popular resistance to outside control, and has been linked to nationalist struggles against colonial domination.

The meaning of the past has very different consequences for

MENSCHENSCHEDELS

vóór het huis van den Radja van Rendeh,
op Soemba.

MEDEDEELINGEN NEDERLANDSCH ZENDELING-GENOOTSCHAP
37ᵉ Jaargang.
Uitgave M. WYT & ZONEN, Rotterdam.

Illus. 2. Etching of a skull tree, reproduced from the diary of a Protestant missionary who visited Rindi, East Sumba in 1892: "In front of the raja's house stood the trophies obtained in war. What did this consist of? Now reader, do not be terrified. They were human heads. There were sixteen of them, all placed on a stake. It was quite a chilling sight when one first encountered it" (Wijngaarden 1893: 371).

each group: the symbolic representation of headhunting is only part of a complex dialectic between "history" and "heritage," and between past and present, in island politics.

Sumba Before Pacification

Neither written sources nor oral histories can take us back more than a hundred years, when conditions in the island's interior began to be recorded by foreign observers, and the fathers and grandfathers of the present generation were engaged in intermittent regional wars. Before this time, Sumba was left in the backwaters of the Dutch colonial empire. Given the name Sandalwood Island during the sixteenth and seventeenth centuries, it was quickly depleted of the aromatic forests that once covered its hills, as the fragrant wood was exported to make incense and clothes chests. The island's other great resource, a small feisty race of "sandalwood horses," was raised on the rolling grasslands left after the forests were cleared, and traded along with textiles and food to foreign ships that brought highly valued cloth, porcelain plates, gold, and metal goods. Arab, Chinese, and Portuguese traders may have been among the first to visit the island. By the nineteenth century, the visitors were mainly British and Dutch.

The trade was centered in the eastern port of Waingapu, where an Arab horse trader had built a small dock to load livestock. Greater access to foreign trade goods and later firearms may have influenced the development of more stratified, autocratic polities in the eastern part of the island, and a more competitive, achievement-oriented system in the west. By the period of the first colonial administration, such differences were already evident, as Versluys has described them:

In the east . . . life is centered on the big houses of the aristocrats, who live with their servants or slaves in a relatively autonomous fashion. . . . Stock breeding is of great importance, and the population is sparse . . . in the west, on the contrary, we see huge plains of wet rice fields and a great many swidden gardens, often layered along the steep slopes of low-lying mountains, and a much denser population. There is greater economic equality, since livestock are distributed over a larger number of owners, and this accords with the total social structure, where the figure of the aristocrat who can live as a separate entity with his family and servants is much rarer. (1941: 436)

Differences in the degree of stratification and the power of individual aristocrats take shape against a background of shared cultural features. All over the island, named corporate groups (*kabisu*) are defined by descent through men, and are attached to fortified villages of sacred houses and ancestral tombs. Local descent groups are segmented and may have branches in several different localities, each of which is usually exogamous. The worship of *marapu* (ancestors, spirits of the land, and deities associated with the clan and village) is centered in the sacred houses, where heirloom objects are stored. Marriage alliances between houses are given great ritual and social importance, but only in the eastern part of the island are they rigorously asymmetric. Complementary exchanges of livestock and gold against pigs and cloth define the relationships of wive-givers and wife-takers at all major rituals, and the wife-giver assumes the superior position.

The Dutch Colonial Project: Problems in Pacification

The earliest Dutch administrators portrayed precolonial Sumba as an island of constant and unregulated violence. Samuel Roos, the first permanent colonial officer stationed on the island, asserted that "there is no other rule than that of the strongest" (Roos 1872: 9), and local warfare and the slave trade had "reduced the value of a human life to a very low level . . . often well below that of a horse" (1872: 10). His successor at the beginning of the twentieth century, A. C. Couvreur, described traditional leaders as, "robber barons and destroyers of their own land" who thought only of self-aggrandizement and made the pursuit of personal power "the most virtuous of goals and the one most widely recognized" (Couvreur 1917: 218).

Couvreur contrasted the Sumbanese warrior ethos with that of the medieval knights bound by the code of chivalry. Whereas the knight was a "chevalier sans peur et sans reproche," both fearless and blameless, the Sumbanese warrior was fearless but hardly blameless. He mercilessly plundered the villages of his enemies, captured women and children to sell into slavery, and destroyed everything in his path. "Respecting no other authority except that of his *marapu* gods, he has no notion of how to keep society at peace . . . or how to cooperate" (1917: 218).

Only one of the early observers noted that Sumbanese domains

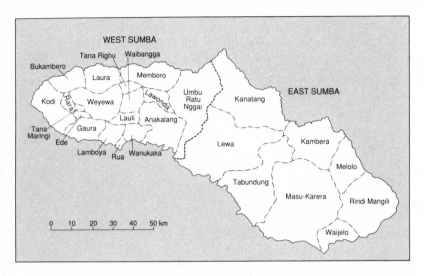

Map 1. The people of East Sumba all speak the Kambera language, while those of West Sumba have ten different languages. Map from Hoskins 1993.

were not always at war with everyone everywhere, but had a carefully articulated system of traditional enmities, and did follow their own standards of honor and rules of combat. A. C. Kruyt (best known as the missionary-ethnographer of Central Sulawesi) documented the fact that some domains (Laura and Tana Rio, Lewa and Tabundung, Lamboya and Wanokaka—to which I would add Kodi and Weyewa) were traditional enemies, and "there could be no question of peace" between them, whereas others had occasional armed clashes but would never take the heads of victims (1922: 557). Headhunting implied a ritualized relationship, and a particular ceremonial code, that distinguished it sharply from other forms of violence, or conflicts with Endehnese slave raiders.

Kruyt noted important differences in the political and social institutions associated with taking heads at the two poles of the island. In the east, war parties were led by a *moni mbani*, or "champion," who might in fact be the raja himself, but who was more often a nobleman who commanded a number of slaves or subordinates (Kruyt 1922: 558). In the west, they were led by members of headhunting clans, whose fortified villages had skull trees in them to show their special role in complex tri- and quadripartite divisions of ceremonial tasks. The leadership of headhunting rituals was delegated to these usually more peripheral villages from the centers of agricultural ceremonies, and there was a more marked division between the war leader (there called the *rato katoda*) and the priest (*rato marapu*). The men that the Dutch writers call the "rajas" were powerful hereditary rulers in the east, whereas in most of the domains of the west there was no central political leader before pacification. The unity of West Sumbanese domains was based on shared ritual allegiance to certain ancestral villages, calendrical prohibitions, and shared language and customs, and was not closely linked to the personality of a conquering lord.

The moral dimension to headhunting escaped its first critics, who saw only an anarchic violence with no rhyme or reason. From 1911 to 1913, Dutch forces that tried to enforce "pacification" paid the price of their ignorance. Headhunters led a resistance movement in Kodi that raided the colonial army for three years, resulting in hundreds of deaths. Popular support for the headhunters made them into heroes, and created an ideal of local autonomy that has remained problematic for the colonial and postcolonial state (Hoskins 1987).

Ritual and Ideology in Headhunting Practices

Headhunting on Sumba, as in other parts of Southeast Asia, was associated with capturing agricultural fertility from enemy peoples and removing the pollution of murder by transforming death into new life (de Josselin de Jong 1937; Downs 1955; George 1991; McKinley 1976). In contrast to the Ilongot as portrayed in rich ethnographic reports (M. Rosaldo 1980; R. Rosaldo 1980, 1989), Sumbanese do not say that they hunt heads because they are driven by grief, anger, or catharsis on a personal level. Headhunts may be undertaken to end the period of mourning for an important person (Hoskins 1989), but their benefits are said to come in a renewal of health and fertility for the whole community.

Headhunting traditions were recorded by Kruyt in 1919–20, just as pacification was taking hold on Sumba (Kruyt 1922), and also by Kapita, an East Sumbanese nobleman and antiquarian historian who has published several volumes on local customs

(Kapita 1976). Comparing Dutch and indigenous sources on East Sumba with those on West Sumba, I discern a difference in orientation—for which I will use the rather loaded term "ideology"—in the way headhunting was carried out at the two ends of the island. I use "ideology" here in the sense not of a consciously articulated doctrine, but of a body of ideas used in support of a political system and implicated in the realization of political goals.

The headhunting rites of West Sumba display an "ideology of vendetta," in which taking a head was primarily an act of revenge, a restoration of balance between foes of equal status. The solidarity of the group was reaffirmed in opposition to an external enemy. In the east, we find an "ideology of encompassment," in which heads were used as tokens of territorial conquest and absorption of one domain by another. In many western districts, the head was brutalized—dragged about on the ground with a thong through its cheek, humiliated, and mocked. In the east, on the contrary, it was honored—addressed with the noble title *umbu* (Lord) and paraded in a procession, held high by the priest, who showed respect for the adversary whose power served to enhance the still greater power of the conqueror. After pacification, the boundaries of domains were frozen into administrative districts, and conquest of new territory became impossible. Headhunting was no longer a part of the constitution of Sumbanese political units. But ideological differences continued to cast a shadow on contemporary evaluations of the violent past, constructing the practice as a living "heritage" or discontinuous "history."

Headhunting East and West

Differences in headhunting in East and West Sumba are found in the composition of raiding parties, festivals to welcome the severed head into the village and process the skull and scalp, and the prevalence of peace covenants or ransom payments. Careful attention to the shifts in the "rules" by which headhunting raids were conducted can give us insight into the underlying strategies that motivated the actors. In the east, the motivation seems to have been territorial expansion; in the west, it was instead control over people and movable wealth.

The Composition of Raiding Parties

Vendetta was given a religious justification in West Sumba, since the ghost of any person killed by enemy forces flew unhappily through the skies causing trouble until the death had been avenged. The close kin and descendants of the victim would be most affected, suffering disease, poor harvests, and other misfortunes until they acted to restore equality and family honor. Ideally, a man's death would be avenged by his clan brothers and sons, guided by famous warriors in villages where the headhunting ritual was centered. The most desirable victim was another brave warrior, and if raiders succeeded in killing an important person, there was no need to continue.[1] In practice, older men and women were often killed because they could be caught more easily. Young women and children were usually spared to be taken as slaves.[2]

[1] In Kodi, I was often told that half of the art of making war lay in creating a fearsome appearance. The war leader was described as a "large boar, a giant monkey, the shining snail shell, the seed of a great tree" (*wawi ryonga, koki njuka, pakole kere mbuku, tambola wu kapaka*). The headhunter himself had to be "beautiful" (*mone kabalaho*)—dressed in a bright red or gold headcloth, wrapped several inches thick around the head and also secured under the chin. He bore weapons decorated with roosters' feathers, horsehair plumes, ivory handles, and even gold inlay. Riding on a splendid horse, he could "dazzle" his opponent and unnerve him, so that the actual battle was already finished once he had been sighted. The "beauty" and "splendor" of the warrior is a theme that has continued in the ritualized combat of the *pasola*, a form of jousting that is now performed yearly in connection with a calendrical feast of renewal (*nale*). In fact, war parties usually left on horseback, but often hid their horses in a secluded place and advanced on unsuspecting victims on foot. Several people described nighttime raids to me, and the ritual couplet that describes the plundering of war suggests that this was the most common strategy. Warriors "advanced at the edge of the day, the deep of the night" (*na waingo a lodo ndango, a hudo ndoko*), and many did not announce their arrival by a thunder of horses' hooves or the jingling of bells on splendidly decorated bridles.

[2] The wives in the village had to follow a series of taboos to protect their husbands on the warpath. The wife was not supposed to leave her home unless absolutely necessary, and then only by a small back path. She was told to pour water onto a small platform attached to the skull tree regularly to assure her husband's safe return, and to dispose of the water as soon as he returned. She could not loosen her hair from her bun during the whole period of his absence, or do any form of women's handiwork—sewing, plaiting, or weaving. The fire in the hearth had to be kept low, and could not be shared with any other house. Kruyt interprets the taboos as "acting as if she were already widowed" (1922: 560), but many of the specifics (such as the firmly bound hair) in fact contradict the taboos of mourning.

I would argue instead that the wife provided an anchoring function to bal-

A raiding party was made up of able-bodied men among the deceased's immediate kin, and a number of hired warriors who would be paid with livestock (*tapo*, "bloodwealth") for casualties they suffered in the course of the attack. These hired warriors would include debtors and people who were economically dependent on an important family, who might use their fierceness in battle to secure their freedom from economic obligations. Raiders could earn horses and buffalo on the warpath to pay bridewealth, and a particularly successful warrior could be rewarded with the ritual honor of his own *katoda*, or "skull tree"—planted in his village from a sapling cut off the trunk of an established katoda. Warfare offered possibilities for social advancement, both in economic rewards and in political influence. A Kodi proverb says, "A fierce youth becomes a wise old man": a successful warrior was considered to have earned a position of social importance and respect.

In East Sumba, the social relations of headhunting were quite different. War leaders commanded forces made up largely of slaves and subordinates, but only hereditary slaves (*ata mema*) were taken on raids to neighboring hostile territories. Several sources say that most of the killing was actually done of slaves by other slaves (Roos 1872: 10; Kruyt 1922: 563). Only a nobleman would dare to confront another nobleman in combat, and there could be no crossing of class barriers. Kapita argues that this was true because "death at the hands of an equal was a dishonor, and would commit one's clan brothers to seek revenge, but dying at the hands of an inferior would be such a great dishonor that the man's ghost and all of his descendants would be cursed" (1976: 170). Only the heads of great warriors (Indonesian *pahlawan*, "heroes")

---

ance the dangerous mobility of her husband. Silent, passive, and contained within the house, she was the counterpart of the wandering warrior, playing a ritual role directly comparable to that of the *rato marapu* or priest, who also stays home, confined within the village, and makes offerings of chickens to pray for the safe return of the war party. Kruyt notes that the "dignified authority" of the priest made him unsuitable as a warrior, since his spiritual power was of a different sort (1922: 562). His stillness empowered the headhunter's aggressive energy; his silence was not broken until the screams and cries when the victorious party reentered the village. Between husband and wife a smaller version of the complementary relations of the warlord (*rato katoda*) and priest (*rato marapu*) were played out, so her dutiful fulfillment of these taboos offered him invisible protection and comfort.

were taken and brought back to the village for an elaborate ritual welcome. Other victims, Kapita implies, were simply left on the battlefield as unworthy (1976: 170). Warfare in East Sumba was a tournament between noble warriors, who led their troops into battle but often stayed at a distance from the combat between their dependents, allowing them to suffer the heaviest losses.

Welcoming the Head and Processing the Skull and Scalp

When a successful raiding party returned to the village, the severed head was displayed as a trophy of victory. In the eastern domains (Kambera, Lewa, and Lakoka, but also Anakalang), the head was cleaned of its flesh and "beautified" before being brought into the village, so that it appeared "pure" and "noble." In western domains (Kodi, Weyewa, Wanokaka, and Lamboya), it was carried in raw and bloody, providing a gruesome spectacle for the victory dances.

All over the island, the head had to be "cooked" or "processed" before it was placed on the skull tree. The soft flesh might be cut off and buried outside of the village, or the whole head could be given a preliminary burial (in Napu, Bokobokat, Weyewa, and Laura) until the fleshy parts had dissolved. In Kambera and Lewa, the head was smoked outside of the village, on a fire prepared above the spot where the flesh, brains, and skin had been buried. In Kodi, Wonokaka, and Lamboya (West Sumba), it was boiled in a special pot until it was "clean," then the skull was removed and the contents of the pot thrown outside the village gates, to the west, "to go down with the setting sun" (Kruyt 1922: 562).

The Sumbanese assert in several ways that they "almost ate their enemies," although symbolic cannibalism was not fully realized (Bloch 1985). In Lewa, once the head was smoked on the fire, the returning warriors roasted pieces of pork for themselves and said, "We are eating human flesh" (Kruyt 1922: 560). In Lakoka, pieces of human flesh were cut off and cooked in an earthenware pot with pork, and then the pot, complete with its contents, was buried in the ground (Kruyt 1922: 562). In Anakalang, the victim's liver was roasted and warriors would pretend to consume it, shouting out "Sweet, sweet!" as they feinted to the mouth and tossed it over their shoulders (Keane 1990: 108). Prayers recited by departing warriors in Kodi and Wanokaka spoke of their hunger for human flesh and their thirst for enemy blood, but once the warriors actually killed a victim, they had to avoid contact with the body.

Such ritual measures betray both an attraction and a revulsion toward the idea of eating one's opponents. Domains at war with each other described their enemies as "eaters of human flesh," although the expression should be interpreted as rhetoric, not reality.[3] Only witches (*tou marango*) on Sumba are believed really to consume human flesh, an ignoble act that no noble warrior would commit. In practice, the headhunter's magical power depended on separating the glory of killing from the contagious impurity of death. The dry, durable parts of the head—the skull and hair—were considered beneficial, whereas the damp, perishable ones—the skin, flesh, and blood—were all extremely dangerous. If the blood from a severed head splattered onto a headhunter in Lewa, he could have no more luck in battle. Contaminated by contact with his victim, he would refuse to take part, saying metaphorically, "I have eaten human flesh" (Kruyt 1922: 561).

In Kodi, the pot and dipper used to boil the head and separate the flesh from the skull could have no other use. They were stored in the loft of the house with other ritual objects and never allowed to come in contact with ordinary cooking vessels. When a death went unavenged for a long time, the skull tree would start to steam with anger, and the pot and dipper would become "hot" to the touch. A diviner would be called to question all the head-processing implements, and, speaking for them in his own voice, would present the need for revenge through the idiom of the hunger of the dipper and pot:

My thirst is not yet quenched,	Njana maghano pango a koko nggu
says the dipper that is never satisfied.	wena a kaco inja magholi
My belly is not yet full,	njana mbanu pango a koko nggu

[3] Symbolic cannibalism is also a common feature of accounts of human sacrifice (Kruyt 1922: 542; Keane 1990: 108; Geinaert-Martin 1987: 114). In Kodi, the liver was the focus of most attention, but in Laboya it seems to have been the brain. Human sacrifice is often reported to have been organized between domains that were once enemies but are now at peace (such as Weyewa and Anakalang or Lauli and Wanokaka; Kruyt 1922: 540–43), and may have replaced hostilities through an exchange of war captives or slaves for sacrifice.

says the pot that is never satiated.	*wena a kamela inja mbanu*
So sound the war cry	*maka pala wungo*
at the base of the skull tree	*ela kere katoda*
steaming in the stone circle	*wyuhuka kalele*
boiling at the skull offering post.	*nyawako katoda*
The cut throats must be avenged.	*tana koko ngole helu*
The limbs must twist in anger.	*tana kalengga langa mbani.*

Verifying the message, the diviner sacrificed a chicken to " raise up the warriors" (*manu kede*) and prepare them for combat, then read its entrails to determine the best time to attack. A story is told of a man in the skull tree house who wanted to curse a rival, and served him a meal of rice cooked in the pot once used for human heads. Just the faintest trace of human flesh remained, but it was enough to pollute the bodies of the man and his descendants. Their internal organs rebelled against the substance, and they were infected with a deep, painful cough. To this day, tuberculosis (known in Kodi as "deep cough," *tengge mandattu*, and said to express a reluctance to eat or swallow certain foods) is said to be passed from father to son among the descendants of this man.

The skulls of human victims were kept in both East and West Sumba as the ancestral treasure of particular houses. In the east, they were hung from the skull tree for the period of hostilities, then buried in the ground when peace was established (Kruyt 1922: 567). In the west, some skulls were returned to the victim's family through elaborate negotiations (Hoskins 1989), but the hair was kept and used in the magical preparations for revenge. In Lamboya, the scalp was take home by the person who killed the enemy, and shared with one or two others, who helped carry the head in the procession around the village. In Wanokaka, it became the possession of the house that had lost a member to the enemy, "replacing" the person whose death the head avenged. In Weyewa, it was tied to a sacred spear, used in divination and as an object of spiritual power (Kruyt 1922: 564–65). The Kodinese called the scalp "the head's leaves" (*rouna kataku*) and hung it in the house, beside the fresh sheaves of paddy and ears of corn brought as harvest offerings.

Both men and women on Sumba traditionally wore their hair bound up in a bun. Men loosened their long hair only to go to battle, and the women loosened theirs only for the period of

Illus. 3. Human skulls stored in a Kodi ancestral village come from victims in the Weyewa highlands. These skulls were unearthed and displayed when the headhunting house was rebuilt in 1980. More feasts and dances followed to commemorate a violent and glorious past. Photograph by Janet Hoskins, 1980.

mourning. Contemporary Sumbanese told me that the long-haired warrior was particularly terrifying because he presented his opponent with an image of himself as a potential victim: "This is how your own leaves [that is, hair] will look hanging on our tree!" was a taunt shouted by raiding parties across the battle lines.

In the more hierarchical societies of East Sumba, ritual treatment of the skulls and hair underscored the temporary ascendancy of a noble lord who had conquered new territory. In the west, it documented the achievement of revenge and the settling of scores between regions. Pushing the analysis a bit further, I argue that in East Sumba, the head represented the idea of sovereignty, the lord as "head" of the domain, one who encompassed and subordinated all others. The blood and flesh graphically represented the conditions of the head's acquisition, the violent taking of human life. Out of deference to the idea of nobility based on bloody conquest, the severed head was "beautified," smoked and darkened until it resembled an ancestral statue stored high in the attic of a traditional house.

In West Sumba, on the other hand, the head represented opposition—the enemy presence as a stimulus to group unity and resistance. It was displayed as stinking and disgusting, and ritually prepared only after the crowd had celebrated its humiliating defeat. The "ideology of vendetta" kept the attackers and defenders at the same level, but insisted on their difference. The "ideology of encompassment" allowed the victor to draw the vanquished across the border and incorporate him as a subject in a new political entity.

Metaphors linking headhunting to collecting the harvest or killing wild animals were common in both regions, but each gave it a different spin. In the east, the enemy was "domesticated" before being brought into the village, and reference to a cannibalistic desire for human flesh occurred only outside the gates. In the west, the memory of murdered ancestors heated the cooking implements in the skull tree house and made them ask for new victims. Hostility was brought inside and the enemy destroyed again as he boiled in the pot.

Peace Covenants, Ransom, and Political Boundaries

Differences in styles of warfare in the eastern and western parts of the island suggest that the more hierarchical eastern groups were concerned with control over land, whereas feuding and warfare in the west mainly concerned control over people. In East Sumba, the conquest of the few coastal areas where wet rice could be planted offered a great advantage to the victor. The conqueror gained control not only of rice fields, but also of vast grasslands used as pastures for his herds of livestock, because horses and buffalo need access to water and could be tended by a few loyal servants or slaves. Territorial conquest also brought human resources: hereditary slaves were attached to ancestral houses and so became the property of the victor.

In West Sumba, by contrast, there were few hereditary slaves, and greater rainfall meant that at the turn of the century good garden land was still available in abundance. Instead, there was a shortage of people to work the land, and of pigs, horses, and buffalo to raise on it. Stealing livestock was a prime motivation for raiding a neighboring region, as was capturing slaves to keep or sell to Endehnese pirates, who operated along the northern coast. War captives were described as "the feet of wild pigs, paddy gathered on horseback" (*wisi wawi ruta, pare pa mandara*: Versluys 1941: 448) and were a form of portable wealth that could be exchanged for metal weapons, imported cloth, gold coins, and even firearms (Needham 1983). Because almost everything of value could be carried away by its conquerors, a village was generally burned and left behind by a victorious war party. Power and wealth were expressed in followers rather than in control of territory, a state of affairs widespread in Southeast Asia before colonial domination (Reid 1988: 120).

These differences show up in the historical sources when we note the absence of peace covenants in the west (where there was little conquest of territory) and their elaboration in the east. Ransom payments, on the other hand, are thoroughly developed in the west, where prisoners were exchanged for wealth. Both peace covenants and ransom payments follow ritual procedures that closely parallel those of marriage, which helps explain why headhunting rhetoric now surfaces in alliance negotiations.

The people of West Sumba describe the enmity between domains as timeless, an opposition that came before history and could never be mediated or resolved. People who did not share a common language or ancestor were "strangers" (*tou heka*), and the cycle of revenge killings between traditional enemies was compared by the West Sumbanese to the slow-burning coals of ironwood and tamarind trees (*api kyomi, api kyaha*), which are never extinguished. In contrast, feuding between people related by descent or marriage was said to be intense but short-lived, like the flames in tall grass or bushes (*api ngingyo, api kahumbu*), which flare up fiercely but just as quickly burn out. The societies of West Sumba have few peace-making rituals, since the territories themselves were said to be "at odds" with each other.

In contrast, in East Sumba, there are several types of peace covenant. The boundaries of headhunting were not marked by linguistic differences, so they had to be ritually marked through a ceremony to erect the skull tree and consecrate it (*pahandango andangu*), naming the enemy whose heads would hang there. When peace was negotiated, the tree was ceremonially uprooted (*butuhu andangu*) and tribute paid to the victors as arms and magical potions were surrendered. Prayers and sacrifices were offered to ask forgiveness of those whose heads once hung there (Kapita 1976: 170).

A second form of peace covenant, called "breaking the bamboo spike" (*pata kanjora*), was performed to end feuding between more closely related groups. Bamboo spears from both sides were shattered and buried together, after a rite to call back the curses exchanged and ask for blessings and cooperation from all who had died in the hostilities (Kapita 1976: 170). An influential man from an area not involved in the hostilities was called in to serve as a go-between. He approached the other side with a gift of cloth and a request for peace. If the other side was willing to negotiate, the man was given betel nut and gold ear pendants (*mamoli*) as a sign of goodwill. Formal meetings between the two sides, using neutral intermediaries, were then arranged. As a sign that an agreement had been reached, it was customary in the east for the victor to present a slave girl to the defeated group, calling her a "replacement for those who have decayed and been lost" (*hilu na na mamohu na mamili*). In return, the vanquished gave the victor a large number of gold valuables. The girl could not be killed or abused, and was expected to marry another slave in the house of the defeated group and bear children for her new masters (Kruyt 1922: 567).

Similarities between a peace covenant and a marriage negotiation were almost exact. Intermediaries were used, a gift of cloth was presented from the bride's side that was answered with a gift of gold, and a woman was transferred. Most important, the victor assumed the superiority of the wife-giver, and placed the defeated group in the subordinate position of wife-takers. After this ceremony was performed, it was assumed that the two groups had friendly relations and could intermarry. The switch from enemy to affine was accomplished by a subtle shift in the proportions of goods exchanged, which opened the way for future, more balanced alliance exchanges.

Similar negotiations were conducted to ransom prisoners (*mai kyahuko*), especially women of noble rank. My informants told me that ransom existed before pacification, but it became increasingly common in the 1920s and 1930s, when the *pax nederlandica* made it safe to travel from one domain to another. The terms were worked out between neutral intermediaries, and involved payments in livestock and gold commensurate with the prisoner's rank. Ransom payments move people back across political boundaries and show the competitive but negotiable political climate of relations between domains in West Sumba. The peace covenants of the east show, on the contrary, a tendency for some territories to absorb others or place them in a relationship of tribute or dependency, as well as to realign boundaries after the victory of a great lord.

The raja of Lewa, for instance, claimed a hereditary right to control the domain of Kambera as well. Since the noble families of East Sumba are closely related, there was some genealogical basis for his claim, and it was backed up by a military conquest of most of the region. In order to keep a firm hand on the newly acquired territory, the raja moved his residence to Kawangu, Kambera, and built a "false skull tree" there. By rights, he could only dedicate captured heads in his own ancestral village in Lewa. But he set up a stick with a coconut shell on top of it as a sign that he could defend the boundaries of his second domain. If his warriors captured a head, they could bring it to his residence and hold a feast to welcome it there, and afterward it would be carried 60 kilometers to his own ancestral village (Kruyt 1922: 566). The raja's military headquarters were shifted to the territory that he had usurped, and in turn-of-the-century Sumba there was no one strong enough to push him back across the boundary into his own home.

When the raja of Lewa seized control of Kambera, he also laid claim to the whole population of royal dependents. He was able to legitimate his claim by pointing out that he shared some ancestry with the former royal family, he owned their treasure of heirloom valuables, and his military success demonstrated superior powers. This pattern of action was not uncommon in Sumba of the late nineteenth century (Couvreur 1917: 208).

Headhunting and Inequality

Historical differences between the political systems associated with headhunting in the east and west still cast long shadows on present practices. In the east, headhunting was used by powerful rulers to enlarge their own territories, and external agents were sucked into power struggles between expansionist war lords. In the west, headhunting remained primarily a way of defending the integrity of the traditional domain, and external agents were pushed back by the local population.[4] In the east, headhunting was tied to the generation of inequality, since violence between domains was the raw form in which hierarchical differences were imposed. In the west, headhunting came to represent an ideal of equality and parity between foes, which used the language of warfare (and later alliance) to express rivalry and a dialectic of challenge and riposte.

Sumbanese are aware of these ideological differences, and articulate them in two myths about the origin of headhunting, one collected by Kruyt in East Sumba (1922: 520), another by Keane in

[4] In the east, the Makassarese-Endehnese pirates were hired as mercenaries to fight for the local rulers, sending troops and ships to help the raja of Kapunduk attack the mountain people of the interior (Needham 1983: 27). They also joined in feuds between Bolo Bokat and Tabundung. Umbu Tunggu of Lewa employed the largest number of Endehnese soldiers, paying them with slaves and plunder. Their virtual monopoly on gunpowder and muskets kept him in power, allowing him to defy Dutch colonial officers at many points (Needham 1983: 33). In the west, the Endehnese were not able to find such powerful rulers, so they formed marauding bands that plundered on their own account, took captives, and sold them overland into Central and East Sumba to work the land. But the Muslim raiders could not establish territorial strongholds in the western districts because of the extent of the popular resistance that they encountered. One retreating mercenary told the Dutch controleur that the people of West Sumba had "bodies which could not be pierced" (Couvreur 1917: 213), because of the superior magic of their "secluded priests" (*ratu sepi*), whose position had not been overshadowed by that of a conquering warlord (Couvreur 1917: 215). I suggest that the more hierarchical political order in the east made the population more docile, subordinated to the power of a few leaders, whereas the "democratic" peoples of the west continued to tap spiritual resources that gave them a military advantage over invading forces.

the western domain of Anakalang (1990: 104–5). The East Sumbanese myth takes place before the people knew the rules for marrying properly, burying the dead, or growing wet rice. A brother
marries his sister and impregnates her, but their child is born
dead, and she dies soon after. He tries to bury her quietly, but huge
thunder and rains express heavenly disapproval. A culture hero
goes up to the great lord of the heavens and is told to dig up the
woman's body and feel her side. Rice seeds fall out, and the hero
plants them. In order to help the rice grow, he is first told to decorate her grave with the heads of field mice, sparrows, a horse, and
buffalo, but the altar is still not "beautiful." He substitutes a
monkey head, and it improves. Finally, he kills the brother and
places his head over the grave, so that it looks out on the rice crop.
"Now, finally, I have made an altar that is beautiful," the hero de-
clares. He divides the rest of the body into two parts: the skin,
stomach, and intestines become the commoners, and the flesh and
bones the nobility.

Three categories of human being are created in the story: outsiders, whose heads may be hunted but who may also become
affines; nobles, who are the form-givers of society and control the
wet-rice fields; and commoners, who provide the labor and protect
the borders. The separation of the incestuous couple in death
highlights the need for exogamy, and the offering of a male head to
promote the fertility of the fields suggests that the complementar-
ity of male and female is expressed in an interdependence of warfare and agriculture. Though it echoes a widespread Southeast
Asian story about the origin of rice from the body of a sacrificed
woman, in this Sumbanese version her death comes as a "natural"
punishment for incest, and her brother's death provides an anti-
dote for the infraction by substituting a head for a sacrifice.

The myth presents a symbolic model of headhunting as an inversion of the reciprocity between affines: if the proper rules are
not respected, those who could be wife-givers and wife-takers become traditional enemies. The blessing of fertility, which is supposed to be given willingly by the bride's family to her husband's
fields and children, can also be extracted violently by the taking of
heads. The Sumbanese argument that revenge is necessary to restore good harvests and to allow for the reproduction of the de-

scent group has its roots in a deeper notion that alliance and enmity are alternate paths that any relationship can take.

In the obviously related West Sumbanese version, the first head taken belongs to a woman. Two daughters, Rabu Dangu the elder and Rabu Dangu the younger, lend out heirloom gongs that are not returned. When their father comes back, he beats the elder daughter to death. Her younger sister demands that the borrowers replace her head with that of their own eldest daughter. The father tries unsuccessfully to sway his remaining daughter with the heads of a chicken, a buffalo, and a monkey, but finally ambushes the borrower's daughter, kills her, and buries her. The spirits tell him that he did well to heed his daughter, but now he must dig up his victim's body, cut off her head, skin it, and hang it in the village square. The killing of a substitute suggests replacement, not retribution: "One might speculate that in taking a head, one appropriates what should have been given but was not, for example, a wife" (Keane 1990: 105). This interpretation is consistent with my view that alliance and enmity are alternative paths for relations between neighboring groups to take. Significantly, the ties to fertility and stratification are absent in this West Sumbanese version, and the logic of vendetta is given a justification.

Transformations Since Pacification

My argument that headhunting and alliance are part of the same system of ideas can be tested by looking at the transformations in the vocabulary and practice of exchange on Sumba since pacification. The strategies and rhetoric once used in warfare are now considered appropriate for the meeting of wife-givers and wife-takers from distant regions. Traditional values of fierceness, military skill, and violent conquest have had to cede to modern ones of rivalrous diplomacy, feasting, and alliance. A transfer of the flow of exchange goods from the warpath (in the form of ransom negotiations) to the alliance path becomes visible in increased interregional relationships.

The ritual format developed to welcome a severed head into the village, the ceremonial dialogue between the priest and the war leader at the gates, is now used to receive any large party from another domain. In modern times, these visitors are probably coming to attend a feast, perhaps bringing contributions of buffalo or pigs that can now be moved, by truck, between domains as distant as Kodi and Anakalang. Now that members of once-warring groups may attend school together in the regency capital of Waikabubak, and may work together in schools or government offices, exchange partnerships have developed between many prominent families. As might be predicted, the tensest alliances are those which bind people from the east to those of the west, because the easterners are afraid that their standards of hierarchical privilege will not be respected, and the westerners refuse to comply with certain restrictions they now describe as "feudalistic." Violence has not been totally removed from the scene of these encounters: in the 1980s, the prisons of Waikabubak held twenty men accused of carrying out murderous vendettas, most of them described as "concerning women" and thus playing on still-tense relations between affines.

Headhunting and Regional Resistance

Pacification in East Sumba was made difficult by problems in communication and the fierce competition among local rulers; but when enough prominent noble men were incorporated into the hierarchy of colonial administration, the subordinate population followed their lead. In the west, however, there was a sustained popular resistance to the imposition of colonial rule. Wona Kaka, a warrior from the headhunting clan of Bongu in Kodi, raided Dutch forces and killed several soldiers in 1911. His actions received the ritual sanction of Ndera Wulla, the Dutch-appointed native ruler, and soon involved the whole region in a three-year guerrilla struggle against the colonial army. Instead of seizing enemy heads, Wona Kaka's warriors seized the Dutch guns, and consecrated them in skull-tree houses as part of their magical preparations to counterattack. The Dutch captured and punished the raja, holding him accountable for the actions of his "subjects," until he died in a Dutch prison. After his death, the whole domain was united in support of the rebels, hiding them and feeding them in the interior. Ordered to leave behind their gardens and settle along the coast, the Sumbanese suffered great hunger and hardship, and hundreds of them were killed in pitched battles that took a much greater toll than several decades of intermittent headhunting had. Finally, in 1913, the rebel forces surrendered in return for a promise of personal safety and were sent into exile (Hoskins 1987).

The particular meaning that headhunting assumed in "history" was the legacy of Wona Kaka's defeat. The warrior leader became the "hero" of a rhetoric of local autonomy—a symbol not of despotic rule but of collective vigor and the desire to repel foreign invaders. Headhunting became a contested tradition, a proving ground for ideological control of the past. The idiom of enmity remained in ritual commemorations of this earlier era, but their content now addressed peaceful rivalry rather than military confrontation.

A man in one of the headhunting villages of Kodi explained how efforts to give Wona Kaka the status of a "hero of anticolonial struggle" have affected the prestige of warrior clans in the region:

Because of Wona Kaka, everyone in Sumba knows how we fought against the Dutch, how our first raja died in a Dutch prison because we refused to accept colonial domination. They want to tell us to do this or that, but we won't be led around by the nose like a herd of water buffalo. The blood of our ancestors was hot, and ours is as well. So it is good to keep these memories alive.

In my village, we have not used the skull tree in two generations. But it still stands in the center of the dancing field, and we "feed" it with rice and meat at our feasts. It cannot start smoking and steaming again because headhunting is now forbidden, but it can remind our enemies of what we are capable of.

The skull tree in East Sumba is interpreted today as an insignia of noble rank (*tanda kebangsawanan*), since it represents the privilege of a few to command many in regional wars. The skull tree in West Sumba, on the contrary, is a popular rallying point and represents resistance to external domination.

But what constitutes an "external force" is a question of the greatest political significance. Kodi oral traditions speak of Wona Kaka as fighting against the "heavy hand of the foreign mother and stranger father" (*inya dawa, bapa dimya*), which in 1911 referred to the Dutch colonial forces. For this reason, there have been efforts to glorify him and his men as heroes in a nationalist struggle against what is often described as "350 years" of colonial domination. Beyond the anachronistic appropriation of a chronology taken from Javanese history into the outer islands, we can also note that the term "foreign mòther and stranger father" is now most often used to refer to the Indonesian government and its representatives who rule from Java or the provincial capital on Timor. Thus, if Wona Kaka was a defender of "village democracy" who opposed subservience to any power from outside the island, his struggle should continue even after Indonesian independence. This is, in fact, the threat that is largely implicit in the brave rhetoric of the present-day leaders of headhunting clans.

Wona Kaka's own descendants see him as a figure in their "heritage," the line of continuity that makes his raid on the Dutch part of a pattern of vengeance killings carried out by his ancestors on anyone who dared to invade their territory. National officials who now honor him want to give him a place in national "history," as the unique initiator of an anticolonial resistance struggle. His descendants insist that they owe him the ritual duty of reburial, and have suggested that the government help pay for such a ceremony. But the plans to place Wona Kaka among the ranks of "national heroes" (*pahlawan nasional*) are charged with ambivalence on both sides.

In effect, the values of history and heritage are forced into direct competition. The officials from Jakarta want to bring Sumbanese history into the history of anticolonialist struggle, which occurred all over the archipelago. The local community in Kodi wants to keep Wona Kaka attached, performing a rite to call his soul back from Java and build him a grave in his ancestral village of Bongu. Their heritage of resistance against outside domination would be lost if Wona Kaka were separated from the land of his ancestors and made a fully "historical" figure. It would mean that the old age of glory was gone forever. Efforts to construct a memorial to Wona Kaka have been paralyzed by the tension between these two contrasting interpretations of the past.[5]

Heads of Enemies and Heads of State

Headhunting rites are no longer practiced in their original form, but the descendants of those villages associated with warfare have maintained certain rules about the performance of the dance of the skull tree (*nenggo katoda*), considered the most elaborate and

[5] Further discussion of these issues can be found in my book, *The Play of Time* (1993).

elegant of Kodi dances. They will not allow their daughters to perform this dance at local feasts, arguing that it can only be done to acknowledge the presence of "outside guests." A recent visit of the regent (*bupati*) was considered a fitting occasion for the dance. Elders of the villages of Bongu, Ratenggaro, and Bondo Kodi helped bring together several dozen dancers to perform a spectacle staged not beside the skull tree but in front of the district office. But the occasion provoked some ironic commentaries from spectators less sympathetic to government aims in the recent electoral campaign. One commented to me in Indonesian: "Earlier, this was the way we welcomed enemy heads, now it is done for the heads of the region" (*Dulu sembut kepala musuh, sekarang kepala daerah*). His words make us question the "honor" that was really being presented. Did the dance represent the regent, as a powerful but hostile force whose presence was not really so welcome? Was the regent, coming from another island, aware of the ambiguous significance of the gesture? What cultural role does the category of "outsider" play in its new extensions?

Headhunting dances mark a boundary that is ambivalently charged. A people's sense of cultural identity is often defined by its relation to hostile outsiders. This was certainly the case when "Kodi culture" became distinct from that of neighboring domains, and heads were taken across borders. It is still the case when the "Other" becomes the distant government, which tries to control the domain. One of the aims of nationalist rhetoric was to shift the boundaries, making the Dutch "the outsiders" and all Indonesians, united in anticolonial struggle, comrades in arms. This aim has been only partially achieved, and there is often local resistance or uneasiness about joining the "imagined community" of the new nation-state.

Today, the descendants of headhunters make predatory raids upon the past to conquer a new goal: an ideal of local self-determination and self-respect. They do not oppose all governmental control; rather, they assert their right to challenge the authority of external rulers. They raise their children to defend the land of their origin and to revere the heritage of their ancestors, who once defended the land with violence. Kodi babies are lulled to sleep with verses that invoke the bloodthirsty deeds of their fathers and grandfathers, and even repeat the characteristic call (*ghogha*,

Illus. 4. Male dancers use the buffalo-hide shields and spears that were part of the headhunter's ritual costume. They mime his terrifying demeanor and lunge in simulated attacks against a line of female dancers. Photograph by Laura Whitney, 1988.

Illus. 5. Female dancers, decorated with gold jewelry and heirloom beads, offer passive resistance to the male dancers, just as the wife of a head-hunter must observe taboos of passivity and inactivity that protect her husband on the warpath. Photograph by Laura Whitney, 1988.

ghogha) of the victorious raiding party when it returned to a village with a severed head.

Sumbanese polities had diverse and shifting boundaries already in the nineteenth century, when they first began sustained interactions with European outsiders. Headhunting served as a "category marker" for a particular kind of distance and enmity that evoked the institutions of raiding, slavetaking, ransom payments, and a barrier to intermarriage. Pacification put an end to violent exchanges of life between domains, and created the conditions for marriage alliances between domains, exchanging women instead of heads. As the system of rules defining hostilities shifted from the borders of the domain to wider categories such as "all Sumbanese," or even "all Indonesians," certain slippages occurred, because there could no longer be the same sense of moral community within these units. The defense of ancestral lands against foreign interference thus assumed a new meaning.

History and Heritage: Ideological Transformations

We can now return to the distinction we established between "history" and "heritage" to see how these materials on the contrasting traditions in East and West Sumba represent different visions of the past. The convention that foreign visitors are welcomed with dramatic dances and song is found all over Indonesia. Its popularity, I would argue, assumes the existence of a "historical" consciousness that separates past and present, seeing each as made of distinct, nonrepetitive events. In East Sumba, where headhunting had been associated with the generation of inequality and the conquering of new territories, the practice is now "history" in a fairly unequivocal fashion. No one expects a revival of bloody raids between regions, and many of the hierarchical differences once represented in warfare are now represented in other ways—through differences in education, government office, and so on.[6] In West Sumba, however, the interests of local autonomy

---

[6] This does not mean, however, that the people in power have changed. On the contrary, in most of East Sumba those noble families who established their power at the end of the nineteenth century through warfare are still quite powerful. The Dutch colonial system of indirect rule through "self-governing territories" (*zelfbesturne landschap*) bolstered the importance of the reigning warlords and gave them more permanent positions in peace time. Present-day regents (*bupati*) and district officers (*camat*) are almost without exception de-

that were defended by headhunters are still in need of defense, so the headhunting dance performed to welcome the regent is still charged with much more ambivalence. Since the people of Kodi (like many others in the west) used to insult and humiliate their captured heads, the display could even be interpreted as an indirect challenge to the authority of the head of local government.

The heritage of headhunting asserts that such enmities are not things of the past, but are still relevant to present concerns. Now that former opponents within Sumba are likely to become in-laws, the agonistic character of alliance negotiations maintains the tensions of an earlier era, but resolves them differently. The heritage of headhunting uses its rhetoric to raid the past for an imagery of fearless confrontations and enduring loyalties to traditional lands. These confrontations can now concern issues of local autonomy, and the preservation of tradition against the encroachments of church and state. New battles are still being fought, although not with the same weapons or in the same terms.

Acknowledgments

This paper was presented to audiences at Princeton University and the University of Bergen, Norway. I am particularly grateful to Valerio Valeri for providing me with helpful comments during the early stages of its composition, and also to Ken George, Hildred Geertz, Clifford Geertz, Signe Howell, Olaf Smedal, and Henning Siverts.

References

Adams, Marie Jeanne
    1969 *System and Meaning in East Sumba Textile Design: A Study in Traditional Indonesian Art.* Cultural Report no. 16. New Haven: Yale University Southeast Asian Series.
Bloch, Maurice
    1985 "Almost Eating the Ancestors." *Man* 20: 631–46.

---

scendants of the warring *rajas* from the end of the nineteenth century. Now, however, they no longer need to incorporate enemy heads to enhance their importance ritually, because other rituals—those of the Indonesian state—are available.

Couvreur, A. C.
1917 "Aard en Wezen der Inlandsche Zelfbesturen op het Eiland Soemba." *Tijdschrift an het Binnenlands Nestuur* 52: 206–19.

De Josselin de Jong, J. P. B.
1937 *Studies on Indonesian Culture.* Vol. 1, *Orata: A Timorese Settlement on Kisar.* Amsterdam: Foris.

De Roo van Alderwerelt, J.
1906 "Historische aanteekeningen over Soemba." *Tijdshrift voor indische Taal-, Land-, en Volkenkunde* 48: 185–316.

Downs, R. E.
1955 "Headhunting in Indonesia." *Bijdragen tot de Taal-, Land-, en Volkenkunde* 111: 40–70.

Forth, Gregory
1981 *Rindi: An Ethnographic Study of a Traditional Domain in Eastern Sumba.* The Hague: Martinus Nijhoff.

Geinaert-Martin, Danielle
1987 "Hunt Pig and Grow Rice: On Food Exchanges and Values in Laboya, West Sumba (Eastern Indonesia)." In J. P. B. de Josselyn de Jong, ed., *The Leiden Tradition in Structural Anthropology.* London: Brill.

George, Kenneth
1991 "Headhunting, History, and Exchange in Upland Sulawesi." *Journal of Asian Studies* 80 (3): 536–54.

Hoskins, Janet
1987 "The Headhunter as Hero: Local Traditions and Their Reinterpretation in National History." *American Ethnologist* 14 (4): 605–22.

1989 "On Losing and Getting a Head: Warfare, Exchange and Alliance in a Changing Sumba, 1888–1988." *American Ethnologist* 16 (3): 419–40.

1993 *The Play of Time: Kodi Perspectives on Calendars, History and Exchange.* Berkeley: University of California Press.

Kapita, Oembu Hina
1976 *Sumba dalam Jangkauan Jaman.* Waingapu: Gereja Kristen Sumba.

Keane, Edward Webb
1990 "The Social Life of Representation in Anakalang." Ph.D. diss., University of Chicago.

Kruyt, Albert C.
1906 *Het Animisme in den Indischen Archipel.* The Hague: Martinus Nijhoff.

1922 "De Soembaneezen." *Bijdragen tot de Taal-, Land-, en Volkenkunde* 78: 466–608.

McKinley, Robert J.
   1976 "Human and Proud of It! A Structural Treatment of Headhunting
      Rites and the Social Definition of Enemies." In G. N. Appell, ed.,
      Studies in Borneo Societies, pp. 92–126. DeKalb, Ill.: Center for
      Southeast Asian Studies, Northern Illinois University.
Needham, Rodney
   1983 *Sumba and the Slave Trade*. Center of Southeast Asian Studies,
      Working Paper no. 31. Melbourne: Monash University.
Reid, Anthony
   1988 *Southeast Asia in the Age of Commerce, 1450–1680*. Vol. 1, *The
      Lands Below the Winds*. New Haven: Yale University Press.
Roos, Samuel
   1872 "Bijdrage tot de kennis an taal-, land- en volk op het eiland
      Soemba." *Verhendelingen van het Bataviaasch Genootschap van
      Kunsten en Wetenschappen* 36: 1–125.
Rosaldo, Michelle
   1980 *Knowledge and Passion*. Cambridge: Cambridge University
      Press.
Rosaldo, Renato
   1980 *Ilongot Headhunting, 1883–1974: A Study in Society and His-
      tory*. Stanford: Stanford University Press.
   1989 "Grief and the Headhunter's Rage." In R. Rosaldo, *Culture and
      Truth: The Remaking of Social Analysis*. Boston: Beacon Press.
Ten Kate, H.
   1894 "Versalg eener Reis en de Timorgroep en Polynesie." *Tijdshrift
      van het Koninklijk Nederlandsche Aardrijkskundig Genootschap*
      11: 194–246.
Versluys, J. I. N.
   1941 "Aanteekeningen omtrent Geld en Goedenverkeer in West
      Soemba." *Koloniale Studien* (Oct.): 433–82.
Wijngaarden, J.
   1893 "Naar Soemba: Dagboekn, Verslagen en Brieven uit de Zending."
      Mededeelingen van het Nederlandsch Zendelinggenootschap 37:
      352–76.
   1894 "Een dooden feest op Soemba." *Indische Gids* 1: 461–63.

Peter Metcalf

Images of Headhunting

"Wittgenstein contends that the very idea of
explaining a practice . . . is a mistake."
—Rodney Needham

Headhunting is a topic that has always attracted
popular attention. For Borneo as for no other part of the world, its
potential for sensationalism has been exploited by travel writers
ranging from the serious to the downright spurious. The common
reader, picking up a book written by professional anthropologists,
might reasonably expect to find something a little more penetrat-
ing, an intelligible explanation of what headhunting is all about.
The common reader is liable to be disappointed.

What concerns me here is why that is so, what special diffi-
culties there are in dealing with this topic. There is, of course, a
currently influential postmodernist position that disavows the
goal of explanation in the social sciences generally (Rosenau 1992:
8). The intractability of the topic preceded this change in intellectual fashions, however; even when less-squeamish paradigms
were dominant, our efforts to account for headhunting were singularly unconvincing.

There is no lack of indigenous explanations recorded in the literature. Severed heads are efficacious, we are told, in making the
crops grow, or securing the foundations of buildings. They establish the virility of young men, or symbolize the subjugation of enemies. In Papua, people were reportedly slaughtered in order to
steal their names along with their heads (Wirz 1922). But where
anthropological approaches have been more successful, it is characteristic that they have gone further than a mere repetition of local rationales, or debates about which of them is the true one. In
the discussion of headhunting, the indigenous rationales themselves have tended to be the focus, and that shows how far we
have to go.

To a large extent, explanation in anthropology is a process of contextualization; a particular belief or practice is seen to make sense as part of a constellation of associated beliefs and practices. But headhunting seems to confound us at the outset, because the appropriate context is often unclear or shifting. How can we contextualize a practice given credence by neighboring peoples of very different cultural backgrounds? Just whose associated beliefs and practices are then relevant, and why is this especially a problem with headhunting?

These are the issues that this essay addresses. They were posed by fieldwork experiences in northwestern Borneo, in the ethnically complex hinterland of the ancient sultanate of Brunei. Living in a Berawan longhouse where traditional religious practices persisted despite widespread conversion to Christianity in the region, I picked up echoes of headhunting coming from different directions. They seemed to emanate from different sources, so that my perceptions became confused.

To sort out these perceptions, I distinguish several different contexts. I begin narrowly, with the community in which I worked. Then I broaden my view, first to a culture area comprising much of central northern Borneo, and finally to the whole island, and beyond. In the process, I reflect on the apparent failures of a mode of interpretation that has become standard in ethnography, and that is sometimes dignified with the altogether too positivistic-sounding label of ritual analysis. I conclude by reaffirming its value, but not before setting out other positions, and my argument is consequently a little complicated, as befits the topic.

A feature of the argument that I find interesting is that having begun above with a structuralist move—the search for meanings beyond indigenous rationales—I end with a poststructuralist notion of multiplex images. This progression, arrived at in working through my ethnographic material, bears out what colleagues in Paris have often remarked: that where American scholars have set a gulf between structuralist and poststructuralist approaches, there is in fact a continuity of ideas.

I speak of "echoes" because headhunting no longer occurs in northwestern Borneo, at least not to my knowledge. Its suppression began at the turn of the century, and indeed provided one justification for colonial annexation. When Alfred Cort Haddon traveled through the area in 1898, on his way home from the famous Torres Straits expedition, the process of "pacification" was nearing completion. Nevertheless, the evidence of former breaches of the peace was clearly to be seen. In his popular account of his travels (1901), Haddon describes his visit to the same communities in which I worked 80 years later. He was struck by the size of the massive communal houses, their floors raised fifteen feet above the ground, and their populations in the hundreds. At Long Teru, he dwells on the human skulls hanging from the rafters "fastened to a circular framework looking something like a ghastly parody on the glass chandeliers of our young days" (1901: 322).

By the mid-1970s, the "chandeliers" were gone. The Berawan of Long Teru lost their stock of skulls in 1956, in a disastrous fire that consumed the entire longhouse. It was an incident that was often recalled, and the poor woman, now elderly, whose kitchen fire started the blaze has never been allowed to forget it. But oddly enough, the loss of the skulls was not lamented. Though it was claimed that the heads had the potential to bring benefits to the community, the service of them was considered onerous. The heads had to be "fed," so it was said, with small offerings, and kept warm with a fire that never went out. Women had to avoid that part of the longhouse veranda, or pass by in a crouched position. Any contact with heads was dreaded, so that only old men, weary of life, would dare move them, whenever the house needed rebuilding.

Moreover, there were those at Long Teru who believed that the skulls lost in the fire were probably too old to convey much benefit, while at the same they retained their quirky power to harm. I do not know just how old the incinerated heads were. I heard stories of killings in the years between the world wars, but details of who and when were not forthcoming. Certainly by the 1950s, all of these heads were decades old. Unlike some other upriver folk, the Berawan did not take advantage of the opportunity to take fresh heads from the Japanese as they were harried by Allied forces in 1946. In the postwar years, the social climate had evidently changed sufficiently that, after the fire, there was no thought at Long Teru of obtaining new heads for the new house.

Nevertheless, the majority of people at Long Teru persisted in their old religion, which is to say they did not convert to any of the new faiths sweeping through the Baram watershed, neither one of the brands of Christianity rapidly making converts in up-river communities, nor the indigenous revival cult called Bungan that tried to compete by eliminating many of the complex obser-vances of the old way, including those of the heads. Staunchly re-jecting apostasy, the community persevered with its headless head rites.

The principal context for these anomalous events was the elab-orate mortuary rituals that I have described in detail elsewhere (1982), rituals that lasted months or years and included secondary treatment of the dead. Consequently, I tried to account for the headhunting rites I witnessed in terms of the same conceptions that I saw as underlying the whole sequence. In particular, I found a pervasive motif of death engendering death, so that only the most strenuous efforts could stop its progress. Headhunting did this by a kind of lateral displacement, so that the problem became someone else's.

This characterization obviously calls for some details by way of justification, and I must pick my way carefully because I am talk-ing simultaneously about at least three epochs: the period since 1956, in which headhunting rites have occurred without heads; the preceding period, after "pacification," but while skulls were still employed; and a more distant time, when fresh heads were sometimes taken.

In recent decades, the taking of heads has appeared only mimet-ically, and it was in this form that I saw headhunting reenacted in the 1970s. Typically, a couple of older men went up and down the house well before dawn, shaking out of their sleep as many young men as they could find. If, as was often the case, a string of all-night festivities had only recently concluded, they might have trouble raising a quorum. Each man was outfitted with what-ever items of military equipment came to hand—spears, swords, shields, and perhaps a war bonnet or two—and eventually a mo-rose band paddled away upriver from the longhouse. The mood lightened, however, with the morning sky, and the soi-disant war party came ashore to look for a certain palm whose leaves (*caang*), torn into long streamers, had been used in the past to decorate

Illus. 1. In the 1970s many Berawan men of the older generation still possessed the panoply of war: short sword, spear, shield, and war bonnet. Photo by the author.

Illus. 2. Tama Jok of Long Teru, wearing a particularly fine war bonnet, decorated with beads, tufts of goat hair, and feathers of argus pheasant and hornbill. Photo by the author.

heads, both fresh ones and those grimy relics that used to hang in the rafters. Nowadays a bundle of the leaves, woven into a rough triangular shape with a ragged tail, substitutes for the head. Two or three were made, and proper form required, I was told, that they be hung up and speared by the young men. I never saw this done, but there was often horseplay and some hazing of the novices. By this time, the sun was fully up, and the party paddled back making as much noise as possible with gongs and war cries, to be met by an answering din from the longhouse.

In the 1970s, these little reenactments were tacked onto the funerals of people of standing in the community, as opposed to those of lesser status. Such grand funerals involved a week or more of exhausting celebration, half party, half ordeal, in which the community passed every night in enforced sociability, and the headhunting rites constituted their last gasp. But not so long before, the headhunting rites had had a more conspicuous role, constituting a separate phase in the mortuary sequence, a phase that, in the nature of things, could not be so neatly scheduled. In the period between the wars, in addition to whatever fresh heads may or may not have been clandestinely taken, old heads were reportedly borrowed from other communities, and this took time to arrange.

The practice of borrowing skulls was encouraged by colonial administrators, who understood the ritual need for them, even as they suppressed headhunting. The district officer primarily responsible for the "pacification" of northwestern Borneo was Charles Hose, and luckily he has left extensive memoirs. He tells us that official collections of heads were kept at "some of the remoter forts" (Hose and McDougall 1912, 2: 38n). These heads were confiscated from unruly communities and loaned out to cooperative ones. Having been utilized, a skull was recovered by the district officer on his next visit, months or years later. This little piece of re-ritualization has its farcical side; one imagines a district officer sorting through his collection for a nice head to lend to a favorite chief, and then perhaps noting the details on a file card for future reference. Note, however, the power that had been assumed by the district officer, not only to supply heads, but also, with evident impunity, to take the dread relics down out of the rafters again whenever he chose.

Prior to the 1950s, the head rites stood alone; that is, they were not tacked onto the conclusion of a funeral. They were then the occasion for a martial festival (ngaalap) in which men proceeded through a hierarchy of warrior ranks. At first participation, young men and boys, regardless of whether they had played any part in obtaining heads, won the right to wear human hair on the sheaths of their swords. At subsequent events, they added various feathers to their war caps, and finally on the fifth occasion they were entitled to pierce their upper earlobes and wear through the holes the teeth of the cloudy leopard, or facsimiles thereof. Many pigs were sacrificed over the several days of the festival, and a special edifice was erected, called belawíng, a tall column covered with the same caang leaves used to decorate skulls.

It seems clear that these were the only rites of the traditional religion that competed in scale with those of secondary treatment of the dead, but the details were already becoming hazy in peoples'

Illus. 3. After a ngaalap rite, some adult men, pleased with their participation, pose by the bundle of caang leaves representing the newly acquired heads. Blood from pigs sacrificed in the rites spatters their clothes and military equipment. Photo by the author.

memories by the 1970s. Nevertheless, ngaalap was still sometimes performed for the boys during the morning following the
mimed raid (ngacaang), and it still roused surprisingly strong passions in the older men. Pouring blood from sacrificed animals over
themselves and the initiates, and screaming war cries, they gave a
convincing display of bloodlust.

If ngaalap was optional in the one-day affair that the headhunting festival had become by the 1970s, other rites were not. The
most intriguing of these involved the erection of a stylized effigy
(ulèng),[1] hardly recognizable as such at first glance. It consisted of
a pole some ten feet long set in the ground at an acute angle, with
two short crossbars tied across it at even intervals, and made
bulky with caang-leaf streamers. Closer inspection revealed fa-
cial features simply indicated on the smoothed upper end. Moreover, the crossbars were referred to as "arms" and "legs." One of
the substitute heads, also made of caang leaves, was hung from
the end. In the rite, a young boy, usually a descendant of the dead
person, climbed up the pole grasping a chicken. He laid the chick-
en's neck across the end of the pole and, with a whoop, cut off its
head. This was the crucial act, though older men also made prayers for the welfare of the community both before and after, sometimes standing astride the ulèng effigy. Later, the chicken's head
was skewered to the top of the post.

Several times I pressed participants to explain who or what the
effigy represented. I got no direct answers; ulèng was, apparently,
indispensable and multivocal. I offer this account: Most obviously,
the effigy represented the victim of the headhunt, and the rite was
yet another reenactment, in even more terse form than the
predawn expedition. The effigy was associated with the victim because a "head" was hung on it—in former times, presumably, the
head was real. The cutting of the chicken's neck replicated the
earlier decapitation, in a form suitable for the very youngest potential warrior. However, this does not exhaust possible identifications. Heads were also hung on the tombs of the deceased villagers for whom the rites were held. (I say "hung" because corpses
were usually housed in wooden vaults raised on columns, like the
longhouse.) Consequently, the effigy might also represent the dead

---

[1] Unfortunately, I elicited no gloss for the term ulèng.

Illus. 4. An ulèng effigy being prepared. On the upper end a "face" has been carved with shallow incisions marking nose and mouth, and a woven caang leaf attached to represent the trophy of a headhunt. There are "arms" and two sets of "legs," making a kind of ladder. Photo by the author.

Illus. 5. The ulèng effigy is being festooned with caang leaves while some of the boys who are about to be initiated in the rites of ngaalap look on. A woman pours water over the putative headhunters. Photo by the author.

Illus. 6. While adult men hold up the ulèng effigy, a young boy is helped to climb it, so that he can sacrifice a chicken on its upper end. Photo by the author.

Illus. 7. The ulèng effigy has been stood up fully, and a man makes prayers in front of it holding a war bonnet. Meanwhile, a melée is beginning nearby, in which men and women smear each other with mud. Photo by the author.

person lying in the tomb, and in that regard it is significant that the ulèng cannot be knocked down or tidied up after the funeral, but must be left to rot like the corpse. In this reading, the chicken stands for the victim of the headhunt, and the child mimes an ultimate act of filial piety.

There is yet a third possibility. The effigy may be a mock victim offered to the "real" victim. By all accounts, even in bloodier times, the rite of standing up the effigy (nínung ulèng, nínung meaning "to erect"), with its little reenactment of headhunting, was performed whenever a new head was brought to the longhouse, weeks or months after the death of a senior person in the community. This is counterintuitive; one might have imagined that a fresh head made any mere playacting superfluous, but the contrary is true. Even the second death, a deliberate murder of someone quite outside the community, called forth another, if in muted form.

No doubt this prescribed mimesis made it all the easier for Berawan after "pacification" to accept the rite of ngacaang in place of former headhunting raids. But I saw in it something more significant, a further expression of themes woven into the entire mortuary sequence.

Those themes were the tendency of death to follow death, and the function of ritual in deflecting and slowing its momentum. They are correlates of broad eschatological concepts most fully expressed in the rites of secondary treatment of the dead (*nulang*). In common with many other peoples worldwide who practice such rites, the Berawan do not see death as the matter of a moment. Instead, it is a slow separation of soul and body, a process whose physical manifestation is the decay of the corpse. The spiritual transition is equally repellent; as the body sinks into corruption, so the soul begins a miserable existence, caught between the lands of the living and the dead. From its dank and lonely exile on the margins of the jungle, it looks back with mounting jealously toward those most dear in life. It is the malice of the recently dead that sets death in motion.

At nulang, the completion of this anxious transition is celebrated in a festival that is genuinely joyful, in contrast to the initial funeral at least a year earlier. The corpse is now dry bones, and the soul is correspondingly transformed into pure spirit, acceptable among the company of the incorruptible ancestors. Its malice has evaporated. At the same time, however, the festival is even more sacred than the funeral, because the ancestors are invited to attend. The contact is both invigorating and dangerous. From the ancestors, all good things flow, but any ritual error during this period of liminal confusion could cause souls of the living to depart along with the ancestors at its conclusion (Metcalf 1982: 207–29). Once again, there is considerable emphasis on the containment of death.

In this overall picture, headhunting appears as one among several techniques of containment. It was possible to extract indigenous explanations for this. In response to a direct question about why heads terminate mourning, some Berawan said that the effort expended is what assuages the anger of the deceased; others, that a slave is thereby provided in the afterward; and still others, that the victim simply provides company. But these rationalizations were produced in an offhand way, without conveying any true conviction, because they did not refer to what was most strongly felt in the rites. A more abstract account comes closer, I believe, to the Berawan conception of it.

In place of a second mortality striking near to home and setting up the conditions for a third and a fourth, promiscuously, headhunting is, as it were, a controlled death, in which the jealously of the recently dead becomes someone else's problem. For it is not the murderer's kin who feel the victim's resentment, but the victim's own relatives. This is confirmed by the necessity to accord full funeral rites to Berawan who fell victim to headhunters from other communities.[2] Regardless of the manner of death, it is the home village that must deal with the consequences of the unquiet soul.

In the headhunting rites, death seems to ebb through a series of ensuing deaths, each moved a little further away from the community:

our death → their death → mock death → animal's death

| *ulèng* = | *ulèng* = | *ulèng* = | chicken = |
| deceased | victim | victim's victim | sacrifice |

In the first and most dramatic, it is inflicted on some other community. Next, it passes to a human fashioned of wood and leaves, and if that remove seems a long step in the imagination, it is lessened by a number of mythic references. One, for instance, tells of a war between a Berawan folk hero and a race of quasihumans who dressed in leaves and ate charcoal. Finally, death becomes the immolation of an animal, in a routine act of sacrifice. At this point, death has withdrawn far enough for normal life to resume. As the headhunting rites conclude, perhaps months after the funeral that occasioned them, the onerous prohibitions (*lumo*) that it imposed on the community, prohibitions against dancing and singing, weddings and joyful events of all kinds, are finally lifted.

Tellingly, the one remaining rite that was always carried was an act of augury (*ngelaké*). It involved "calling" the eagle *Ictinaetus*

[2] Another way of saying this is that death at the hands of headhunters is not "bad death," a concept discussed below.

malayensis, in Berawan *plaké*. I have described elsewhere the prayers for summoning the bird, and the manner in which omens are read from its flight (1989: 184–213). Suffice it to say that this is the most serious form of divination employed by the Berawan, one used only in matters of life and death. As the headhunting rites came to a close, there could only be one question: is the dying finished, or will more deaths in the community follow? The augur sat at his post by the riverbank, day after day if necessary, until an eagle appeared. Only some appalling omen earlier in the proceedings would prompt cancellation, the cause then being judged hopeless.[3] When a bird appeared, tension mounted suddenly in the longhouse, and everyone ran to witness an outcome that until this moment in the long mortuary sequence remained always in doubt.

I leave it to the reader to decide just how convincing this account is. There are naturally several ways in which it might be criticized. In the contemporary intellectual climate, it might be faulted for preferring imputed meanings to indigenous rationales, however superficial. This criticism is not new, however. In the 1960s, just as interest in ritual was reawakening within anthropology, Victor Turner felt the need to defend himself against similar charges. In a famous essay, he unpacks meanings of the *mudyi* tree that go well beyond those that can be elicited directly from Ndembu informants. Can there be meanings, he asks, of which the participants in ritual are unaware? How can the outside observer know better than they? His answers are that the deepest premises of ritual are often unspoken, if not unsayable, and that the ethnographer may elucidate them by careful and self-conscious collation of a wide range of material, in a manner not usual among those who live a culture as an everyday reality (Turner 1967: 20–25). Since I have followed these principles in addressing Berawan death rituals, I apply them also to the headhunting rites.

[3] For instance, if a negative result has already been received in the augury made earlier in the funeral. At the singing of the death song, called *tíjun*, a simple divination is carried out for each member of the community to make sure that his or her soul has not departed with the ancestors. It is so simple that it very seldom fails to produce a reassuring result. But I have seen it do so, and then another death is expected, and further augury is pointless.

Setting aside for the moment the broad epistemological issues, there is a special difficulty related to the topic of headhunting that bothered me from the outset. Here I have produced an account that ties headhunting into some very specific Berawan ideas and practices surrounding death. But headhunting is found throughout central northern Borneo; secondary treatment of the dead is not. It seems that I am guilty of explaining the general from the particular.

Central northern Borneo is a region of considerable ethnic diversity, but there are a great number of cultural continuities in mode of residence, economy, social organization, and religion, enough to make out a distinctive culture area, of which Jérôme Rousseau has provided a useful overview. Among other things, he shows that headhunting existed everywhere in much the same form, and with similar ritual functions. With the rest of Borneo there are discontinuities, he argues. For instance, the Iban to the south evinced an endless demand for heads, whereas people in central northern Borneo generally preferred to have only a few, and even gave away surplus heads to neighboring communities (Rousseau 1990: 264–81).

There is one cultural feature, however, that is not at all continuous across central northern Borneo, and neither is it a mere detail. In the communities that practiced it, secondary treatment of the dead furnished the occasion for the largest gatherings and the grandest rituals, as it did for the Berawan. In the other communities, this manipulation of corpses and their remains was generally viewed with disgust, as I learned from upriver visitors to Long Teru. In this radical difference of attitudes, the proponents of secondary treatment were in the minority; their communities comprise a band that I have labeled the nulang arc, running along the western and northern fringes of the culture area (Metcalf 1975).

The peculiar distribution of secondary treatment in central northern Borneo has ethnological significance, but the problem here is what sense it makes to base an account of headhunting on rites that are relatively uncommon in the region. I see *three possible responses*, each of which will take a couple of paragraphs to explore, even briefly.

First, I might argue in the manner of the *Année sociologique* school that Berawan death rites provide a special case, a "well-controlled experiment," that illuminates a wider context. Robert Hertz uses this approach in a celebrated essay, arguing that rites of secondary treatment, wherever found, shed light on the collective representation of death in general (1960 [1907]). My claim would be more modest, that in one corner of Borneo the rites of a minority tell us something about the beliefs of the majority.

There is a plausibility to this, in view of the linguistic connections described by Robert Blust (1972), in particular, cohesions that he calls Lower Baram and Kenyah. Speakers of Lower Baram languages include the Berawan and several other communities along the nulang arc. Speakers of Kenyah languages live further upriver, and did not in historical times practice secondary treatment of the dead. Putting this in temporal perspective, Blust considers that the ancestors of all these peoples arrived on the northwest coast of Borneo some three thousand years ago, and then spread east and south (Blust 1976: 214). Oral histories that I collected suggest that the current distribution of the Lower Baram speakers at the fringes of the culture area may have come about as a result of a move back toward the west.

What matters here, however, is that secondary treatment of the dead may well have been part of the cultural repertoire of the common ancestors of the Kenyah and Lower Baram speakers. The practice is an ancient one, found widely throughout western Austronesia (Bellwood 1985). It is more likely that the Kenyah peoples dropped the practice in recent centuries than that the Berawan and others acquired it, and consequently the Kenyah may well share pervasive sentiments concerning death that receive their fullest expression in the rites of secondary treatment. So it is that across the length and breadth of central northern Borneo, heads were required in order to terminate mourning for aristocrats and leaders (Elshout 1926: 232; Hose and McDougall 1912; 2: 38).

In further support of the claim, it might be pointed out that even among the Berawan, only a few individuals ever receive full rites of secondary treatment. For most, there is a less costly, abridged sequence that nevertheless addresses the same conception of transitions of the soul (Metcalf and Huntington 1991: 94–97). As Dianne Tillotson has argued, it is easy to exaggerate the dichotomy between cultures with extended death rites and those without; often, similar notions are manifest in both (Tillotson 1989: 58).

If the considerations make the claim plausible, they do not establish it, however. In his scathing dismissal of the special-case method, E. Evans-Pritchard (1965: 58) accuses Émile Durkheim of using it to disguise inconvenient counterexamples. In order to support the notion that some concept of deflecting recurrent death is associated with headhunting throughout central northern Borneo, it would be necessary to repeat the analysis for at least some of the communities not practicing secondary treatment, and to find in them something akin to the ambiguous ulèng effigy. This can be done, I believe, utilizing in particular J. M. Elshout's detailed account of Kenyah headhunting rites observed between 1913 and 1915 (Elshout 1926: 281–332); but I leave that point-by-point comparison for another occasion.[4]

The *second* possible response is to see the need for an account of headhunting that applies across central northern Borneo, but to doubt that one based on death rites, extended or otherwise, is the right one. What commends this view is that the termination of mourning is only one of three motives or ritual functions for headhunting that are widely reported across the region. The other two, as reported by Rousseau (1990: 275), are a renewal of fertility in people and land, and the consecration of a new longhouse. A priori, there is not reason to believe that one ritual function provides the pattern for the other two, nor is it obvious how my description of displaced death applies to housebuilding and fertility. My tendency to privilege eschatological notions might be no more than an artifact of how headhunting happened to have echoed in Berawan ritual, long after the suppression of the actual practice.

Against this, it must be noted that the multiple ritual functions of headhunting widely observed across the region constitute a problem for any general account that tries to show how all three

---

[4] Rodney Needham (personal communication) points out that Kenyah belawing have many points of similarity with Berawan ulèng. Berawan also made belawing, which were much larger constructions than ulèng, and there was an intermediate size called *kedamen* as well. All these had faces carved on their upper ends, and Needham remarks that these are simply apotropaic. But that does not explain the "arms" and "legs"; moreover, Berawan do not much employ the human face as an artistic motif.

derive from some underlying concept or concepts. My version relies on a notion of death tending to follow death. Once the process is halted, the benefits that follow are what A. M. Hocart (1952) called simply "life:" health, vigor, longevity, and, for good measure, bountiful crops, many children, and security in new houses.

To test that proposition, it would be useful to know whether, before the turn of the century, Berawan ever took heads outside the context of mortuary rites, just to give the community a recharge of fertility, or just to secure a new longhouse. The evidence, of course, is lacking. But even if I had a list of occasions, a headhunter's diary, the issue would not be resolved. As was remarked to me, if fresh heads are available, there are bound to be recently deceased to whom they can be dedicated.

Not all affliction is attributed to the recently dead, however, and at first sight this militates against my account. A frequently cited cause of illness, for instance, is the wandering of souls in dreams, when they are liable to be ambushed by all manner of unknown spirits. It is the business of shamans to locate and liberate these souls, a process that often results in new information about the identities of spirits. But it is often discovered that these malign spirits came from long-ago inhabitants of the vicinity, and it was even suggested to me that all such malevolent spirits are ultimately of human origin.

This suggestion was made during a discussion of "bad death," a belief that the souls of people who die in certain especially unpleasant ways cannot go to the land of the dead as others do. Instead, they are caught between worlds, just like the newly dead, and remain spiteful indefinitely. Consequently, no funerals are held for them. Instead, their corpses are dragged away without ceremony into the jungle and buried hurriedly. Women who die in childbirth are the most feared; but note that casualties of warfare and headhunting do not die bad deaths, and so do receive rites to allay the malice of their souls (Metcalf 1982: 254–56).

The bad dead provide a bridging category between the recently dead and other malign influences that might help to explain why heads were necessary to new house construction. The argument would be that similar notions of bad death are held across central northern Borneo (and, in fact, beyond), and that the accumulation of malicious spirits of the bad dead is a reason given for abandon-

ing an old longhouse site. Conversely, when settling in a new territory, a special need for heads was felt (Southwell 1959: 41) because there was no way to tell whose bad dead might still be in
residence.

The argument is not entirely convincing, however, and the multiple ritual functions of heads remain a problem. Since the bad
dead are irredeemable, they receive no funerals. Some say that
they eventually gain entry to the land of the dead, and lose their
awful character; others say that they never do. But it is not explained why their malice is assuaged by headhunting.

The *third* possible response is to accept my account of Berawan
headhunting rites, but to deny that it has any relevance for communities lacking secondary treatment of the dead. In this view,
the peoples of the nulang arc simply comprise another culture
area separate from the truly central Bornean communities. Indeed, I was told more than once that the practice of headhunting
itself was borrowed from the Kenyah. If true, this would seem to
make the Berawan rites an insecure base on which to build an account of headhunting across the region.

There is more to tell, however. Berawan say that long ago they
were the only inhabitants of a huge tract of jungle in the lower
Baram watershed. Lacking any available enemies, during major
death rites they killed marginal members of the community—
slaves, and those without kin—instead of raiding for heads.[5] Moreover, the practice was revived, so it was said, after colonial rule
was imposed, because deaths within the community were less
likely to result in a complaint to the district officer than a murder
perpetrated elsewhere. W. H. Furness reports a vivid account that
he was given in a Berawan village of the death of an old slave
woman at the hands of those she had served for years (Furness
1902: 62–63). Moreover, the substitution of human sacrifice for
the taking of heads, and vice versa, is found throughout central
northern Borneo, so that the latter can be seen as a variety of the
former. In this the Berawan do not appear in any way atypical.
Cases were even reported in which the two merged: slaves were

[5] Susan McKinnon (personal communication) points out that the killing of
members of the community fails to export the recurrence of death to a different community. But the victims—slaves or old women—were selected because they had no kin in the longhouse, and consequently no particular person
there became the focus of danger.

purchased from other communities, and later decapitated (Burns 1849; Hose 1927: 48–49).

Nevertheless, it makes perfectly good sense to set apart the peoples of the nulang arc as a separate culture area, since such units are nothing more than heuristic devices anyway. But why stop there? As described above, the Berawan language belongs to a group that Blust (1972) calls Lower Baram, which is related to the Kenyah languages. The communities in the northern section of the nulang arc speak more remotely related languages of the Kelabitic variety; those to the south use languages related to Melanau. On those grounds we might distinguish at least four culture areas, which are also not uniform. There is no reason to stop the process of discrimination until we arrive back where we started: with the Berawan, and with the logical problem of explaining the general from the particular.

Having come full circle, the interpretation of ritual seems to have played us false. If we pay attention to the details of particular rites, we cannot see the big picture. In searching for the general explanation, all the purchase that we gain from specifics is lost.

These perplexities make one sympathetic to the critique of symbolic analyses made by Renato Rosaldo (1984: 178). Explicating culture "through the gradual thickening of symbolic webs of meaning" only works, he argues, in the "densest forest of symbols." But in his work on the Ilongot of northern Luzon, Philippines, Rosaldo found this approach thwarted by a lack of "cultural elaboration." The Ilongot were until recently infamous headhunters, and the practice was evidently central to their sense of identity. Yet they offer nothing but one-line explanations for it. Severing and tossing away the victim's head allows them to alleviate the rage that they feel at the death of a loved one; that much they say, and no more. The truth of the statement is for them beyond further explication.

The same self-evident quality is apparent in the indigenous rationales reported from central northern Borneo. As A. M. Elshout found, "The information to be had from the Kenyah himself, when one asks him why headhunting played quite so important a part in his past, and on what ground the worship of heads really rests, is very scarce, and one is surprised to find that he can say practically nothing about it" (1926: 211).[6] The first thing to note is that failure to elicit explanations is, in itself, nothing new. On the contrary, at the turn of the century, anthropologists made much of the lack of dogma in "primitive religions." Indeed, it might be taken as a defining characteristic, so that we might speak instead of the "nontheological religions." Since superficial inquiries into the meanings of ritual often produced nothing more than the invocation of precedent, the conclusion was easily reached that the primitives were subject to an inflexible "rule of custom," which in turn explained why they persisted in error and superstition generation after generation. In this way, paucity of dogma provided a key premise in evolutionary and intellectualist approaches to comparative religion.

The reaction in the twentieth century against these views has inevitably involved undermining the premise. With the data of fieldwork, it was easy to show that ritual had profound social significance. Later, semiotic techniques revealed meanings that were unstated but deeply felt, and the results of their application constitute the distinctive contribution of contemporary anthropology to the comparative study of religion.

The problem in the case of headhunting is not, however, that there are no explanations at all, but that we are offered rationales so terse and repetitive that semiotic techniques can find no purchase. Typically, practitioners or the descendants of practitioners do not refer to custom at all, but to some palpable goal. As the Sebop, near neighbors of the Berawan, told William Furness, headhunting brings "blessings, plentiful harvests, and keeps off sickness, and pains" (1902: 59). This contrasts with the way both Berawan and Sebop go about explaining, for example, their death rites, or even such details as the ulèng effigy discussed above. In justification of these things, the ways of the ancestors are immediately invoked, sometimes followed by a rambling and idiosyncratic discussion. This is what we have come to regard as normal; what is baffling about headhunting is that its indigenous explanations are so pat, so ready to hand.

Rosaldo's solution is to rely on the force of emotion, which he sees as the principal shaper of human behavior. He presents this as a novel move, but I see it as a very old one, the familiar appeal to

---

[6] Quoted in Needham 1983; his translation from Dutch.

the psychic unity of humankind. Having failed for a decade, he says, to make any sense of Ilongot headhunting, he suddenly comprehends it following the tragic death of his wife while doing fieldwork elsewhere in the Philippines. It is the experience of his own overwhelming emotions that allows him to appreciate directly the rage that comes with grief. One cannot doubt the sincerity of his reaction, but note that the insight that it furnishes depends entirely on the assumption that Ilongot ways of experiencing the world are at some basic level identical to his own. The problem with this is obvious. Having resorted to universals, there is no room left for cultural differences. Even if we allow the presumption of a uniform human reaction to loss of close kin, which is dubious, we still have no explanation for why that reaction is expressed institutionally in such diverse ways. If Rosaldo sees murder as the "natural" outlet of a universal emotion, he only shifts the problem of explanation to those societies that do not practice headhunting, like our own, or that abhor violence, like the Zuni. There is something very nineteenth-century about all this: culture as a veneer of restraint over the barbarity of uninhibited savages. We should remember that empathy was a favorite device of Edward Burnett Tylor, who thought he could use it to see directly into the mind of primitive man.

A uniformitarian view of emotion cannot be allowed, however. We know very well that people respond differently to the same situations, and manifest the same behavior while feeling all manner of emotions. Imagine an Ilongot man who is not in fact deeply moved by the death of his wife; would it follow that he felt no compulsion to engage in headhunting? Might it not be simply the thing expected of him, just as Americans are expected to adopt restrained manners and dark clothing?

As Gregory Bateson (1936) made clear half a century ago, there is a sharp distinction to be drawn between personal emotions and cultural ethos. Emotions are a slippery basis on which to stand a theory of culture precisely because of the lability that Rosaldo noticed. Grief may turn into rage, and, as everyone knows, love into hate. But that says next to nothing about the prevalence of family violence in different societies. Whatever chaotic forces may well up in the individual can only be named, accounted for, expressed, or reproved through cultural understandings.

In her study of the Ilongot, Michelle Rosaldo (1980) shows a careful concern for the social construction of emotional states. She describes normative behavior among teenage males that includes constant moodiness and sudden bouts of pointless destructiveness. No doubt this behavior is trying for the parents, but the point is that it is not evaluated in negative, or wholly negative, terms; it is for parents a sign of maturation without which they would fear for the future vitality of their sons. It shows their "passion" (*liget*), without which the "knowledge" (*beya*) that they will acquire as adults would be ineffective. Consequently, the violence to which youths are prone, as an expression of their animal vigor, takes on a positive aesthetic.

Renato Rosaldo's simple reductionism tries to explain the particular from the general—a worse problem than the one with which we started. Michelle Rosaldo preserves the advantages of revealing a particular cultural configuration. But neither makes much mention of ritual, and it appears that the Ilongot are unritualistic to a degree that makes them atypical of Southeast Asia in general. Since the Rosaldos have between them written two monographs bearing on headhunting, the Ilongot tend to be viewed as a type case, yet there are none of the cults so prominent elsewhere in the region. Indeed, if we think of headhunting as the collection of heads, the Ilongot did not practice headhunting at all. Their practice was simply to throw the severed head into the air, let out a yell of triumph, and abandon it at the site of the murder—no riotous return, no installation rites, no festival.

It follows that the kind of reritualization that occurred in Borneo after "pacification" was not possible for the Ilongot. More subtly, the elaboration of the symbolism of headhunting was stilted, as Renato Rosaldo noticed. In Borneo, the emphasis seems to have been on the acquisition of heads as raw material that would realize its potential only after ritual processing—a notion that closely parallels the processing of corpses in mortuary rites. Just how heads were obtained was of secondary concern. I was told that Kayan and Kenyah folk even broke into Berawan mausoleums to steal skulls. The emphasis among the Ilongot is, by comparison, on murder. One wonders how contingent the business of decapitation actually was; if violence had a kind of feral beauty in it, would not a knife thrust through the heart have done just as well?

If catharsis were the goal, why not hack the victim to pieces? In either event, it is plain why the final suppression or abandonment of murder was for the Ilongot a complete break with the past, as Michelle Rosaldo describes (1980: 32–33).

The Ilongot are not a good comparative case for the Berawan. There are, it is true, echoes among the latter of the modal personality that Michelle Rosaldo describes: vigorous, alert, even quick-tempered young men are much admired, and old folk remark that the hopes of the community reside in them. But the virtues of the warrior are not the only traits that are privileged. Emphasis is also placed on cheerfulness, generosity, and cooperation, and the sullen youth prone to vandalism is certainly not appreciated in the longhouse. As for the purging of emotion, it is hard to see how standing up an effigy does much to vent a consuming rage, and one can only wonder what Ilongot would make of headless head rites. Generalizing unwisely, Renato Rosaldo has been misled into discounting the force of ritual in peoples' lives.

We come back, then, to the bald assertions that questions about headhunting so often elicit, and it is Rodney Needham (1983) who has addressed their implications most directly. Beginning with the Kenyah of Borneo, he cites cases over a wide area of South and Southeast Asia, from Assam in the west to Yunnan in the north, of peoples who associate skulls with fertility. What Needham wants to show is that there is no intermediate term in this association, as observers have constantly been led to assume, beginning with the Dutch missionary ethnographer A. C. Kruyt (1906), who attributed to the Toraja of Sulawesi the notion of *levensfluide* (life-fluid) or *zielestof* (soul-substance).

Needham argues convincingly that such intermediate terms only appear to resolve the problem by giving the causal connection a physical form of the type familiar to Western science, as if vitality were a kind of electricity. These terms may give us the comfortable illusion of comprehension, but there is no reason to believe that they play any part in the thinking of Southeast Asian peoples. Kruyt made no claim that either of his terms glossed any expression in the Toraja language, and later he abandoned both. Maurice Bloch (1982: 229) is the latest to succumb to the temptation to explain headhunting by some alienable stock of "life."

The effect of Needham's demonstration is to oblige us to confront squarely the perception of causality in other cultures. He quotes Lucien Lévy-Bruhl's statement of the question: "We still have to use the word 'cause.' But let us avoid supposing that the primitive mentality uses it with the same atmosphere that it has for us, and let us try to find out precisely what goes on in them [the primitives] when they use their corresponding word" (1949: 35). To this Needham adds tartly: "How far we are from that stage of investigation is shown by the fact that we do not yet know whether there is a Kenyah word corresponding to 'cause'" (1983: 83).

This is a deep issue, and it appears to block further progress on the significance of headhunting. But perhaps we can in part circumvent it. First, the indigenous rationale that Needham finds all over Southeast Asia is not, as we have seen, the only one that is offered. The Ilongot make no direct connection between heads and fertility, for instance. One could argue that an increase in vigor is for them associated in a roundabout way with headhunting, but there is no mysterious causality here. Were I to say to a troubled teenager: "Join the army, it'll make a man of you!" no one would imagine that the act of signing up or putting on a uniform was what brought about the alleged maturation. As it happens, the Ilongot offer a quite different one-line rationale, and we do not know how many more of these there may be worldwide.

As for the Berawan, they will agree readily enough with the proposition that heads bring renewed vitality to the community. But if asked simply what is the use (íno guné?) of headhunting, they almost invariably respond that new heads finish mourning.[7] Again, it is possible to subsume the second rationale under the first, but the point is that Berawan do not put it that way. Similarly, the first rationale is not completely without ritual expression, but if my account of the headhunting rites has any validity, it is not what is foremost in their minds.

These multiple indigenous explanations lead me to wonder whether the impenetrability of one of them has not too much concerned us. We are not unfamiliar, after all, with statements whose chain of causality will not stand examination. I may assert that aspirin cures headaches, and yet be quite unable to say how. It would

---

[7] To be precise, mourning is finished for the community as a whole. Close family members may continue with their observances for up to a year.

take Madison Avenue to come up with some spurious mediating term—"Doctor-Power," or some such. I might volunteer that it has something to do with biochemistry, but that only states a general cultural premise, equivalent to the proposition that people do not prosper without proper ritual. It might be objected that the knowledge of just how aspirin works is available somewhere in our society, even if restricted to specialists. But I am told that this is not in fact so; medical researchers have not worked out the detailed reactions. Like us, doctors take the effectiveness of aspirin, and many others cures, as a simple fact.

The force of Needham's argument is that the conundrum of headhunting is reduced to two terms, heads and fertility, which stands in the same relationship in cultures spread across a huge geographical area. Other features of these cultures, all the details that make each unique, are necessarily set aside. Consequently, our attention is drawn away from cultural specifics, toward an element of beliefs that has a quasi-universal nature. This is a well-trod path. It might lead, for instance, to some aspect of the "primitive thought" of which Lucien Lévy-Bruhl spoke. It might even lead to an archetype in the Jungian mode, some product of human phylogeny made manifest in the dreams of "modern man" and the rituals of "the primitive" (June 1964: 107, passim). Archetypes have been erected on less substantial grounds. I do not mean to associate Needham with either application; in fact, he specifically disavows both (personal communication).[8] The tension remains, however, between culturally specific contexts and quasi-universals. My purpose is to insist on the former.

There is a feature of the explanations of headhunting that has been too easily taken for granted, however, and that is that they take a cause-and-effect form in the first place. The "explanations" comprise statements of consequences, but this is not how anthropologists' accounts generally work. Instead, we set about a much broader task of contextualization, the goal of which is some kind of image phrased in indigenous terms.

[8] Needham draws on the work of Lévy-Bruhl, but on the later writing in the *Carnets*, after Lévy-Bruhl had abandoned the ideas expressed in *Primitive Mentality* (1923).

I speak of an image in the sense of a metaphor or simile, but also a concatenation of such, a nexus of metaphorical extensions through which a cultural feature is perceived indigenously.[9] The most ready example for me to give concerns the mortuary practice already mentioned, secondary treatment, and I discuss it again here only to emphasize what might be gained from ritual analysis.

The central metaphor that I discerned in Berawan death rites can be stated simply enough. If I may be forgiven for quoting my own ethnography:

The character of the soul in the period following upon death is best understood by viewing it as metaphorically linked with the corpse. The connection is not physical; the soul is not in any sense in, or tied to, the body. Indeed . . . even in life the soul is thought to be able to separate itself from its mortal vehicle and travel about in other worlds. At death, the physical association only becomes looser. Now the soul cannot reenter or reanimate the body; that is what makes it a corpse. Instead, the relationship between body and soul becomes one of shared fates. As the abandoned body sinks into ruinous corruption, the soul also changes its nature, and not for the better. Progressively it takes on a dreadfulness of its own. . . . Only the passage of time can alleviate this condition; the slow ebbing of putrescence, leaving dry bones, hard and imperishable. (1982: 94–95)

From this metaphor, an expanding series of implications and elaborations of meaning radiate into each phase of the death rites, and further, into other facets of Berawan culture.

The Berawan image of secondary treatment is no doubt unique if we consider all its intricacies. But the opposite is true if we pay attention to broad features. Echoes can be detected in very different places and social environments, and the parallels are sometimes striking. Donald Tuzin, who worked among the Arapesh in northern New Guinea, once told me after a talk that virtually everything I had said about Berawan eschatology applied verbatim to the Arapesh. This was additionally remarkable in that his own

[9] Roy Wagner (1972: 6–7) uses the term "ideology" in a very similar sense. He argues that cultures typically encompass contrasting and inconsistent ideologies, and he assigns a creative role to such inconsistency. I make the same argument below concerning coexisting images, but I prefer to avoid the term "ideology" because it already has established connotations that make its use in a new sense somewhat clumsy. Meanwhile, I employ "image" in a way not unfamiliar in poetics.

account of their beliefs proceeded from a very different standpoint (Tuzin 1975).

Based on the Berawan image, it would be possible to produce a considerable list of beliefs and practices that might be found associated with secondary burial. In a brief comparison of cases in Southeast Asia, I paid attention to half a dozen items that seemed basic: the notions that dying is a slow transition between spiritual states and that the process is disagreeable; an emphasis on the symbolism of decomposition; fear of the recently dead and of invasion of the corpses by nonhuman agencies; an assumption that the malice of the recently dead, somehow hovering nearby, is slowly replaced by the benign influence of the ancestors, acting at a distance (Metcalf and Huntington 1991: 97).

To this list we could add items less directly related to the central metaphor. For example, a widow or widower is often subjected to privations that appear unreasonable to us. A surviving Berawan spouse is cooped up in a tiny and deliberately uncomfortable house of mats right next to the corpse and fed rotten food; surely a strange way to comfort a bereaved husband or wife! But the privations are not viewed as punitive; on the contrary; they are the only means to deflect the malice of the deceased from its most likely target. Only by imitating the corpse can the spouse escape joining it (Metcalf 1982: 73–77, 103–4). Consequently, the image of death comments ironically on the institutions of kinship and marriage.

Again, there is a strange association between decomposition and wealth. When the corpse is displayed on the verandah of the longhouse, valuable cloths, beads, and golden ornaments are hung about it. We might expect that the proximity of death would only pollute these things, but that does not take into account the link that a deceased individual will eventually make with the ancestors, from whom all such wealth proceeds. A death in the community, though a disaster, is at the same time a golden opportunity. The type of communication that it allows is similar to, but more potent than, that which occurs in the sacrifice of animals (Metcalf 1982: 107–10). In this way, the ideology of secondary treatment influences Berawan understandings of sacrifice.

Further examples could be adduced, but I must emphasize that there is no suggestion here of a fixed or inevitable correspondence between secondary treatment and any set slate of ideas. Were we told nothing of a society but that secondary burial was practiced, we might reasonably make a whole series of guesses about other practices and related beliefs. In some cases, all our guesses might be wrong. It is more likely, however, that some would be confirmed, and others not. That is all that we have gained, but it is a considerable gain.

I do not suggest that the corpse is a "natural symbol," a phrase some have used. On the contrary, a general finding of the study of symbolism is, as Needham succinctly puts it, that "anything can be made to stand for anything else" (1985: 169). There is always the possibility that metaphors completely different from those we have traced could be erected on the practice of secondary treatment. Among the Bara of Madagascar, for instance, the Berawan concern for eschatology as such is almost completely absent, and a quite different emphasis is put on the transition of the corpse. Moreover, similar metaphors can be mobilized in cultures that lack secondary treatment per se. For example, the Mambai of Timor have even more elaborate symbolism of corruption than the Berawan do, relating it to the very creation of the world (Metcalf and Huntington 1991: 105–30; Traube 1986: 200–236).

The point of this excursion into secondary burial is to contrast the images that we have of it with the various explanations of headhunting. For the former, it is possible both to explore the particular way that different cultures elaborate the metaphorical links between body and soul, and to pursue a comparative project in which we see partial similarities here and there across a region. As to why these similarities exist, I can do no better than E. B. Tylor, who, a century ago, concluded that they are proof either "of blood relationship or of intercourse, direct or indirect," or alternatively, where diffusion could be ruled out, as the result of "like action of men's minds under like conditions" (1964 [1878]: 3). As regards the latter, we have no more need to invoke the action of the unconscious than did Tylor.

The flat statements of consequences that comprise the rationales of headhunting have no such yields; instead of opening up connections for us to explore, they close them off. The alternative

is to compare the nuances of diverse images of headhunting specific to one cultural cohesion or another.[10] Such images are not exclusive of one another. It is possible, indeed likely, that there is
some unique aspect or emphasis in the Berawan image, though it
nevertheless shares features with many others found across central northern Borneo. This was really the issue discussed in the
section beginning on page 264 above, although it was phrased
there as a dilemma of false generalization. I am inclined to believe
that a notion of the necessity to contain death is characteristic of
the region, and widely incorporated into images of headhunting,
but whether or not that turns out to be true, the way to proceed is
plain enough.

Another way of saying this is that various images of headhunting
may overlap in a particular cultural context. This was dramati-
cally brought home to me during fieldwork. At the beginning of
the paper, I remarked that echoes of headhunting came to me
from different directions during fieldwork. Not only did I observe
the headless head rites described above, but I was also caught up
in the midst of a panic in which Berawan thought that vague outside forces were sending assassins to take their heads.

When I first became aware in July 1974 of paranoia spreading
through the lower Baram region, my first reaction was irritation.
Life in the longhouse lost its usual free-and-easy sociality. People
barred the doors of their rooms soon after sundown. I was warned
not to travel alone or go where I was not known. Strangers of all
kinds were suspect, especially foreigners.

The warnings turned out to be well founded. After a month or
so of nightly alarms, I decided to go inland to the farms for a
respite—as I thought. On my way, I skirted a community of long-
settled Penan, people who had close ties with Long Teru and knew
all about my presence there. Nevertheless, my sudden appearance

---

[10] This is not to preclude the possibility of a distinct image of headhunting
held by Berawan women. In the nineteenth century, women figured prominently in the practice, as victims. This seems to have been the case not because they were specially selected—all heads were of equal worth—but because they were more vulnerable. Old women, for instance, were often sent
out alone to collect firewood in the forest. Women also had special roles in the
rituals of headhunting, only a few of which are noted above. The gender aspects of the rites are interesting and important, but I have found it impossible
to treat them properly here without obstructing the main line of argument.

on a jungle path took them by surprise, and one lad fired his shot-
gun at me, luckily without taking very good aim, before I had realized that he was there. The situation was soon smoothed over. I
said it was my fault for not making a nice loud *lalu*—a sort of yo-
del—to let them know I was coming. They said the boy who fired
at me had seen the tin box that I carried on my back, and jumped
to the conclusion that it was for putting heads in—this despite
the fact that these boxes are standard items among upriver folk,
useful for keeping gear dry in a leaky canoe. We parted warily, and
I went on my way, nursing my own paranoias. At the farms, there
was even more uproar than at the longhouse.

What people feared were *penyamun*, a Malay word meaning
"robber" or "bandit," but understood throughout Borneo to imply
"headhunter." When I asked who these penyamun were, it was
hinted that they were most likely Iban in the pay of the state government. The homeland of the Iban lies to the south, but they are
numerous, and have expanded northward, displacing or absorbing
the smaller ethnic groups in their path. That Berawan suspicions
should fall on them is understandable, in view of the constant
friction over land rights in recent decades. But the headhunting
scare had much the same effect in Iban communities, and I do not
know who fulfilled the role of penyamun for them.

For many people, however, penyamun took on an extrahuman
quality. Bands of heavily armed soldiers wearing camouflage uniforms appeared and disappeared mysteriously near the lake that
lay behind the longhouse. They resembled army units that have in
recent years come upriver, usually in launches or landing craft.
Some of these forays were in response to unrest among upriver
people about land claims or the depredations of the logging industry, and others were related to a nagging communist insurgency
that flares up from time to time. But the approach of regular army
units was always detected well in advance. Moreover, the spectral
soldiers seen at the lake were reported to have no badges on their
uniforms, and this was taken as evidence of evil intentions.

On one occasion, a group of women collecting firewood near a
riverbank suddenly saw a number of men hiding in the branches of
a large tree. Screaming, they fled towards their canoes. The only
man present ran back with his *parang* (work knife or short sword)
drawn, but he saw nothing, and later scoffed at the fears of the

women. This man was, in fact, one of the few skeptics in the long-house who doubted all the penyamun stories. Other men repeated them with every bit as much credulousness as the women. Never-theless, it was an older woman who presented me with a view of penyamun as nonhuman, indeed as inverted humans. They slept all day, she said, hanging by their knees from the lower branches of trees. If I saw any, I was to kill them at once.

In the context of the longhouse, penyamun seemed to focus a range of fears related to the uncontrollable world outside the community: Iban immigrants engulfing Berawan lands, the gov-ernment making decisions in which they had no say, and even an inkling of the workings of international capitalism.

In addition, there were perhaps some more elemental fears. The phantasmal penyamun hinted at dread of the jungle itself, para-doxical in a people that we see as living in the jungle. But that is not the Berawan view of it at all; they live *beside* the jungle. Most Berawan do not in fact care to spend a night in the jungle if it can be avoided, and they think it positively uncivilized to sleep on the ground. I was even rebuked for lying on the ground. Souls of the recently dead are often talked of as hovering on the margins of the forest. In my experience, the only people in central northern Borneo who think of themselves as living *in* the jungle are the hunting and gathering Penan, and that may help to explain why, despite their unwarlike and retiring reputation, they have put up a better fight against the voracious lumber industry than any other of the interior folk.

The literal inversion of the penyamun in one account has a couple of associations. Hanging by the knees, penyamun resemble the huge fruit bats (*pawat*), with wingspans up to six feet, that roost in trees during the day and fly out in great numbers at sun-set. A taboo prevents the husband of a pregnant woman from dis-turbing fruit bats, least the child be born deformed. This taboo is one of a long series, but it makes the pawat a suitable transforma-tion of penyamun. Again, inversion is itself a symbol of otherness. I was reminded of John Middleton's account (1960: 230–38) of the annular worldview of the Lugbara of Uganda, in which humanity decreases with distance from the home community. From beyond the horizon came the Europeans, who ran the colony of Uganda at that time, and Lugbara insisted that in their country (and when no Lugbara were looking) Europeans walked around on their hands.

My informant in fact hinted that her roosting penyamun were Europeans.

After the scare had lasted several weeks, I sought to avoid the confusion by escaping downriver for a while. At the Catholic mission station in Marudi, a small bazaar a day's travel upriver from the coast, and later in the coastal town of Miri, I discussed the panic with priests, some of whom had the advantage of long residence in Sarawak. Their reaction was professionally cool; they had seen these outbreaks before, always the same, the result of malicious rumor-mongering among a simple people.

The impression of uniformity was reinforced by a survey that I conducted by mail of missionaries across Sarawak. Each of the half-dozen respondents described a rumor arriving from upriver or down, it hardly mattered which, and taking hold among town people and spreading to upriver folk, or the reverse. Often it was whispered that a headless corpse had been found in a village some way off, but that the police had hushed up the matter. Houses were fortified at night, and the fear slowly ebbed after two or three months.

What is most significant about these accounts is that the panic spread with equal facility among the descendants of headhunters and those who had no such traditions at all. Nor was the scare restricted to the interior. On the coast there are large populations of Chinese whose forebears had migrated in the nineteenth century, and indigenous peoples whose ancestors had accepted Islam many generations ago. In Sarawak, the latter are called Malays, an ethnic label that is synonymous with Islam. For both these populations, headhunting is culturally alien, yet the penyamun scare swept through the cities on the coast just as it did through the interior. The rumors may indeed have started on the coast.

Consequently, it is obvious that we must once again radically expand the context of our inquiries. There must be a state-wide image of headhunting, in addition to whatever local ones exist, and it will clearly have little to do with headhunting rituals, headless or otherwise. Instead, it must relate to historical experiences that are shared by Berawan and Chinese, Kenyah and Malay alike.

As is widely known, Sarawak was ruled by three generations of English adventurers who carved out for themselves a personal fief in Borneo. The first of these, Raja James Brooke, was kept busy during his reign suppressing piracy and warfare along the coast. Iban ferocity became infamous. Headhunting was involved in this violence, and it is said that Malays were implicated, in that they organized raids in which they kept the spoils and their Iban followers took skulls (Pringle 1970: 46–55). Building on James's successes, the second raja, Charles, greatly increased the size of the state and established a firm basis of administration (Crisswell 1978).

It is during Charles Brooke's reign that we hear the first reports of penyamun scares. Here is a description given by A. C. Haddon:

During the greater part of the year 1894 a remarkable and widely distrib-uted panic spread over Sarawak, and all the races of the Raj, Chinese, Malays, Sea Dayaks [Iban], and various inland tribes were alike affected. The Malays of Sarawak and Brunei started a rumour all through the coun-try that the Rajah was anxious to obtain a number of human heads to lay in the foundations of the new high-level reservoir at Kuching, and that men were sent out at night to procure them. (Haddon 1901: 338–39)

Haddon's account is very similar to those I received from mission-aries all over the country in 1974, and the *Sarawak Gazette* re-cords outbreaks throughout the intervening 80 years.

As in 1894, what evidently triggered the outbreak in 1974 was major construction work, in this case the massive derricks that were being erected in the sea to exploit offshore oil fields. They are just visible from the beaches near Miri: great, gaunt structures looming out of the haze. It is not necessary to be descended from headhunters to wonder what it is that keeps them so improbably standing there in the middle of the sea.

We might jump to the conclusion that the answer provided by the penyamun rumor was taken from the practices of Iban head-hunting, about which people on the coast had opportunities to learn earlier in the nineteenth century. But, as noted above, Iban images of headhunting are not identical to those found in central northern Borneo, among such people as the Berawan and Kenyah. In particular, Iban do not seem to have used heads when building new longhouses, which are anyway more flimsy that those built by their neighbors to the north. In his account of the founding of a new house, Derek Freeman (1970: 120–23) makes no mention of heads.

Meanwhile, Haddon himself points out that as the trans-

Siberian railway approached the northern borders of the Chinese empire, a rumor broke out in Peking that the Russian ambassador had applied to the emperor for two thousand children to be buried in the roadbed, in order to secure its foundations (Haddon 1901: 339). Perhaps this idea of how to secure new construction arrived from China with the immigrants, mostly poor laborers. True, a particularly Bornean slant has been put on the idea in restricting the human material purportedly required to heads, but that is a small modification.

What is plain, however, is that the construction that triggers penyamun rumors is not of a traditional type, such as the building of longhouses, but something quite unprecedented. To Raja Charles, a reservoir undoubtedly signaled progress for his little capital city. To the government of Sarawak, and even more to the federal government of Malaysia in Kuala Lumpur, which receives the lion's share of revenues, the oil wells certainly connote development. To many ordinary people in Sarawak, they evidently mean something else.

Ever since colonial "pacification," the peoples of Sarawak have had little to fear from each other. Interethnic violence has been minimal, and this is to the credit of the successive regimes of the Brooke Raj, direct colonial rule from London, and postindependence governments. Nevertheless, the peoples of Sarawak have seen their control over their own lives progressively eroded, as they have been drawn ever tighter into a world system. This is their shared experience. In this context, penyamun scares can be read as a commentary on indigenous attitudes to the "progress" that has been foisted on them willy-nilly.

These circumstances suggest comparison with another, and more celebrated, form of social ferment, which has a similar brushfire quality. Like the penyamun rumors, the millenarian mass movements called "cargo cults" in Melanesia spread rapidly from one ethnic group to another.[11] Jean Guiart (1951) saw this as

[11] In Melanesian cargo cults, a prophet typically appears who announces the imminent return of the ancestors, bringing with them all the material wealth—the "cargo"—that Melanesians see belonging to Westerners. Sometimes the ancestors are expected to arrive by spectral ship, sometimes in airplanes. Often the enthusiasm triggered by these prophecies causes people to destroy their property in expectation that everything will be replaced by the ancestors.

their key feature, and explained it as a kind of protonationalism. Whatever their seeming irrationality, he argued, Melanesians achieved through cargo-cult activity an awareness of themselves at a supratribal level, as a people against their colonial masters. Consequently, the cults prepared the way for later political movements organized in a fully rational way. E. J. Hobsbawm (1959) extended Guiart's argument to millenarian movements in general, as well as to banditry and secret societies.

The evolutionary and Marxist underpinnings of Guiart's and Hobsbawm's arguments require them to see cargo cults as forerunners of greater things. But the penyamun scares have recurred unchanged for almost a century. Hobsbawm might respond that circumstances in Sarawak have been such as to frustrate a fuller self-awareness. Robert Pringle (1970: 54) remarks that the yoke of Brooke rule rested, on the whole, very lightly on their subjects. The Brookes firmly believed in a kind of Victorian benign despotism. They did not encourage European settlement or plantation agriculture, and they restricted missionaries. This light touch was sufficient to provoke the fear of outside forces unconsciously expressed in penyamun rumors, but nothing more. Direct rule from Westminster did not occur until the British empire was in decline after the Second World War, and only mild pressure was exerted toward more rapid economic development, with its resulting disruption. Only in the postindependence era did the pace quicken, but Sarawak was by then a junior partner in the Federation of Malaysia.

Against these arguments, it might be urged that cargo cults have hardly prefigured national unity in independent New Guinea. The country is wracked with internal tensions, and cargo cults persist, as do the penyamun scares. Perhaps Wagner has a better view of it when he remarks in *The Invention of Culture* (1981: 31) that cargo cults are best seen as a kind of "reverse anthropology," an attempt to literalize the metaphors of modern consumer society from the standpoint of tribal culture. They should, he says, be called "culture cults." This fits neatly with an obvious feature of penyamun scares, one that Haddon noticed at the turn of the century. We see Borneans as the headhunters; they see it the other way around.

In just one corner of the globe we find a historic tradition of ritualized murder; mimetic performance of the same associated with the bloody or blackening trophies, or with cobwebby skulls, long dry, or with no head at all; accompanied by persistent fear of head-hunting by others that builds occasionally to a panic originating among, or spreading to, peoples outside both the area and the tradition. What these various beliefs and practices imply is a number of coexisting images of headhunting. Whether or not my account of them is adequate does not affect the essence of my argument. The point is that we should turn away from the supposed consequences of headhunting, those indigenous rationales that have preoccupied us, and instead focus upon specific contexts appropriate to its many superimposed images.

Acknowledgments

I thank Clare Kinney, Susan McKinnon, and Rodney Needham for their helpful comments on earlier drafts of this paper.

References

Bateson, Gregory
   1936 *Naven*. Stanford: Stanford University Press.
Bellwood, Peter
   1985 *Prehistory of the Indo-Malaysian Archipelago*. New York: Academic.
Bloch, Maurice
   1982 "Death, Women and Power." In M. Bloch and J. Parry, eds., *Death and the Regeneration of Life*. Cambridge University Press.
Blust, Robert
   1972 "Report of Linguistic Fieldwork Undertaken in Sarawak." *Borneo Research Bulletin* 4: 12–14.
   1976 "Language and Culture History: Two Case Studies." *Asian Perspectives* 27: 205–28.
Burns, Robert
   1849 "The Kayans of North-west Borneo." *Journal of the Indian Archipelago and Eastern Asia* 3: 140–52.
Crisswell, Colin
   1978 *Rajah Charles Brooke: Monarch of All He Surveyed*. Kuala Lumpur: Oxford University Press.
Elshout, J. M.
   1926 *De Kenja-Dajaks uit het Apo-Kajan-gebied: Bijdragen tot de Kennis van Centraal-Borneo*. The Hague: Martinus Nijhoff.

Evans-Pritchard, E. E.

1965 *Theories of Primitive Religion.* Oxford: Clarendon.

Freeman, Derek

1970 *Report on the Iban.* New York: Athlone.

Furness, William H.

1902 *The Home-Life of Borneo Head-Hunters.* Philadelphia: Lippincott.

Guiart, Jean

1951 "Forerunners of Melanesian Nationalism." *Oceania* 22: 81–100.

Haddon, Alfred Cort

1901 *Headhunters Black, White, and Brown.* London: Methuen.

Hertz, Robert

1960 [1907] "A Contribution to the Study of the Collective Representation of Death." In *Death and the Right Hand,* translated from the
French by Rodney and Claudia Needham. New York: Free Press.

Hobsbawm, Eric

1959 *Primitive Rebels: Studies in Archaic Forms of Social Movement.*
New York: Norton.

Hocart, Arthur Maurice

1952 *The Life-Giving Myth.* New York: Grove.

Hose, Charles

1927 *Fifty Years of Romance and Research: Or, a Jungle-Wallah at
Large.* London: Hutchinson.

Hose, Charles, and William McDougall

1912 *The Pagan Tribes of Borneo.* 2 vols. London: Macmillan.

Jung, Carl

1964 *Man and His Symbols.* New York: Doubleday.

Kruyt, A. C.

1906 *Het Animisme in den Indischen Archipel.* The Hague: Martinus
Nijhoff.

Lévy-Bruhl, Lucien

1949 *Les Carnets de Lucien Lévy-Bruhl.* Paris: Librarie Plon.

Metcalf, Peter

1975 "Who Are the Berawan? Ethnic Classification and the Distribution of Secondary Treatment of the Dead in Central North Borneo."
Oceania 47: 85–105.

1982 *A Borneo Journey into Death: Berawan Eschatology from Its Rituals.* Philadelphia: University of Pennsylvania Press.

1989 *Where Are YOU/SPIRITS: Style and Theme in Berawan Prayer.*
Washington, D.C.: Smithsonian Institution Press.

Metcalf, Peter, and Richard Huntington

1991 *Celebrations of Death: The Anthropology of Mortuary Ritual.*
2d ed. Cambridge: Cambridge University Press.

Middleton, John
  1960 *Lugbara Religion: Ritual and Authority Among an East African People*. Oxford: Oxford University Press.
Needham, Rodney
  1983 "Skulls and Causality." In Needham, *Against the Tranquility of Axioms*, pp. 66–92. Berkeley: University of California Press.
  1985 *Exemplars*. Berkeley: University of California Press.
Pollard, F. H., and E. Banks
  1937 "Teknonymy and Other Customs Among Kayans, Kenyah, Kelamantans and Others." *Sarawak Museum Journal* 4: 223–27.
Pringle, Robert
  1970 *Rajahs and Rebels: The Ibans of Sarawak Under Brooke Rule, 1841–1941*. Ithaca, N.Y.: Cornell University Press.
Rosaldo, Michelle
  1980 *Knowledge and Passion: Ilongot Notions of Self and Social Life*. Cambridge: Cambridge University Press.
Rosaldo, Renato
  1984 "Grief and a Headhunter's Rage: on the Culture Force of Emotions." In E. Bruner, ed., *Text, Play, and Story: The Construction and Reconstruction of Self and Society*, pp. 178–98. Washington, D.C.: American Ethnological Society.
Rosenau, Pauline M.
  1992 *Post-Modernism and the Social Sciences: Insights, Inroads and Intrusions*. Princeton: Princeton University Press.
Rousseau, Jérôme
  1990 *Central Borneo: Ethnic Identity and Social Life in a Stratified Society*. Oxford: Clarendon.
Southwell, C. H.
  1959 "The Kayans and Kenyahs." In T. Harrisson, ed., *The Peoples of Sarawak*. Kuching: Sarawak Museum.
Tillotson, Dianne
  1989 "The Graves of the Rice Ancestors: Changing Mortuary Patterns in Southeast Asia." Ph.D. diss., Australian National University, Canberra.
Traube, Elizabeth
  1986 *Cosmology and Social Life: Ritual Exchange Among the Mambai of East Timor*. Chicago: University of Chicago Press.
Turner, Victor
  1967 *The Forest of Symbols: Aspects of Ndembu Ritual*. Ithaca, N.Y.: Cornell University Press.
Tuzin, Donald
  1975 "The Breath of a Ghost: Dreams and the Fear of the Dead." *Ethos* 3: 555–78.

Tylor, Edward Burnett

1964 [1878] *Researches into the Early History of Mankind*. Chicago: University of Chicago Press.

Wagner, Roy

1972 *Habu: The Innovation of Meaning in Daribi Religion*. Chicago: University of Chicago Press.

1981 *The Invention of Culture*. 2d ed. Chicago: University of Chicago Press.

Wirz, Paul

1922 *Religion und Mythus der Marind Anim von Hollandisch-Sud-Neu-Guinea*. Hamburg: Friedrichsen.

Index

Index

Library of Congress Cataloging-in-Publication Data

Headhunting and the social imagination in Southeast Asia / edited by
Janet Hoskins.
    p.   cm.
   Includes bibliographical references and index.
   ISBN 0-8047-2574-8 (cloth : alk. paper). — ISBN 0-8047-2575-6
(pbk. : alk. paper)
    1. Headhunters—Asia, Southeastern—History—Sources. 2. Rites
and ceremonies—Asia, Southeastern. 3. Body, Human—Symbolic
aspects—Asia, Southeastern. 4. Violence—Southeastern Asia.
5. Asia, Southeastern—Economic conditions. 6. Asia, Southeastern—
Social life and customs. I. Hoskins, Janet.
GN635.S58H42   1996
394—dc20   95-23128
                                              CIP

Original printing 1996
Last figure below indicates year of this printing:
05 04 03 02 01 00 99 98 97 96